No Word of a Lie

No Word of a Lie

DAVE EDWARDS

ATHENA PRESS
LONDON

ISBN 978 1 84748 471 0

First published 2009 by
ATHENA PRESS
Queen's House, 2 Holly Road
Twickenham TW1 4EG
United Kingdom

Printed for Athena Press

I wish to thank Diana, without whose help this book would have never been written. I thank you!

In memory of Peter Hazell.
Pete was a nice bloke; he never had a bad bone in his body, but what little luck he had ran out.
Rest in peace, mate.

If this book ever gets published, every penny of my profit will go to my local cancer charity, the Cherry Tree Lodge. This you have my word on, and you can carve that in stone!
No word of a lie!

This book is dedicated to those I share the moon with, and they know who they are!

Foreword

Fuck! Now that I have your undivided attention it's time to tell you about this book so you don't have to waste your time reading it, although I hope you do take the time to read it.

First things first: all the events in this book actually happened and the people are real people. I have changed some of the names for obvious reasons – and some I haven't for obvious reasons. Nevertheless everything written is true, no word of a lie. And those events that I did not personally witness have been corroborated by those who did.

I never set out to write a book; it was just the way it happened and it seemed a good idea at the time! It actually started out by accident. A close friend of mine, named Margaret, and I were conversing about our childhoods – how hers and mine were poles apart – and during the course of the conversation I told her about two particularly fun, memorable incidents I encountered in my youth, and surprisingly her reaction was a fit of hysterical laughter, as was her friends'. Surprisingly, she suggested that I should capture such incidents by writing them down, so after giving her suggestion much thought and getting over my initial response, which was 'me? Write a book? Nah!' I thought to myself, why not – and here I am.

I am no Shakespeare or Wordsworth or even a wordsmith, having never been good with words, but I do know some real whoppers: words like Dendrochronology and, of course, Paracetamoxyfursenbenroneocyin; but how often do you get to drop that into a conversation? But anyway, I write how I speak and I hope you understand what I am trying to say. I know swearing is a sign of lack of education, but Elsie Fuck-Fuck was her name. And sometimes a well-placed 'fuck off' helps people know exactly what you mean. It's international and worked in every country I have been to!

I am not an educated man by any stretch of the imagination; I have no certificates of academic achievements or qualifications. I am just me and this is my story. I hope it makes you smile just once, and if it does I will be happy with my endeavour to produce the book.

My story… Well, it seemed a good idea at the time!

No word of a lie!

One

Remember being seven?

This will make you smile nostalgically and wish you were seven all over again.

According to today's regulators and bureaucrats, those of us who were kids in the 1950s, 60s and 70s probably shouldn't have survived.

Our baby cots were covered with brightly coloured lead-based paint, which was promptly chewed and licked.

We had no childproof lids on medicine bottles, or latches on doors or cabinets, and it was fine to play with pots and pans.

When we rode our bikes we wore no helmets, just flip-flops and fluorescent 'clackers' on our wheels.

As children, we would ride in cars with no seat belts or air-bags. Riding in the passenger seat was a treat.

We drank water from the garden hose and not from a bottle. It tasted the same.

We ate dripping sandwiches, bread and butter pudding, and drank fizzy pop with sugar in it, but were never overweight because we were always outside playing.

We shared one drink with four friends, from one bottle or a can, and no one actually died from this.

We would spend hours building go-carts from scraps and then went top speed down the hill, only to find out we'd forgotten the brakes.

After running into stinging nettles a few times, we learned to solve the problem.

We would leave home in the morning and play all day, as long as we were back before dark. No one was able to reach us all day, and no one minded.

We didn't have PlayStations or Xboxes, no video games at all. No ninety-nine channels on TV, no DVDs, no surround sound, no mobile phones, no personal computers and no Internet chat rooms. We had friends. We went outside and found them.

We played elastics and street rounders, and sometimes that ball really hurt. We fell out of trees, got cut and broke bones and teeth, and there were no lawsuits. They were accidents and we learned not to do the same things again.

We had fights, punched each other hard and got black and blue. We learned to get over it.

We walked to friends' homes.

We made up games with sticks and tennis balls and ate live stuff, and although we were told it would happen, we didn't have many eyes out nor did the live stuff live inside us for ever.

We rode bikes in packs of seven and wore our coats by only the hood. Our actions were our own and consequences were expected. The idea of a parent bailing us if we broke a law was unheard of. They actually sided with the law. Imagine that!

This generation has produced some of the best risk-takers, problem solvers and inventors ever. The past fifty years have been an explosion of innovation and new ideas.

We had freedom, failure, success and responsibility, and we learned how to deal with it all.

And you're one of them. Congratulations! Anonymous.

I have been reliably informed that I was born on a very wet Saturday afternoon on 24 November 1956. However, I have no recollection of this momentous occasion whatsoever!

My earliest memory of my life is that of happiness and joy. My mum and dad were my world and I think this is the best time to tell you what I know of them. So, ladies first. My mum, Catherine (Katie), was born on 6 April 1922 in a place called Tourmakeady in County Mayo, Eire. She was born and brought up in a small house with some land for farming, which was by all accounts totally inadequate to support them, and I have been told on more than one occasion the hardships that her family endured, like having to walk for miles to school in their bare feet.

I feel that I should mention at this point that for many years I harboured the illusion that such levels of poverty were confined exclusively to rural Ireland. However, my unquenchable thirst for knowledge and in particular my passion for history has led me on a lifelong quest to discover as much as possible about whatever captures my interest and imagination. Consequently, those who know me can testify that I am a mine of useless information. It's rather like what Winston Churchill said: 'People always ask me what I don't know.' Anyway, back to the point... During my quest for knowledge, I realised that the level of poverty and all that goes with abject poverty, such as ill health, high rates of infant mortality and crime, was just as extreme in London's East End at this time. The East End was a shining example of abject poverty, and that was in the capital city of the greatest empire in the world, and that's a fact.

My mum's father died when she was very young, leaving my grandmother with three children: Mum, Tommy and John. After my grandfather died, my grandmother remarried – a man named Jimmy Welsh – and had three more children. So the family now had six children and times were getting harder, so Jimmy left for England to find work. He finally found a job in Scotland and it was there he died of a heart attack not long after, leaving a wife and six children with no breadwinner and no income support, and, need I say, life was tough.

Despite the poverty Mum's family, as well as many others, experienced, she has always said that even during the hardest times she never knew hunger in Ireland, tough as things were. I suppose this was because she lived on a farm and had access to the basics: chickens = eggs; cows = milk and cheese, et cetera. With this in mind I could never understand, especially as a child on holiday, why Irish children would say to me, 'Oh, the famine! The bad English!' And, without fail, I would always find myself in a fight over it. As an Englishman, needless to say I am very patriotic and have been so since a very young age. I don't know why – the Queen never made me a cup of tea or even sent me a Christmas card – but it's just the way I am. Anyway, so I'd find myself fighting with these kids because I couldn't get my head around why they blamed the British for the famine; I mean, we didn't start it. It happened, that's nature, and my argument was that 'If it wasn't for an Englishman, Sir Walter Raleigh, you wouldn't even have had the fucking potato in the first place...' Smack! 'Anyway, the country's a fucking island! Never heard of fishing?' Wallop! I was never strong on diplomacy, even at the age of ten or twelve, and I'm still not today. However, I pride myself on having excelled in the use of bad language. I never swore in front of Mum and Dad, though, for obvious reasons, but being brought up in the council flats meant that swearing was totally accepted.

In the summer of 1938, when my mum was at the tender age of fifteen, she decided to seek her fame and fortune; in other words she set out for England. With the help of a distant cousin and a postal for the grand total of £2, which was a considerable sum of money in those days, she booked her passage on a ship to this Royal Throne of Kings, this Sceptred Isle, this Precious Stone set in a Silver Sea; she came to England!

While on board she met another young girl who was also embarking on a new life. They were to remain friends for over sixty years. Her name was Lillian, known as Lilly – Auntie Lilly to me. I will tell you what little I know about her and her life. She was from Kinsale, which was a fishing community in those days. As far as I know, Auntie Lilly had lost her father, two brothers and her brother-in-law when a boat sunk sometime shortly before she came to England. She also lost her sister soon after this tragic incident when she died in childbirth. Unbelievably the baby died too, and Lilly's mother died just months later, supposedly from a broken heart – I wonder why! Despite such overwhelming circumstances, Lilly found the will to go on and she came to England to make a fresh start, she married and had a son. However, she hadn't seen the last of her bad luck. Her husband was a terrible man, a wife-beating drunk! Auntie Lilly would often walk into doors and get black eyes; their son would wet the bed each night for fear of beatings. His traumatic upbringing had a massive impact on him, and as a result he spent many years of his short life in prison. In fact it was in prison that he died, shortly after his mother's death.

It often makes me wonder how some people's lives are: some have never had pain, so to speak, yet others' lives are filled with nothing but pain and sorrow. But that's how it goes.

When my mum got to England she found gainful employment in a guest house and was employed by people of the Jewish faith, not that it makes any difference, but by all accounts she was treated exceptionally well and they always had her welfare and safety as a priority.

The day Mum would never forget was Sunday, 9 September 1939, the day Britain entered the Second World War, the greatest conflict in the history of humankind! As she recalls, all the residents and the owners, as well as the staff, gathered in the dining room of the guest house to listen to the radio announcement: 'We are now at war with Germany.' As a young girl, Mum did not comprehend the magnitude of the statement; for that matter, who did? The responses of the people gathered around were varied. For some it was a calm assertion of 'it will be over by Christmas' – hopeful optimism!

According to Mum, things did not change much; there was the implementation of the blackout and rationing, but life carried on as normal. Mum, like other people, did not know what to expect – Germans walking down Piccadilly? It was not until 1940, when the 'phoney war' was well and truly over, that things really began to change. The Blitz was something Mum remembers vividly, watching dogfights in the sky over Croydon when visiting her cousin.

It was about this time that Mum had some friends who worked in the ammunition factories and were earning money. It was for this reason my mum was persuaded to join them. However, it was not long before she realised that she had made a big mistake! While she was in service she ate well, just as the guests did, had her washing done by the laundry service, had no bills to pay and still got her wages, however small, once a week without fail. This is why she soon began to regret her hasty decision to work in the factories, but she says it seemed a good idea at the time and I suppose we have all been guilty of not thinking things through at some time or other in our lives.

So Mum does her bit for the war effort, and after the Blitz was over it was full steam ahead on the home front. Mum recalls one of the happiest moments of her life as being on her way to the Shepherd's Bush Empire to see a show with Auntie Lilly and the tram stopped dead in the street and someone shouted, 'The war is over!' Their joy knew no bounds; they hugged each other and cried with joy. So, to hell with the show, Mum and Auntie Lilly made their way to Buckingham Palace, on foot, to join the thousands of others in celebration. Mum says it was the happiest time in her life; she felt so proud to be British. 'But she's Irish' – who cares! However, the story does not have such a happy ending. When Mum and Auntie Lilly arrived back at their digs, the landlady was inconsolable because she had received a telegram that morning revealing the immortal words 'It is with deep regret that we have to inform you that Pte Smith was killed in action on… et cetera.' Her only son had been killed just two days before the end of the war. It just seems to me that some people, for whatever reason, have a charmed life, whether it be in love, wealth, health or happiness, and some, or should I say a few, have these in small portions during their lives; and then there are those unfortunate souls who for some unknown reason know nothing but pain, sorrow and heartbreak.

So after all that, let's get back to Mum and Dad. I've mentioned all there is to about my mum and now it's my dad's turn. Dad was born in the family terrace house on 9 September 1935 in Wales. He came from a normal-sized family. He had two brothers: John, the eldest; then Dad; then David, the youngest. He also had a little sister, Mary. My granddad was a painter and decorator by trade and this was to be the career path my dad would follow in years to come, unlike his two brothers, who decided to work in the pits, mining. The town Dad was born and raised in was, at a time when Britain was largely industrial, a strong mining community and, as such, mining was the biggest local employer.

For a short time my Uncle John, known as Big John, worked in a glove factory and it was there that he made friends with a young lad who loved to sing: that young lad was to become the famous singer, Tom Jones.

For reasons unknown to me, Dad eventually decided to leave the valleys and go to London. Maybe it was the bright lights or the opportunity of greater work prospects that tempted him; somehow I think it was the latter.

So Mum and Dad met at a dance hall, their relationship developed, they married and I came along. So that's about before I got here. Next up's my childhood memories.

Two

1959. My earliest memory was when I was about three years old. At the time we lived in some basement rooms at No. 5 Windermere Road, Archway. My bed, or cot I should say, was a suitcase suspended by rope between a chest of drawers and my mum and dad's bed. I have often wondered, if I was analysed by some kind of psychoanalyst, whether or not they would discover if sleeping in a suitcase affected me subconsciously, perhaps resulting in my love of travel. Or would they more than likely say that it mentally traumatised me and such profound effects have led me to suffer from a degree of claustrophobia – to which I would simply say: 'Bollocks!'

The road on which I lived was a dead end; there was very little traffic and consequently the road was my playground, as it was for many other kids. I have many happy memories of watching my dad walking down the road after work, and he would always bring me an ice lolly.

At the top of the road was Holloway Road, and if you turned left onto it, about the fourth shop down was a sweetshop and tobacconist. It was a proper sweetshop, selling sherbet lemons, rhubarb custards, cola cubes, aniseed twists, liquorice allsorts – and of course, Fisherman's Friend. But alas, this emporium of tooth decay has long since gone and I believe it is now a continental mini-supermarket selling curious strange-shaped vegetables, one-day bus passes and a huge assortment of various alcoholic drinks at a very low price; all of which are advertised by marker pen on luminous star-shaped cards. The customers who patronise such establishments are usually small, red-faced men called Patsy or Jima, who drink copious amounts of this mindbending strong lager, which is commonly known as electric soup, and once the required volume is consumed they spend their time shouting at cars and urinating in doorways.

The basement rooms we lived in were warm and cosy, rented

to Mum and Dad by a Greek called Ekonnic. Anyway, my dad did a deal with him. The deal was that Dad would decorate the house and this 'favour' would be reflected in the rent, OK!

However, although my dad kept his part of the bargain, the part involving the rent reduction soon became questionable. At this time I was happily playing in the garden and the massive garden wall fell on me and rendered me unconscious. As luck had it, my mum caught sight of this catastrophe and rescued me from beneath the small mountain of rubble. I had blood gushing from my head and I was wrapped in a towel and carried in the direction of the Whittington Hospital. Fortunately, a kind motorist stopped when he saw us and drove us the rest of the way. I still carry that scar to this day.

Anyway, Mum and Dad were evicted from the basement dwelling shortly after this incident. I remember all of us walking down the road, laden with suitcases. There was no Citizens Advice Bureau and resorting to legal action was only an option for those with money.

As a result of our eviction I was taken to Wales to live with my grandparents until Mum and Dad could secure a home for us back in London. Well, that was the plan – a plan no one saw fit to inform me of.

We travelled to Wales on the longest-ever train journey to visit my nanny. *Hang on! What's a nanny?* I thought. We soon arrived at a small terraced house and – surprise, surprise – it was raining! Well, it was Wales. I was smothered in kisses and hugs by this strange lady who was my 'nanny' whom I had never seen before, but going by the hugs and kisses she must have liked me.

I don't remember much about my time in Wales, but I do remember that I fell asleep and when I woke up and asked where my mum and dad were was told that they had gone! *Gone? Gone! Where? Why? What about me? Mum! Dad!*

I can't even begin to tell you how I felt. I felt so alone and abandoned. I suppose that's because I was! The empty, lonely feeling was awful. Through a veil of tears I was comforted by my nanny. She had large soft arms and my head rested on her breast, snivelling and crying. But all the consoling and comforting could not erase the blow I had suffered. Nevertheless, despite the veil of tears and hiccups I finally fell asleep. Like I said, I don't recall much of those early days in Wales, but with the love of my nanny I was soon back to my old self, whatever that was.

My nanny's name was Hilda. She was quite a small woman, but as I was only three years old, everyone seemed big to me. When I next saw her, when I was an adult, she was tiny and had the most wonderful feminine Welsh accent. She loved me and was very kind to me and I grew to love her very much indeed. My nanny, to the best of my limited knowledge, had been married no less than five times, which in those days was a considerable amount, and not even a rock star!

My granddad at the time, or let's say my nanny's husband at the time, was called Bert. He was good and kind to me, as my nanny was. I remember that each morning he would have his tea and would dunk his buttered toast into it – novel. Well, if the French can eat snails, need I say more? But, having said that, I followed his lead and it was lovely. However, with the wisdom of age I can now safely say that it was not exactly a culinary delight.

Time passed by and I settled into a normal life; well, as normal as one can be given the circumstances. There are a few things that always remind me of Wales: hills, rain and the smoke of open coal fires. I always seemed to be walking, and no matter where I was going it was always uphill, and it was always raining. Many years later I was travelling down China's Yangtze River and I was hit by that smell of Wales: it was damp; there was the smell of coal fires. I have read that the sense of smell provokes memories much faster than sight or sound. Must be true.

On some rare occasions we would go and visit Granny Parfit. I was never quite sure whose nanny she was, but anyway, she lived in a house which was situated on the top of a very steep hill and we always visited her in the rain. She was bedridden and always dressed in black and was very old indeed, which explains why her face was so full of wrinkles – to the extent that she shared an uncanny resemblance to a dried prune.

Granny Parfit's house was full of stuff. It was so cluttered and I was absolutely fascinated by one particular item, a huge clock that chimed every hour on the hour. It was massive. Strangely, I don't recall ever speaking to Granny Parfit, but I remember quite clearly that whenever an announcement was made that we were to visit her, I was overcome by a feeling of dread as we walked, in the rain, up the hill to her house.

Almost every day I was sent to the shop to buy my granddad cigarettes. This was normal and quite acceptable in those days, as I don't remember any law that forbade the sale of tobacco to three-year-olds. Well, I was nearly four anyway – practically a man!

It was quite a simple task. My granddad would scribble on a piece of paper which, once produced to the shopkeeper, was exchanged for a packet of twenty Senior Service cigarettes, which were placed in my tiny hands. I had not yet grasped the concept of money, and I still haven't. The shopkeeper proceeded to make a note in a large book, and this form of payment was known as 'on tick'.

Sometimes, while going through this procedure, I would be given the cigarettes and an ice lolly as a token of gratitude from my granddad for being a good boy.

It was not long before I decided to exploit his generosity. Each time I was dispatched to obtain his cigarettes, I would find myself pointing to a brightly coloured chart with various illustrations of ice lollies et cetera. I would point to the desired item and watch as the shopkeeper made a meticulous note in, what seemed to be, the world's biggest book. I would then devour the culinary delight as quickly as I could, always careful to remove any evidence, such as traces of raspberry ripple from my face with the sleeve of my jumper before returning with the cigarettes to my granddad.

Well, the game was up! Nothing was ever said to me, but one day I again tried my luck in the shop and I was refused! *How dare he! I will take my fraud elsewhere!*

I was happy in Wales. I started infants or some form of early education at the local school, which was located at the top of a hill. I knew this was important because I was bought a coat. It was a grey duffel coat and I was taken to the big red-bricked building – school – by my Auntie Mary. My name was written on a label and I was left in the playground. I had no idea what to expect, but it was not long before a bell was rung and all us kids were rounded up and herded into a large hall, which smelt strongly of wood polish, and after a lot of names had been called out I found myself alone in this huge hall, wondering what to do. Thankfully a lady came along and asked me my name, which I told her. She took me by my hand and led me to an office and, after what seemed like an age, I was taken to a classroom and I spent the rest of my time playing in a sandpit, which was fun, but I found it hard to understand what the other children were saying as I couldn't grasp the Welsh accent at all! I don't recall much else about my time at this school; in fact I don't think I spent much time there.

One morning I was woken by my Auntie Mary and was told that I had visitors. Intrigued and puzzled, I rubbed the sleep from my eyes and descended the steep wooden staircase down to the kitchen, and to my great surprise I saw my mum and dad there. My joy knew no bounds; the sense of joy was unbelievable. And to add to this overwhelming joy, they had brought me a toy garage with cars and everything! This was, without doubt, one of the happiest memories of my life. There were hugs and cuddles, but within no time at all it was time to go. My heart was broken and I could hardly breathe for the stream of tears running down my face. Sorrow engulfed my very being. They left and the door went clunk. They had gone. I ran upstairs and cried on my bed. My Auntie Mary came to comfort me with my new toy garage, but it suddenly meant nothing to me.

After what seemed like a long time afterwards, I could hear voices in the kitchen: it was my mum and dad. I ran down the stairs as fast as my legs would carry me and into my mum's open arms. They had got as far as the station and could not leave without me, so they came back for me! I was once more on the longest-train-journey-ever back to London, back home; well, home was where my mum and dad were.

I don't recall the method of transport we employed to get to my new home, but I imagine it was a bus. Mum and Dad had rented two rooms at the top of a house in Junction Road, and of course they had to share the kitchen and bathroom. My bath, though, was a tin tub, which was hung on the back of the door when not in use so this didn't bother me too much.

At this time, my mum worked in a paint factory and I was dispatched to a childminder, which I hated, and all I can really remember about this is that I was made to lie down on a sofa, facing inwards all the time. It wasn't just me, though; it was the other inmate too. My time there seemed endless and the only happy time I ever spent there was at Christmas, when the other inmate and I were allowed into the enormous living room, which had a huge Christmas tree in the corner, and we sat around it watching television until our parents came to collect us, at which our joy and relief failed to cease.

Well, that was the end of 1959, the year Castro took power in Cuba, the rock-and-roll star Buddy Holly died in a plane crash, the Hollywood legend Errol Flynn died at the age of fifty, and the era of the Teddy Boys was in full swing!

As my mum and dad worked, I was once again sent to a childminder. Her name was Margaret and I came to know her as Auntie Margaret. She lived in Draton Park and she had a son who was my age, called Boujay. Why? Fuck knows, 'cause I don't! But nevertheless I felt loved and I was happy there. The highlight of my week was Saturday, when my dad would take me to the cinema in Victoria, which played cartoons continuously. I loved them, but I think my dad had even more fun than I did. Unfortunately, however, we always seemed to be home in time to catch the wrestling and football results, which seemed to go on for ever. The object of this exercise was to check the Pools, which even to this day I don't fully grasp. I think you had to predict a team to win or draw. I will endeavour to outline the concept: West Brom 1–Rovers 2; Harrogate 2–West Ham 1; Arsenal 3 – and so forth. If you predicted the results correctly you could win a large amount of money. Well, that was the plan! And like most of life's plans they go bollocks.

Anyway, we did not stay in Junction Road for long, if my memory serves me correctly. It was a bright sunny day that we moved to a house on the Tithe Farm estate in Dunstable, which was miles away in Bedfordshire – or more Luton, really. It was a brand new house; we had our own bathroom and toilet – an inside toilet at that. Things were looking good!

My dad had a motorbike and would travel miles to work.

Work was scarce in his chosen profession as a painter and decorator, and he ended up working for a major car manufacturer in Bedford. Meanwhile my mum would go picking potatoes with other women from the local area, and I would always accompany her. I remember being so cold doing this work with my mum, and the days always seemed as though they would never end. On occasion the farmer would give us a lift on a flat trailer to the main road, where we would then walk the rest of the way home.

Summer turned into autumn and autumn into winter, which meant only one thing – my birthday. I got a cowboy suit complete with a hat and a pair of guns and I thought I was the dog's bollocks. It's funny how some things stick in your mind.

Not far from us lived a family whose name does not matter, but I remember that they were skint. We were skint, but they were really skint. I can remember my dad bringing home small cuts of wood which he had painted in various colours that were available to him, and within no time there were quite a few brightly coloured wooden blocks and they turned out to be a present for the skint family's little girl, Lilly. She was over the moon with her set of building blocks that Christmas. That same year I got a metal toy ambulance, which lasted for years.

In early January my dad brought home a puppy, which we named Lassie. How original! Lassie's sole function was to chew up everything in sight and then shit all over the place. It was also in January that I was sent to my new school, which was miles away. It was a new school and I had fun there, despite the fact that all I seemed to do was cut pictures out of catalogues to make bigger pictures and a big mess in the process. As for learning stuff, that was not part of the plan and I did not stay in this school for long because it was not Catholic.

So now I am on school number three, which was a whole different ball game. It involved learning things like the alphabet, which seemed like a waste of time to me. As long as you knew all the letters did it matter which order they went in?

So there I was with my grey short trousers, snake belt, V-neck jumper and duffel coat, and of course not forgetting the sensible shoes. What the fuck are sensible shoes anyway? Ones that talk polite, or what? Anyway, as it was winter I was made to wear a balaclava. Itchy thing – I hated wearing it.

I remember quite clearly having to learn the days of the week. You know Monday is followed by Tuesday and so on, but me – I just couldn't grasp it and I did my level best to keep a low profile when the teacher went around the class pointing at people to recite the days of the week. Anyway, I managed that all right, but then came the months of the year. Fuck! There are twelve of them and some of them are really long words. My luck ran out as far as keeping a low profile went and I was pointed at to recite the months of the year, so it was 'Monday, Tuesday, April, May, Saturday and June.' Not what she wanted to hear, but it got a great laugh.

At this time in my life, things were quite good, except for the lack of money, that is. When winter came, so did the snow, and Dad could not get to work and life became increasingly difficult, but we managed somehow. The thing is, if you're skint and everybody else is skint, you don't really know you're skint because you're all in the same boat. The estate we lived on was so new that the shops hadn't even been completed and a couple of times a week a converted bus would arrive at the end of the road to serve as a mobile shop. It sold bread, milk, sugar, et cetera. But most importantly it sold sweets, and when the bus would turn up I was in for a Wagon Wheel – lovely jubley! In addition to this mobile shop, there was also a bread van, which would come around. It also sold cakes. I remember one time in particular my mum bought a chocolate cake, which was to be eaten on Sunday after Mass. Well, that seemed ages away, but Sunday finally came at last and dinner was eaten with great haste and I made sure to leave plenty of room for the chocolate cake. So I get a slice and poke it in my gob, and while doing my squirrel impression I started to choke, cough, splutter, spit and cough. My eyes were full of water and my dad slapped me on the back and told me that I shouldn't have 'eaten so fast', or words to that effect, and eventually my entire mouthful of cake ended up on the floor and with it there was a nice bright shiny screw. There had been a screw in the cake! That was what I had almost choked to death on – a fucking wood screw!

Winter turned into spring, and spring into summer and where we lived was a paradise playground because it was one big building site. There were mountains of sand, scaffolding, piles of bricks. It was a great place to play, and as for school, I hated it. I just couldn't see the point of it – why? But I had no choice; I just had to put up with it, as you do. I lived to play outside with the other kids, bikes, toy cars; it was what a child should do.

One morning I woke up to great excitement: Lassie had puppies! There were four beautiful bundles of fluff, eyes still closed. We kept them for a while, but eventually my mum gave them away to good homes and life was much the same, until the big shop opened. That was a big event. It was called 'Wavy Line' and it soon became the focal point of the estate. The thing I remember most about it was a cunning marketing ploy, which was that if you were at a cash till when the bell rang, you would be given a pair of stockings. What if you were a bloke? But anyway, I would be sent to the shop for errands – milk and bread and suchlike – and I was always told that if the bell rang while I was at the cash till I was to get size 11 American tan. It was almost a mantra, and yes it did ring, and I got it right.

So ended 1960. Other events of that year were the death of Clark Gable at the age of fifty-nine and the Sharpeville Massacre in South Africa. The following year, 1961, saw John F Kennedy become US president; Alan Sheppard became the first American in space; Spurs became the first team in the twentieth century to win the cup double; the Berlin Wall started to go up; George Formby and Gary Cooper passed away and Ernest Hemingway committed suicide.

Three

1962 started and it turned out to be a very memorable year for James Hanratty because he was hanged for murder; Chris Bonington became the first Briton to ascend the North Wall of the Eiger; and Marilyn Monroe died.

Despite all of these momentous events, what I remember most about that year was the day my dad came home from work early! This was so unusual and became even more so when we went to a church that had just been built and did not yet even have any chairs. I could not work out why; it wasn't even Sunday. It turns out that it was the day of the Cuban Missile Crisis, when the world was on the edge of World War Three. Even as a child I could sense the unease of the people in the church. Personally I couldn't give a fuck; I just wanted to go out and play. Needless to say my education was not at the top of my agenda. I just couldn't be arsed with it – times tables and all that. I just had no interest whatsoever.

Then one day Mum and Dad told me that we were moving back to London. 'But why?' I asked. 'I like it here.' I had no say in the matter, of course. So in November 1962 we moved back to London. We had what was known as a 'transfer'. We got a two-bedroom council flat, and they got a brand-new semi-detached three-bedroom house. A fair deal if you ask me!

We moved into No. 80 Leyden Mansions in a place called Hornsey Rise, North London on a very wet Saturday afternoon. Mum and I sat in the back of the lorry all the way from Luton to London, which was a long journey – a dark one too. We arrived at our new home at last, just as darkness fell, and we were met by one of Mum's friends, Lily Brooks. She had been friends with Mum since the war and lived close by in Finsbury Park.

The flats were built in the 1920s and looked like a prison, but it was our new home. The ground floor consisted of a toilet, a kitchen and a living room and an enclosed staircase, which led upstairs to two bedrooms and a bathroom with just a bath and no toilet or sink – just the bath! The living room had an open fire, as did the bedrooms, and the coal was stored in a cupboard under the stairs. In the hallway, high up, were two meters, one for the electric and the other for gas, both of which were fed by coins.

The flat had a layout like the ground-floor maisonettes, flats with an upstairs! The first-floor level were ordinary flats on one level. These were reached by a stone staircase from the ground-floor arch, which was situated either side of the yard. Access to the first-floor flats was by a long balcony, which went all the way around the front of the building. The second floor was the same format as the ground-floor maisonettes.

I kinda felt a warming to this place; it felt secure, in a strange way. The flats had lots of kids around all the time, all different ages, which was great, I had someone to play with, and the neighbours introduced themselves to us as we unloaded our few belongings into our humble new abode.

Our neighbours to our left at No. 79 were a very old couple; they had a daughter living with them and she seemed really old too! Her name was Dorothy. They would have massive arguments and we could hear every word they screamed at each other, but, as young as I was, I was sure Dorothy was as mad as a box of frogs!

On occasion her dad would beckon me to him when I was out playing in the yard and ask me to do the 'dust', which was to carry an enormous metal bucket – well it seemed enormous to me! – full of ashes from the coal fire, which was the most common form of heating in the flats for everyone. (Central heating was to me pure science fiction!) So I would stagger down the yard with both steady little hands clasped around the handle of this bucket, and ascend a stone flight of stairs to the shoots and empty the lot down the hatch, trying not to get absolutely covered in coal ash, and then return the empty bucket to its rightful owner. And for this immense labour-intensive task I would be paid the princely sum of 2d! Which I would immediately go and squander on as many sweets as possible!

I remember on one occasion I was asked to do the 'dust' and was invited into the parlour, as he called it – it was just a posh word for the front room – while he went and got the money to pay me for my labours. And I remember, quite clearly, looking at eye level, as a six-year-old, into a glass cabinet, where inside lay a row of medals, which were so shiny! And of which he was so very proud. He told me he had won them in the Great War. The cabinet housed a small collection of old photos of him as a young man in his army uniform, and other artefacts, which in later life I was to find out were known as trench art – things made by soldiers in the trenches. It is very collectable, so I am led to believe. And I remember one day I did the 'dust' and he had his medals out, polishing them, and he even let me touch them. I was so impressed. He must have been a very brave man to get all them medals from the king!

Our other immediate neighbours were a couple called Reg and Mable. Reg was a bus driver, and Mable was one of the first traffic wardens. They had three children – two boys and a girl – whose names I just can't recall.

Next to them lived 'Old Bill', who was old and his name was Bill, so that makes sense. Bill was a retired postman, who had been in WWI and had fought at the battle of the Somme! He would say things like, when it was raining, 'Cor, boy, nothing like the Somme, boy!' Bill lived with his younger brother Frank, and he was a postman too! Ran in the family! He was a veteran of WWII and was captured at Dunkirk. So zee war is over for you, Tommy! Well, in his case, Frank.

If at any time you were skint, you could always knock on Old Bill's door and say the immortal words, 'Do you want your ashes done?' And nine times out of ten he would, or at least he would give you a penny. He was a nice old boy. To this day I have two gold watches he left to my mum, for her kindness to him. All Mum would do every now and then, when cooking a dinner, was allow for an extra portion, and I would be tasked to take it to Bill, which I did, and he was always grateful. But that's the way it was then in the flat that I lived in. Often you would get a knock on the door, and one of the kids would say, 'Mum said have you got a cup of sugar till tomorrow?' Or the other one was 'Have you got a shilling for the gas meter?' And you always did, and you would always get paid back, because if you didn't they would be fucked next time around! Everybody did it sometime or another; that's the way life was and nothing to be ashamed of. If anything, I am proud to have come from such a community; it was a true sense of belonging.

One time I was invited into Old Bill's flat to carry out some rubbish for him. It was, as one might say, a nice little earner. Well, it was my first time inside his home. I was honoured! The place was stacked floor to ceiling with nice neat piles of newspapers, thousands of them. You had to navigate your way around them to do anything; they were everywhere: hallway, kitchen, everywhere! He had no TV and not even a radio! The silence was deafening! He just sat and read papers all day every day! Well, whatever makes you happy!

Friday was always a good day. If you were lucky enough, he or Frank would call you from their front door and ask you to go up the chippa for them. Well, of course you would – it was a nice earner – and the order was always the same: cod and chips twice. And he would give you three shillings to buy the stuff with. The chippa was miles away. Well, it seemed that way; it was up Hazelville Road, which to a seven-year-old was a long walk, but I somehow didn't mind the walk: it was the queue outside the chippa that pissed me off. It seemed to take ages! It seemed the whole world had fish and chips on a Friday night! The only nice part about it was that wonderful aroma that wafted its way down the street, enticing you to buy fish and chips. So once you got the nice neat bundle of white paper, you would bestow thyself with speed to Old Bill, and your reward would be a sixpence, which you would promptly piss up the wall on sweets!

The flats were full of characters; everybody knew everybody. It was such a friendly place: children played safely; there was no traffic; there was always someone standing in a doorway or leaning over the balcony talking to someone! Some people tend to stick out in your mind more then others, like Eddie Omo. Well, that wasn't his real name; that what everybody called him, and I will tell you why!

Eddie was his name. He was a short bloke with thick black curly hair, and was deaf in one ear. Well, if he wasn't, he should've been with the amount of cotton wool he had in it! He

29

was from Wales, I think. And Mrs Omo, known as Cathy, was without a doubt the most ugly woman I have ever seen, and I have seen a few!

Eddie's chosen profession was a dustman, and he wore 'cor blimey' trousers, and he did live in a council flat, and he wore these massive hobnailed boots which made a crunchy sound when he walked. He always wore a brown leather jerkin, which was held together with string, and wore gloves with no fingers. Eddie was a Dustman!

He had three daughters: Ann, Susan and Paula. Anyway, Eddie's old woman fucked off and left Eddie with the three girls and a load of bills. To fuck off from the old man and the girls is one thing, but to fuck off and leave a load of debt is another. As they said, that was taking the piss! So Eddie is left with the girls on his own. No such thing as social services to help him: he just got on with it! Saturday night was bath night. (People just didn't bath every day then; it was the way it was. When I think about it, I always recall the story of Queen Elizabeth I. She had a bath once a month whether she needed it or not! No wonder she was the Virgin Queen: she must have hummed!) So bath night in the Omo house was Omo night. He used washing powder in the bath, hence the name Omo! For fuck's sake, if you did that now they'd lock you up for child abuse! But what I will say, it didn't do them any harm that I know of anyway. But having said that, I didn't fare that much better: I used to have Dettol in my bath.

Eddie was a nice man. Sometimes you would see him coming home from the local boozer, 'The Favourite', pissed, walking along with rubber legs. He was like a ball bearing in a pinball machine, bouncing from inanimate objects on his way home. I never heard a bad word said about Eddie, ever. OK, he got monged and pissed – so what? It's not a crime, and trying to bring up three girls on his own in the early 1960s was not an easy thing to do. So with the passage of time, Eddie gets himself a house-keeper. Her name was Stella. I fuckin' hated her. I don't know why, but I did. She was a hard-faced cow; she always seemed to beat the girls at any given chance. I remember once the three girls were sitting on the stairs in the archway leading to the yard; I asked them what was up? They were my friends. And little Susan said, 'We just don't want to go home. She's horrible to us.' My heart broke for them. The poor fuckers never had a chance!

Eddie's house was like Steptoe's yard, of the popular TV series *Steptoe & Son*. He was always bringing stuff home from the Dust. It was about Christmas time when you would get a knock on the door, people flogging bent gear, all sorts of stuff which would have been 'liberated' from a warehouse or lorry, all kinds of stuff slippers, books and records. But most of all, booze, which everybody bought: martini, sherry, all the festive forms of booze. That's the way it was; it was the way of life. I can say without any fear of contradiction that I never ever knew anyone to be a victim of theft in the flats where we lived, ever! This was for two reasons. One, people had fuck all to nick anyway. (Most people had slot TVs which you would feed money into, but we did own our TV; we were lucky.) And the second reason was that it was the unwritten law: you never stole from your own, ever!

Somehow or other, Stella had loads of Babycham, which was a very popular beverage at the time. It was obviously nicked – unless Stella had decided to open up a local off-licence, dealing exclusively with one product. It was a very sophisticated drink, I'll have you know. In hindsight it was an early form of alcopop.

Her place was full of it, ceiling to floor, crates upon crates, and she was knocking it out for 3d a bottle. She was doing a roaring trade; couldn't move the stuff fast enough. Even the kids were drinking it. (Well, it was cheaper than Tizer.) So it was all sold, stock ran out and so did Stella – with the Christmas Club money. This was where people would pay in a couple of bob each week, towards their added extra expense of Christmas. Well, that was the plan. People did not have bank accounts then – well, not in my flats, as far as I was aware. It was for 'those' people. My mum used the post office to save what she could – a wise woman.

So, Babycham sold, Stella fucked off with the Christmas Club money. She was a very popular person – everyone was asking after her. So the balloon had gone up. Poor Eddie didn't have a clue; she had turned him over too! Eddie was left to deal with a lot of highly pissed-off people knocking on his door, poor fucker! But none called the 'Old Bill' about it. That's the way it was.

Other people in my block were the Gasons: Mr Gason (Dick),

Mrs Gason, Peter, John, Carol, David, Diane, and last, but not least, Sharon. Six kids in a three-bedroom flat.

Dick never seemed to work; why I don't know. The eldest son, Peter, had been 'inside' a few times. John I think had done a borstal sentence and decided to take the path of the straight and narrow, but I have never known anyone to have so many jobs. He would change his job every week, but at least he had a job. Carol worked in a shoe factory. David and Diane were twins and were exactly three years older than me to the day, 24 November, and Sharon was the baby of the family.

I remember when Peter escaped from borstal or some government residential institution, and the Old Bill turned up, knocking on the front door looking for Peter. Mrs Gason opened the upstairs window above the front door and said, 'If you don't fuck off I'll pour this piss pot over you!' Well, they didn't, and she did! Peter tried to leg it out of the ground-floor window and was caught and sent back to the nick.

On the first floor lived Milly and Jack Webber. They had two children: Michael, who was a lot older then me, and Theresa, who was younger then me. They were nice people. Milly was a short woman and rather round in shape, and seemed to spend all her day leaning over the balcony, smoking endless cigarettes and talking to other neighbours who were leaning over the balcony. Michael was a hard worker. I arrived at this conclusion by logic deduction, as he always came home filthy, so evidence would suggest it was hard manual labour that he did.

Along the balcony from them were a father and son, Dick and Charlie Alsop. Dick was retired, and Charlie... well, he could never keep a job down. Why? Fuck knows, but what he did do was piss all his lot up the wall on model Airfix kits and records. Well, it was his money, but he was thirty-two! But he was a happy soul and a very kind person, and that's what matters.

On the top floor were a few families: the Huckles, the Bamseas, and a woman whose real name escapes me, but she was commonly known as Elsie Fuck-Fuck, not because she was easy with her sexual favours but because every other word was 'fuck'. 'It was fucking cold today'; 'I'm going down the fucking road.' Honest to God, every other word was 'fuck'. The trouble was, it became quite infectious; you started saying it too, which in my case would result in getting a glowing red ear caused by a well-placed smack on the side of my head from Mum! In 2005 a female comedian, Catherine Tate, brought 'Nan' to our TV screens. Well, that was Elsie Fuck-Fuck.

Not long after we had moved in the flats, I started my new school. This was school number four. It was St Joseph's Roman Catholic Primary School, which was situated halfway up Highgate Hill. I was bought a complete new school uniform: grey short trousers, a blue-and-white snake belt, grey socks and, of course, sensible shoes again; a grey shirt, a grey V-neck jumper, the compulsory school tie, which was blue and white, and a school blazer with the school badge emblazed on the pocket. Even if I say so myself, it was very smart. I even smelt new, as new clothes do.

Each morning I would walk to school from my humble abode. It seemed miles away, but I soon kinda got used to it. Well I had no fucking choice in the matter. I was the only kid in my flat to go to this school; most of, or I should say all, the other kids attended more local schools, but they were not catholic, and I was.

The school was an old school, which I would say was built in the 1850s. It had loads of character and I loved it – the building that is, not the education aspect. Each morning the playground would be full of kids playing: some playing hopscotch, girls with skipping ropes, boys playing football, and me. At nine o'clock a teacher would ring a hand bell, and we would all form up in our classes. Once we were all formed up, we would all march off to the school hall, where we had assembly and school prayers, which was followed by any important announcements. Once that was done we would all smartly march off to our designated classroom to have the register called. It was more like a roll call!

Then it was down to business – education – and I fucking hated it. I just could not get a grasp of it. It seemed most of the lessons were religious based: Bible stories, New Testament, Old Testament. Lots of emphasis on religion.

At eleven o'clock it was break time, and the milk monitors would hand out to each of us a small bottle of milk, which you had to drink, and it was nearly always warm. I fucking hate milk!

But if you didn't drink it you would be reported by the milk monitors, the chosen few. Things people do to wear a badge! And even worse is a badge that gives power, a sign of authority which equals power, which equal bollocks to me. I have never been impressed by rank – ever. I never wanted to have power or rank; I just want to be happy.

So after you stuck the milk down your neck, you could go out to play. When possible, I would stay behind and look at the books, even though I could not read a word. My reading was shit, but I could look at the pictures in the book. Besides, I hated football; I just could not see the sense in it.

Sometimes we would play war! Fucking great! Making noises like a machine gun or hand-grenade noises. That was for me!

After play it was more learning stuff, which I hated; it was so boring. I could not wait until lunchtime just to get out. We would be marched over to the dinner hall and made to eat dinner, and you had to clear your plate. Once it was cleared you would have to go and stack your plate up, and by the pile of empty plates was a nun. We had some nuns as teachers, but her job was to make sure you cleared your plate.

I hated mash potatoes with a passion, so what I would do was stuff my pockets with them, go up to the 'Duty Penguin' get the all clear, and promptly empty my pockets. Sorted!

When I got home I would have my proper dinner, but for some of my schoolmates the school dinner was their main meal of the day.

Friday was the best day for school dinner: it was always fish and chips. I am sure the school meals were well planned for their nutritious value, but they tasted shit to me.

On Tuesday the whole school was marched up the hill in twos, all holding hands, boys next to boys and girls next to girls, up the hill to the church for confession; after confession was lunch.

After lunch, two or three coaches would turn up to take all the boys off to some place in Highgate to play football all fucking afternoon. I hate football…

As I had no football kit I was made to stand on the side and watch the game, every Tuesday. I would have to watch a load of little schoolboys kick a ball between two sticks. My joy knew no bounds!

Wednesday was Mass day; once more hand in hand up the hill to go to Mass.

Now this is true: when I was young we had to fast prior to receiving Holy Communion. Anyway, there was a boy in my class called Gary. His mum and dad owned a boozer, and Gary always had money, which he would blow in the school tuck shop at morning break. But even with all his loot he stank of piss, and nearly every time we walked up the hill I was his partner.

So you would be kneeling down, hands clasped in prayer as you do, and more often than not Gary would do one of two things: piss himself or faint. Or if it was a good day he would do both!

So you would be on a direct line to God, and then you would feel your knees getting wet, and then sometimes you would hear a clunk, and that was the sound of Gary fainting. To add to this he would be manhandled out of the church.

And I saw a nun once, beating him to the rhythm: you – *smack* – must – *smack* – not – *smack* – faint – *smack* – in – church – *smack*! On the back of his bare legs.

So not only has the poor fucker wet himself and fainted; for good measure he's been beaten up by a dwarf nun, poor fucker! I wonder what ever happened to him. If you did that to a child today you would be locked up.

Thursday was my favourite day. It was the day we always had art in the morning, and after lunch we had swimming. I loved swimming. It was the highlight of my week, off to Hornsey Road swimming pool.

On Friday it was up the hill again to Benediction, column of twos. This was my favourite service, I loved the smell of the burning incense; it was almost intoxicating and had a great sense of occasion. But after Benediction it was home time and freedom!

On a Friday evening one of the local schools had the Penny Club. This was a place to go and play. You paid your penny and they let you in, hence the name; not rocket science. You could play on the coconut mats, the big wooden horse, climb ropes, play on the apparatus, and you could play rounders, but for some reason or other you could not play football. There is a God!

So I meet a pal of mine, called David, and he was in a shit state. He was, one might say, rather distressed. What had happened? He had borrowed his older brother's football – of course without his consent – and it had been confiscated by the dreaded 'Carrie', the school caretaker. So if he goes home without the ball, his bigger brother is going to turn him into a pile of snot and blood! So Davy boy is shitting himself.

So he asked me to help him. What could I do but say yes: he was a mate. So off we go. To say I was a bit apprehensive was somewhat of an understatement.

According to our intelligence, the ball was held in the 'Carrie's Hole'. Let me elaborate on that: it was kept in the caretaker's office, which was situated at the back of the school, where there were piles of coal. Between the mountains of coal was a stone staircase, which led to a long corridor, at the end of which was a door which was the Carrie's office, The Carrie was a tall bloke – well, he was tall to us, but we were only kids. He wore a peaked cap and had a limp, and always seemed to be shouting at people, mostly at us. He was a feared man! And we were about to enter his lair! My part of the mission was to keep dog (keep watch). Well, that was the plan, and I was not at all comfortable with it. At all. My bottle was going; I was terrified. But I was here now, so 'let's do it' was the attitude that prevailed. It soon dawned on me that this was isolated cover! If he turned up, we were fucked: nowhere to run. This was not a good plan! So Dave descends the stairs to the office on tiptoes, and for some reason or other I find myself right behind him. I don't know why, I just did. Probably the safety-in-numbers instinct. So we are both on tiptoes past the mountain of carbolic soap, past the massive pile of shiny arse-paper, God! That corridor seemed miles long; my heart was pounding. I am mentally screaming *come on, come on!* Closer now. We are next to a huge pile of tins of floor polish. *Come on, come on!* My bottle was going big style, I can tell you! At last we get to the door. *Hang on: what if it's locked?* races through my mind. Too late now: we are at the door. As Dave clasped the handle, it turned and made the loudest squeaking sound in the world as he opened the door. *Come on, come on!* The door is opened at last, and in the 'office' is a load of books and loads of crap but, in the corner on a desk, was the ball! I say, 'Just get the fucking ball and get the fuck out of here! Come on, come on!' He grabs the ball, and that's it: we are ready to go!

As we are about to break the land speed record, he says, 'Stop!' Me, incredulously, 'What?' I can't believe my ears. Stop? What the fuck for? My heart is fit to bust. In the corner of the office was an old sink, which had shaving kit, the usual razor, brush and soap, and towel, and a toothbrush, so he picks up the toothbrush and heads past me. Why? What I had failed to notice was just opposite the office door was a pile of old blankets from the first-aid room. Ah! But on that bundle of blankets was what must have been the oldest dog in the world. It was also the fattest dog in the world, fast asleep, thank god! So what did Dave do? He picked the dog's tail up and stuck the business end of the toothbrush up the dog's arse! Yep! And the dog didn't even wake up! He then put the toothbrush back in the cup. I was in hysterics; I couldn't run for laughing as we ran along that long corridor, but I had this mental image of him brushing his teeth and turning to Mrs Carrie and saying, 'Where did you buy this toothpaste?'

Saturday was pocket-money day. My dad would say 'Here's your spending money.' I would think to myself, well, what else am I supposed do with it? I would head off to Jarman's in Crouch Hill and buy toy soldiers, as you do.

My mum got a job in the kitchen at the Whittington Hospital, working nights. It was here that she made some firm friends, one of which was Ann Brooks – I always called her Auntie Ann. She was from Germany, and had met her husband Bill just after the war, and they got married. She was a wonderful person and I liked her very much. They had two children: a daughter called Peppie and a son called Verna.

By all accounts, or I am led to believe and the story goes, during the war Bill served in the Royal Navy, and after the war he and some of his chums got in the supply-and-demand trade: people demanded and he supplied. Well, in other words, he was smuggling, one might say life's luxuries, from France to England, with the aide of an MTB – a motor torpedo boat – that he and his chums acquired from a port in North Africa. By all accounts he did quite well and decided to quit while he was ahead. The secret is to know when you're ahead, but this is what I was led to believe. How true it is I don't know.

On Sunday morning at ridiculous o'clock, Uncle Bill and the kids would turn up, and we would all go off to Petticoat Lane. It was an amazing place. We would walk down Club Row and look at all the animals for sale; it was like a zoo. But it also had some strange-looking people. Some were street entertainers. I remember one bloke who was tied up in chains and put in a sack, and within a few moments he was free. I was fascinated. Then there was this other geezer; he was an old man with a beard, and he would push this pram with a great big gramophone playing music. Strange, very odd, but it takes all sorts.

So it was almost Christmas time again and the table was in the front room. Mum would do dinner and whisky, and Dad and I did Tizer. This was the life! That Christmas I got a train set, which Dad and I had great fun with lying on the floor watching a train go around and around in front of the open fire. And it was the traditional dinner – big dead bird. What I can't work out is if turkey is so wonderful, why do we only have it at Christmas? I didn't and don't like turkey, but yet we have it every Christmas.

Four

So ended 1962 and 1963 started. This was the year the Labour Party came to power, Beeching did the rail cuts, and there was the Great Train Robbery. Ian Fleming's James Bond came to the silver screen with *Dr No*, and the Beatles found fame with *Please, Please Me*. *Dr Finlay's Casebook* was prime-time viewing, along with *Emergency Ward 10*; Richard Greene was Robin Hood.

Saturday afternoon was perpetual day TV: horse racing and then wrestling, which usually came from some town hall north of Watford and had such famous names as Jackie Pallo, Mick McManus, Les Kellet and Billy Two Rivers, to name but a few. These blokes would go at it big style, but what always made me laugh was the old women sitting ringside in the front row, screaming and shouting insults. And if the 'Baddie' was thrown out of the ring they would lay into him with their handbags. All very ladylike.

After the never-ending football results would be *The Adventures of Robin Hood*, which was compulsory viewing for all eight-year-old boys. After this was the BBC *Dixon of Dock Green*, which stared Jack Warner as a good old-fashioned Metropolitan police sergeant, and each episode had a moral to it. It was all bollocks anyway. Later in the evening was the *Black and White Minstrel Show*. Now, work this out. You have a load of white blokes, blacked up and dressed up as Negroes, singing songs that were written in the 1850s! What was all that about? And this was prime-time Saturday-night viewing?

Life was pretty much the same week in week out. School was the same; I still hated it. But this was the time I joined the Cubs, the 59th Holly Park. Now I want you to imagine the scene: Baden-Powell, sitting in his local boozer, and he says to his mates, 'I got a great idea! I am gonna get a lot of little boys, get them to wear short trousers, take them up the woods and give them a woggle! What do you reckon, mate?' Whose response, I would imagine, would be, 'Fuck off, you'll get fifteen years for that!

No, but on a serious note, I think the Cubs and Scouts, Boys' Brigade and Brownies and Guides do truly wonderful work with young people. I had a great time doing all sorts of Cub stuff, but I never seemed to earn any badge. I just was not interested. It was about fun, which it was.

I learned to swim and loved it, but before I actually learned to swim I almost drowned. I remember it as if it was only yesterday. I was in the pool, obviously, and I don't know exactly what happened, but I lost my footing, and I flapped. I panicked, and then I went all drowsy, and I kinda felt at peace with myself, is the best way I can describe it. And then I blacked out. The next thing I know I was being pumped out on the side! I didn't know you could drink that much. Well, in fact I'd been drowning. So I am sorted, sitting on the side, with a towel around my shoulders, and as I was sitting there my mate Eddie Heinz says to me, 'You OK? Do you want a glass of water?' Do I wanna glass of water? I nearly drowned! And he asks me do I wanna glass of fucking water! Eddie, Fuck off! After this I learned to swim and eventually got so good that I gained awards.

Once a week at school we all traipsed across to the big hall for PE and we would do all sorts of stuff on benches and big coconut mats, all very energetic stuff, running around in our bare feet. But every now and again, we would do country dancing. Fuck knows why – we just did. The format was as follows: there would be a line of four boys and a line of four girls who would face each other and on the given command would do required steps. Simple. Oh, yeah! I don't know what type of dance it was, some form of barn dance I think, but for sure it was not a tango or foxtrot. Anyway, I am standing next to a geezer called Gerry, who was a tall boy, and I know I was thick at the education stuff, but Gerry was really thick! At least I could write my name, but Gerry was not even at that level.

So we are all standing ready to dance, and the teacher says 'Left hand out', so we all put our left hand out. So far so good! Then she says 'Now your left foot forward.' We all comply, but Gerry plonks his right foot down. Then the teacher comes over and says to Gerry, 'Show me your right hand!' and Gerry does, then she says, 'Show left hand' and Gerry shows her his left hand.' Well, I am thinking, he hasn't got a lot of options, so he shows her his left hand. Her response was 'Good' and she walks away. Then she says 'Left foot forward' and we all do it, but not Gerry. He plonks down his right foot. This time the teacher has got the right arse! And she shouts at Gerry, 'Show me your left foot!' And Gerry just burst into tears and, through a veil of snot and tears, proclaims, 'No one showed me the feet!' The poor fucker could not get to grips that left was left, whether it was feet or hands. But she sorted it for him.

Before I knew it, it was Christmas time again, and just before Christmas, Mum and Dad bought a brand-new electric fire. This was wonderful: it meant almost instant heat. No more waiting for the coal fire to heat the place; it was sheer luxury. And to add to that, Mum and Dad bought a carpet. Yep, a carpet. Well, it was a big rug, but it was a million times better than lino on your cold feet. Life was looking good.

That Christmas morning, when I awoke, Santa had brought me a nice big red shiny fire engine. It was fantastic; I was over the moon. Christmas and birthday was the only time of the year I got toys from Mum and Dad, just the same as all the other kids. It was a time to look forward to.

So once more the kitchen table was in the front room, and more copious amounts of dead bird were consumed by all. It was the only time of the year we all sat at the table together and ate; that's the way it was. Mum would cook the dinner and have the occasional nip of whisky. That was the only time Mum had a drink. Dad just might go potty and push the boat out and treat himself to a light ale, but more often than not he was a Tizer or Corona man. He just didn't have that thirst for alcohol, thank God!

So ended 1963, and the new year was upon us. If my memory serves me well, that winter we had rather a lot of snow. I love the snow even now. Snow has a silence about it; I don't know why, but it does, and I love it. I love the sound of the noise it makes when you walk on new snow.

Where I lived is a place known as the Wooden Bridge, and it

was an abandoned railway line that had a wood bridge across it, hence its name: simple! It is now a nature walk from Highgate to Finsbury Park.

The Wooden Bridge was our playground, and it was brilliant. We spent many happy hours playing there as kids. But the Wooden Bridge was not just a bridge to us; it was, one might say, a rite of passage. What you had to do was climb up onto the brick pier at the end of the bridge, and tightrope across the bridge on the very narrow parapet wall. It was a true test of 'Bottle'. We all done it, once.

There was this massive tree which had a rope swing on it, and a massive knot tied at the end, which was our seat, and we would all jump on it, four or five of us, swinging out, as the tree was on a cutting. When the swing swung out, it seemed to go so high. It was real fun. We would swing out and jump, the object of the exercise being to see how far you could jump. Ah, but to do this you needed to gain as much altitude as possible. It was a true test of personal courage or stupidity! But we did it, and I don't recall anyone actually breaking any bones. But boy! I have seen some classic landings that any stuntman would be proud of!

Sometimes when we were out playing over the Wooden Bridge, we would play Robin Hood, as you do. So we would all go off on a bottle hunt. Let me elaborate on this. In those days, when you bought a bottle of fizzy drink – R Whites, Corona, and of course Tizer – you had to pay a deposit on the bottle of 3p (old money, of course), so we would go off on a bottle hunt. But my mate Rob said, 'Fuck this. I got a better idea!' And the plan was to climb over a load of gardens that led to the back of Harry Harvey's.

Harry Harvey's was a local papershop that sold newspapers, sweets, fags – all the usual stuff sweetshops sold. But this was the only sweetshop that never sold fireworks, the reason being, some years before they did, and I don't know what actually happened but the lot went up on a Friday evening. Yep, the lot! Rockets, bangers, Catherine wheels, the full monty! Nice firework display! It was going to happen sooner or later, as the shop was owned by three brothers who always seemed to have a fag in their gobs.

So we climb over the gardens to get to the back of Harvey's, over the wall – which I might add, had a load of broken glass imbedded in cement on the top of the wall, which was a real pain to climb over but we did – and passed a load of empty bottles over, and then brought them in the shop for the return deposit. It worked like a dream. Nice one, Rob.

So, once financially solvent, we would head off down the paraffin shop, which was on Hazelville Road. It was the local hardware store, and it sold paraffin, hence its name. At that time we had a lot of West Indians living in Ashley Road and they all seemed to use paraffin as a source of heating. The paraffin shop sold all sorts of stuff, as one might expect, but the focus of our attention was the lengths of bamboo that you could buy for 2p, a length of string, and a long, narrow green cane. So with a bit of elbow power you could make a serviceable longbow, which was the object of the exercise. So for 3p you got your bamboo, a length of string and an arrow. Job done.

So we were all kitted out, and to make it more fun we would sharpen the end of our arrows on a brick wall, and then divide up into two groups and fire sharpened arrows at each other. Great fun!

But one time – for some reason I was not involved in this game – one of the lads fired an arrow and it hit Alan, my mate, right in the eye! It stuck in his eye, ouch! He was taken to hospital and nearly lost his eye. That put a downer on that game for a while. Well, at least a couple of weeks anyway.

I loved the winter months, but especially November, for the following reasons. One was Guy Fawkes. This was when the Boggies came out! Let me tell you what a Boggie is. It's a cart with two pairs of old pram wheels, a cut-down length of scaffold board, and a steering mechanism made from a large nut and bolt and controlled by a length of washing line. Primitive but effective. And of course no brake, except your feet.

All the kids in all the flats would go 'Wooding'. This was an annual event where every kid took part. The idea was to collect as much burnable material as possible. We would go into what we called 'bombed' houses. Well, in fact any house that was empty was fair game to us. We would descend on it like a plague of locusts, and if it was burnable it was looted. Loads of kids all ages.

It would resemble a medieval carnival: kids dragging doors, wheeling old tyres; you name it, we had it away! But once we got the firewood, we would have to hide it, because there was fierce competition between each block of flats as to who would have the biggest bonfire, and therefore we had to hide it and that was a real problem, but we always managed to, in all sorts of places.

But every year, Blythe Mansions always had the biggest fire by far. This was down to two important factors. One, Blythe was a massive block of flats, and therefore had more kids, which equals more labour to gather wood. And two: they had flat roofs on their flats and it was an ideal place to hide their wood, which they did! Sometimes all the kids from Blythe would go on a wood raid. They would muster a small army of kids and charge into Leyden Mansions and loot all our wood! Bastards!

The other enjoyable aspect was going 'Guying'. This an acceptable form of begging. What we would do – and you always seemed to do it with a mate, one to guard the Guy and the other to speak – was to say 'Penny for the Guy, mister?' The average Guy was an old pair of pyjamas stuffed with old rags or old newspapers, and a papier-mâché mask, and that was your Guy!

When I think about it, Guy 'Guido' Fawkes was a seventeenth-century soldier of fortune and a very brave man, and it is said he was the only man to enter parliament with honourable intentions. He suffered under immense torture and died for what he believed in, but I bet he would be mega pissed off to be remembered as an old teddy bear with a papier-mâché mask.

This brings to mind one of the funny stories of my youth. Me and my mate Dave decided to go Guying, made the Guy and off we go, but all the best pitches are taken, outside the local boozers and bus stops. It was the first come, first served basic, and we were out of luck, so it was fuck this!

So we dump the Guy, and head off down the road to Seven Sisters Road. And we find ourselves outside the local department store, which was called B B Evans. So we decide to have a look around. And then Dave says we'll nick the fireworks. I wasn't too happy with it, but I go along with it. So we go up to the toy department, and it's on the top floor, and it was gearing up for

Christmas, and loads of toys; and more important it was here they sold the fireworks.

This was the plan. I keep the big fat bird busy. The sales woman was a massive old woman, with blond hair and really thick glasses. They were like the bottom of milk bottles, and when you asked the price of anything she would hold the item right up close to look at the price. In other words she was blind as a bat, which was well handy for us. Dave was gonna get on all fours, tuck his school jumper in his trousers crawl along behind the glass cabinet to the display of fireworks and loot as much stuff as he could. When he was loaded, he would jump up and make a dash for the fire-exit door, down the stairs, and away. Good plan. So I go up to fat bird and ask her how much was that big Lego set – yeah, the one on the top shelf. So she huffs and puffs and goes off to get a stepladder. Yep, it's all going to plan so far so good. Well, she's halfway up the ladder, and Dave jumps up and legs it to the fire doors. I am right behind him! The doors are flung open with a loud crash, and we're off! Jumping down flights of stairs in one leap. Then we hit ground floor. Bang wallop, the doors are banged open, and we are legging it up the road like a pair of lunatics, legs like pistons, hearts pumping; turn a corner and dive into a front garden and hide behind a privet hedge in complete silence, except for our beating hearts. We are looking at each other, not a word said, just in case we are being chased, and any sound would give our hiding place away. The silence was deafening, but nothing. We had got away with it! YES!

So we decided to divvy up the loot – well, in this case the fireworks – so Dave pulls his jumper out, and all the swag hits the deck with a muffled clutter, and to my surprise and horror was a massive firework. It was huge! It cost 12/6, which was an absolute fortune then – 52p in today's money. But that was a vast amount for a firework. 12/6, fucking 12/6! It was like a fucking car battery with a fuse!

But what are we gonna do with it? Fuck knows, was my suggestion. And then Dave said, 'I know. Follow me.' Well, I did. And we come to this telephone box, and he just looked at me with such a grin on his face. I could almost read his mind. Yep, we would set it off in the phone box!

Good plan. So we go up to this telephone box, and it was an old-style phone box; you needed the biceps of a weight lifter to open the door. So we tug it open, and as usual it stank of piss and stale tobacco. It was one of the old Bakelite phones; you had to press button A; then, when you got the ring tone, you had to press button B. Simple.

So we lit the blue touchpaper, or fuse, and ran across the road to wait for the show to start!

FUCK! To our sheer horror, this old boy goes into the phone box. Me and Dave just looked at each other in terror, shock, and most of all fear!

Then all hell breaks loose! *Wiz, whoosh, bang, boom, whizzz, freerrr...* The sounds were amazing, but the colours and light – it was a light show to behold, even though it was a rather confined indoor extravaganza! All we could see was the bloke's hands through a veil of purple smoke. It was like a mime artist, with hands frantically trying to find the door! And to our great relief, he bimbles out of the box, smouldering, and the look of horror on his face! Just think about it: you're in a phone box – 'Hello dear, I am—' Crash, bang, *whizz, whoosh,* what the FUCK! We looked at each other and ran for our lives!

On Bonfire Night, in the late afternoon after school, all the kids would be out. All hands, no matter how tiny, would help build the fire. It was a sight to see, and at about six it was lit. Everyone seemed to come out to watch the fire. Mums and dads would read instructions and stand well back and watch the fireworks go off. It was a real community thing. But us boys would do all sorts of crazy things. The most popular was getting hold of a small scaffold pipe; place a rocket in it, light it and point it at your target, and whoosh! You've got yourself a bazooka. Great fun!

The other sport of the evening was firing Roman Candles at each other. That was fun too! Madness, but fun!

In the next block of flats in Leyden lived a young girl, Carol. She was a nice kid, and her dad was a bus driver, a small man, but again a nice bloke. So he comes home from a hard day driving a No. 14 bus, with this massive box of fireworks under his arm. Little Carol was so excited! She just couldn't wait for her dad to have his tea and then come out to join in the festivities, of course with the massive box of fireworks.

So, tea consumed, Carol's dad emerges with the box. So he opens the box. Carol can hardly contain her excitement, and her dad goes off to light one of them. As he is doing this, the whole box goes up! The whole lot! Whoosh, bang, whizz, nice display! What must have happened was her dad always smoked, and he must have dropped some hot ash into it. That was the only explanation I could come up with. Carol was devastated!

I loved the smell in the air the morning after Bonfire Night. It was a wonderful smell.

The next big date for me was the Lord Mayor's Show. Uncle Bill would come and collect me, and Peppy, Verna and I would head off to watch this wonderful show. It was fantastic: all the floats, the soldier, sailors. It was a great day out. We would always stand under the bridge at Ludgate Hill and freeze, but at least we were dry, as it always seemed to rain.

And then it was my birthday, and I got a toy castle, for my ever-increasing collection of toy soldiers.

At school, things were pretty much the same, and we started to gear up for Christmas, making endless paper chains, and all sorts of decorations for our class and the school hall.

But the main event in the school calendar was the Nativity Play. This seemed to take a massive amount of preparation, making the scenery, costumes and props. It was all labour-intensive stuff, but anything was better then school work. Anything, anything.

I always got the part of the bloke at the back with a tea towel on his head and that was fine by me. I never got a speaking part, but that was fine by me too. I didn't have to learn any lines.

This epic was performed on two consecutive nights, which gave all the mums and dads a chance to see the show. It was always a full house, and, after the production, mums and dads would be invited to come to the class and see our work, which in my case was not a lot!

I was not allowed to watch TV until five o'clock. I don't know why, but that's the way it was. My favourite programme was *Blue*

Peter. I loved the show, the way it was presented; they would tell you interesting stories and how to make things. But what always pissed me off was that you always needed sticky-backed plastic, and I could never find a place that sold it!

I would try and make the Advent Candle, and it always turned out to be a pile of shit! I am sure they had a professional Advent Candle maker!

The other programmes I would enjoy was *Mr Pastry* and *I Love Lucy*, but most of the time I was out running around, playing with my mates. My mum worked nights and I would spend time with her before she would go to work. Dad was always sitting by the fire with his head stuck in the paper, and I would play with my toys in front of the fire. Heavenly bliss.

I still could not grasp the concept of reading, but I had comics: *The Beano*, the *Dandy*, and the *Topper*. I could not read a word, but I would look at the pictures and make up my own stories. Mum and Dad had no input on that front whatsoever. Why I don't know; that was the school's job? And it was Christmas time once again, table in the front room, and more dead bird! That year I got a machine gun. It was great; it had batteries and made a real loud noise, with flashing lights. I made as much noise as possible. Well, it was Christmas!

I was lucky compared to some of my mates in the flats. One of my mates' parents virtually lived in the boozer, and his dad would come home pissed up and knock his wife about on a regular basis. One Christmas I will never forget. My mate – I will not mention his name – all he got for Christmas was a small jigsaw. His mum and dad go down the pub and leave him on his own! They come back, pissed up; his dad kicks the jigsaw all over the place, throws the dinner all up the wall, and gave his mum a black eye for good measure! Happy Fucking Christmas! The poor fucker never had a chance in life. I can still see him sitting on the steps of the pub with a packet of crisps and a bottle of Coca-Cola. Other than his free school milk and school dinners that was his basic diet.

What I do know is, as soon as he could, he joined the army, where he owned his first full set of clothes. Last I heard he done well. Well, he could not have got worse!

Five

So started 1964. We had Harold Wilson in power, with a Labour government, and the US found itself heavily involved in a foreign war, called Vietnam. Some things don't change. And Nelson Mandela, goes to jail for a long, long time! This was when the greatest Englishman after Nelson died – the death of Winston Churchill. The Moors Murders shocked and horrified the country. And the Beatles got an MBE.

This was the time I was taken to Ireland, by my mum, on a boat-train. It was the first time she had returned to her native land since 1939, twenty-six years. We got the boat-train to Holyhead, which seemed to be the world's longest train journey ever! With what seemed hundreds of other people we boarded the boat. It was absolutely packed, but we managed to secure a seat in the lounge, and then we headed off to the restaurant for some grub, and I remember I had an enormous plate of egg and chips. It was, to coin a phrase, handsome! Not long out of the port, the sea turned rough, and boy it was! Everybody was staggering around like Eddie Omo on a Saturday night. I have never seen so many sick people at any one time, ever. People were vomiting all over the place; the toilets were full. It was horrendous. But for some reason or other I was not sick at all, even with a belly of egg and chips! The journey seemed to last a lifetime, though it was only a few hours. But it seemed a lifetime, especially for those poor souls hanging over the side being sick.

We docked at last – dry land. But we then ran into another problem – there was a train strike and we were stranded. It was havoc, I can tell you! But with a bit of good fortune, Mum heard someone say Castlebar. Castlebar? That was our destination, so Mum goes over to the man who said the magic word, Castlebar, and started to talk to him. He was with his wife, and they were trying to get to Castlebar, in Mayo, and the plan was to hire a cab. So the man was talking to another man, who was gonna be our cab, and the man agreed to share the cab with Mum – at a price, of course. So Mum and the man hand over a load of dosh to the cab man, who goes off to get some petrol. Well, that's what he said! And he's gone a long, long time and eventually returns, and he's pissed, wankered, monged out of his nut! He would have to drive because he was in no fit state to walk!

The man who did the deal with Mum was not best pleased, to say the least; so a right row starts, shouting and pushing. Anyway, we get our money back off the drunk, and then the plan was to hire a car, which we did, and drove for hours to Castlebar, and we finally get there. It was in the middle of the night, so Mum phones her friend and he came to collect us. It had been a very long journey, and I was ready for my bed, or anyone's bed for that matter!

At last the car headlights fell upon this single-storey house, which was whitewashed and had a thatched roof. It was real picture-postcard, typical Irish cottage. The house, one might say, was innocent of luxury. It had a stone floor, and they cooked on an open fire with a massive pot, just like a witch's one, and my nanny was sitting by the fire. She was an old, old lady, dressed in black, with a very hairy chin, and had a funny smell, and to add to this she was smoking a pipe! This was nothing like my Nanny Hilda.

The house was situated on the side of the road. It was very small and had no inside toilet and no running water. The water that was needed had to be brought up from the well, which was at the end of the field, and was brought up to the house in a bucket.

I would be sent down to the well to fetch the water with a big metal bucket, so I would bimble down to the well, lean over it and do my very best to fill the metal bucket. It weighed a fucking ton! I would then stagger back, holding it with both hands, and the sharp metal edge of the bucket would cut into my exposed legs and of course I would spill it all over myself. So I was wet, cut, and very pissed off!

There was absolutely nothing to do but look out of the window and watch the rain. The high point of the day was midday, when the radio was turned on and it would take time to warm up, and at the precise time the angelus bell would ring, and everyone would say their prayers. This was very strange to me, but I had to join in this twice-daily ritual, every day! To relieve my boredom I would go and watch one of my relatives milking a cow. I had never seen a real cow up close. They're fucking enormous smelly things, and all they do is shit all the time!

What I want to know is what was the first man doing to a cow when he discovered you could get milk out of it? Just give it a thought for a few moments. Yep. Odd, or what! Once the cows were milked they had to be mucked out. The place was full of cow shit and straw, and I had this enormous pair of wellies on that belonged to my Uncle Martin. But they were size 52! Well, they seemed that size to me. So, as necessity is the mother of invention, they put a load of crunched-up newspaper in them so they would fit me. Well, it was better than wearing sandals, trust me!

I don't think I have ever been so bored in my whole life, ever! After dinner in the evening, Mum and her neighbours would go off visiting people in the village, but it didn't seem a normal village. The houses were miles apart, and it was always the same formula at each house that we visited: tea and biscuits, and end up on the 'fire water'. Whiskey!

They would talk for hours and hours, yap, yap; it was mind-blowing boring. You would not believe it!

When it didn't rain I would walk up to the Burkes. They lived up the road and it was the local village shop. It was the type of shop that sold everything, from shotguns to coffins, and that's no word of a lie! But what I do recall about the shop was it seemed to have the highest counter in the world. You had to stand on your tiptoes to be seen to get served, and anything you bought was always wrapped in brown paper by Mrs Burke. I wonder did they wrap up the coffins?

The Burkes were a large family and a wide range of age. I think I recall four boys and three girls, so nine in total, the average size of an Irish family in those days. I would walk up and play with the children, but they always seemed to be at school or studying. Well, I suppose there was fuck all else to do! But when we did play, it was great fun, playing in the barns and other assorted outbuildings. They never seemed to have toys like I did but managed to occupy themselves. They were wonderful kids, not one bad bone in any of their bodies; smashing kids.

Just down from the Burkes was the Gibbons family. There was Corrie Gibbons, a large jolly woman who was always smoking; she was a very kind woman. She had four sons, and I think three daughters. Corrie was a single parent. I don't know if she was a widow, or if her old man was working in England, or if he'd just fucked off. Fuck knows. But what I do know was that they had fuck all. But they were as kind and loving as anyone I have had the pleasure to meet. It's a funny thing: I have been fortunate to have done some travelling in my life, and I have seen poor people in Africa and in South America, and the poorest people seem to be the nicest to be with.

In 2007 I was in the Sahara Desert, as I love the desert and feel quite at home in that environment. I love it. There is something about the place; it makes me feel so humble with the magnitude of it all. And as for the desert sky at night… well, I can't find the words to describe it! Anyway, I decided to do my level best to try and stop smoking again, and only took a few packets of fags. So puff, puff away as you do. So this night I am sitting around the fire with our guides and try to communicate with them. I loved to watch them talk over the flames of the open fire, their ebony faces weathered by the sun, and their teeth looking like pearls in their mouths as they yapped away. So I open my last packet of fags and take out a fag, and, as I do, one of the boys asks me for a fag by using sign language, but I had thrown the empty packet on the fire. I then broke my last fag in half and we had half each. He was chuffed to bits. So I have my half-fag and decided to hit my scratcher (get in my sleeping bag). I always sleep in the open, never use a tent, because you can't see the stars at night if you're in a tent. As the sun came over the horizon, which is a sight to behold, I was woken by my mate the smoker, with 'aiwar, aiwar, aiwar.' He had made a brew, just for me. How kind: what a nice gesture. It still tastes like camel piss, but we became mates. He had no English, and I had no Arabic, but we were kinda mates.

Well, it's not what's in a man's pocket: it's what's in his heart. And the window to a man's soul is his eyes!

But, having said that, I did have a couple of fights with some kids. What it was, because I was English, I hated anyone bad mouthing my England! I don't think they disliked me as a person, but the 'English' generally. They would bang on about the bad English, the Black and Tans, Oliver Cromwell, but the one that got me was the issue of the famine. For fuck sake, we didn't start the fucking famine! And if it wasn't for an Englishman, Sir Walter Raleigh, they would never have had the potato in the first place! And it's a fucking island. Ever heard of fishing? Der!

It was always so cold and wet. A lot of the time I would find myself standing on a chair, turning the handle of the butter churn around and around, endless turning. All this to make butter. For fuck sake why don't you just go up the shop and buy it like normal people? I would spend hours looking out of the window, looking at the lake – it was called Loch Mask – which was only a field away, but what can you do with it? Nuffink!

On occasion it might get really exciting and I might even see a boat on the lake. I could hardly contain my excitement. Fishing, I am sure, is a great sport to some people, but me, I don't get it. You stand there for a lifetime with a big stick and some string with a hook on the end of it, trying to catch a fish. Why not buy one and save a lot of time and effort? I suppose it's a way of doing nothing and looking like you are doing something. Well, that's my reasoning!

Just by the lake was Paddy Welsh's. This was the local boozer. Mum and I would walk down to Paddy's at night with the aid of an old lamp, and me in my massive wellies, in the rain of course. What a laugh!

So I would find myself sitting in the corner of this tiny pub with a packet of crisps and a bottle of Cidona, which was an apple-tasting soft drink, watching a load of people talking, most of whom wore flat caps and drank a drink called porter. My joy knew no bounds!

Sunday was Mass day. It was best clothes on, shoes polished, and a very long walk to the local church, which to me was miles away. God, I could not wait to get back to London!

What I remember most about Ireland, apart from being bored senseless, was one night I was taken up to one of the nearby farms by car. Yep, me in a car in Ireland. Things were looking up; I was getting the prick of all this walking stuff. Anyway, I witnessed the birth of some piglets, from a massive mummy pig, obviously! It was very noisy and very smelly. Apart from that, I was not impressed whatsoever.

At last came the day we were going home. At last! The train strike was over and London here we come.

So it was back to school and all that education stuff, Mass and football, but at least it was England.

The event of the year was the death of Winston Churchill. I was glued to the TV, watching his funeral. I was so impressed with all the pomp. And this was the year that a new pop music show came to our TV screens: *Ready, Steady, Go!* It sounded all very sporty to me, but it was so popular; it had pop stars like the Rolling Stones and the Dave Clarke Five, just to mention a few. Yeah, it was OK – for girls!

I was jumping about on the furniture as you do. Well, Mum was in bed after a night shift, so I don't know what happened but I end up going arse over tit and hear a crack. It's my arm. Did it hurt or what? So I stagger up the stairs, whimpering in a veil of tears and snot as you do, and wake her up.

And she goes into one for waking her up. Walloped for waking her up! This was not my day! And then she realised something was not quite right, like I had a broken arm!

So we go and get the 210 bus to the Whittington Hospital and wait a lifetime to be seen – nothing's changed there you'll be glad to know – and I end up having my arm set in plaster of Paris up to my elbow, which was a real pisser. It meant I could go to school, but alas no swimming. FUCK!

The highlight of the TV viewing was on a Sunday night. It would be Roger Moore as the Saint, which was followed by *Sunday Night at the London Palladium*, with a line-up of top stars, such as Charlie 'Hellow My Darlings' Drake, a popular Irish group called The Bachelors, and this entertainment extravaganza was hosted by Bruce 'Nice to see you, to see you nice!' Forsyth. Other popular TV programmes were *The Baron*, *The Rag Trade*, and *Bootsy and Snug*, which was a situation comedy about National Service.

But my favourites were *The Beverly Hillbillies*, and *Hogan's Heroes*, which was set in a German prisoner-of-war camp.

After the school summer holidays I was put in Miss O'Conner's class. She was great; she actually took time out with me and realised something was not quite right. What I mean was I always sat at the back of the class. Well, you would do if you had a Dinky toy car in your pocket! But I was transferred to the front row. Shit!

Anyway, I would copy stuff off the blackboard, and I still got it wrong. One day she gave me a letter to give to my dad, which I did. So I go home and give Dad the letter, when he's having his dinner, and I go into the front room to watch TV. Then Dad comes to me and says, 'David, count the bars on the budgie cage.' So I go one, two, three, four, et cetera. Then he announces, 'There's nothing wrong with your eyes!' and rips the letter up! And that was the end of that! Now, have you ever tried to count the bars on a budgie cage? Well, think about it!

However, the school doctor comes to the school and I have an eye test, and not a budgie cage in sight! So I am sent to Manor Gardens to the optician's – I might add under great protest. I hated that place. The last time I was in Manor Gardens, I had had a mouthful of fillings without any anaesthetic. Fuck, that hurt! So just the words Manor Gardens struck fear into me.

So the day came and my mum takes me, and I need glasses. It was like someone turned the light on. OK, I had to wear these awful pink fucking glasses; they were the National Health issue glasses. But now I could see what was on the blackboard, and things started to change for me. I actually developed an interest in things, like history, and with the help of Miss O'Conner things began to change. I was able to read the Janet and John books, which were a wonderful Ladybird series. Basic storylines, but at least it was a start. I think my reading age was two!

Things started to fall into place, and I developed a real passion for history, and Miss O'Conner came up with the novel idea that if I liked history, she would encourage me to read history. Good plan! And I started to read when I was nine.

Well, as for maths and sums, I am fucking useless. I know two and two aren't yellow, and how much is that? Is this enough? We had to learn our times tables, which wasn't rocket science; all you needed was a good memory.

Once more it was my birthday, and I got a model by Airfix of the sailing ship the *Royal Sovereign*, which looked fantastic on the box, but when you opened it, it was a pile of brown plastic. But my dad made the kit with me and after a few evenings it was completed.

It was Christmas Show time at school, and it was all hectic stuff, rehearsals and dressing up, and of course not a sign of a speaking part, thank God!

My dad had a workmate whose son was in the Scouts, and he seemed a lot older then me, and was big time into the Scouting bit. He had loads of badges up his uniform arm, and did all the camping bit. And he got Dad and me tickets to the 'Gang Show', which was a show put on by the Scout movement. It was very professional stuff, I'll have you know. It was a wonderful evening; they sang all the well-known songs like 'Riding Along on the Crest of a Wave'. It was a night to remember.

Six

So ended 1965, and 1966 began.

The most memorable event of that year was when England won the World Cup. Big Deal! I remember it quite well. I went out to play and the place was like a ghost town. The only thing missing was the tumbleweed blowing down the road! And I am sure it was very important to a lot of people who wear bobble hats; but me, I would rather watch paint dry – any colour!

It was also the year that the master of the silver screen released the classic film *Dr Zhivago*, a wonderful film which I didn't see till I was much older.

My only real experience of the silver screen was the bedlam of Saturday morning pictures, which each of the local cinemas showed on a Saturday morning from nine till twelve. It cost 6d to get in. The place would be absolutely packed with hundreds of screaming kids. The format of the morning would be some short cartoons, a short film by the British Children's Film Foundation, which always seemed to have Melvyn Hayes in it and all real goodie-two-shoes shit, and then a serial, and then the main feature, which always seemed to be a Hollywood B-movie about cowboys and Indians.

Sometimes the film would break down and the place would go mad! All the kids would stamp their feet and boo!

During the interval there would be competitions up on the stage, with kids doing hula hoop and all sorts of things, but I was too busy sucking the life out of my jubilee lolly.

In the afternoon I would take myself off to the local swimming pool in Hornsey Road, where I would spend as long as possible until my time was up, and then walk home with red eyes and a neatly rolled-up, chlorine-smelling towel, eating a bag of chips. This was the life.

Then one day at school, something happened that I would remember till the day I die!

I had a good mate in my class called Eddie Heinz. We had the same mindset, if you get my drift. We had no interest in education whatsoever, and we always played together. We always seemed to be in trouble; nothing major – playing-with-our-Matchbox-cars-during-the-lesson type of thing or being caught playing marbles in the cloakroom during assembly. Nothing worth capital punishment!

It was absolutely pissing down with rain, and it was playtime, and when the weather was that bad we were kept in class; fair one. We used to have these wooden desks and they were old and very heavy. The lid opened, and you kept your books and Dinky cars inside! There was a girl in our class; her name was Eve. She had blonde hair and the bluest eyes you ever did see. And to add to her beauty she was a great drawer. But she was a girl! Yuck!

What sticks out in my mind is that she was left-handed. Now this may not sound relevant, but it was when we had PE and if it was rounders, because if Eve was on your side, you would win! She would whack that ball for miles – well, at least over the far fence, which meant someone would have to walk over and climb the fence to get the ball, which meant you could have a leisurely plod around the post. It took them ages to get the ball – a bit like cricket without the wicket, and you didn't have to wear big white jumpers. I could never work out why they didn't have anyone fielding over the fence? DER!

So back to the chase. Anyway, her desk was opened and the next thing it's gone whack slap bang on her little hands. OUCH! That's a big ouch, right across her fingers. She hit the roof. Well, she would have done if her fingers weren't trapped in the desk!

She was honking big style, tears and snot, the lot! Why do you always get a head full of snot when you cry?

So she's taken off to casualty, just down the road, in a veil of tears and hiccups. To say it went 'Loud' is an understatement. So now there's a full investigation as to what happened.

This must have been serious. Now, we were taught by Penguins (nuns) and the headmistress was a Madame Paula, and she turns up, and she summoned Mr O'Conner, who was her deputy and who was a very strict teacher, and in no way related to my teacher, Miss O'Conner, who for some reason was not in that day. God, I wished she was!

So Mr O'Conner got a face like a smacked arse. And the next thing I know is there was a lot of little fingers pointing at me. 'It was David Edwards, sir!'

It was me? I was in the frame and I didn't do nuffink – 'onest!

So I am told to go and wait outside the office. This was a very bad sign; this did not look good!

All the indications were I was in for swift and merciless punishment. I just had this bad feeling in my blood! I was terrified. I am standing outside the office. I felt like the only person in the world, and I felt this is going to be painful!

So I am looking out of the window and I saw my class go in a column of twos to the big hall. Strange, it's not PE day. And then they're followed by another class, and then another class. This is looking bad. I don't know why, but it did; maybe because every eye was falling on me.

Then after what seemed an age, two prefects came for me, so now I am under escort to the main hall. My bottle is going, but I had to keep a grip!

As I enter the big hall, all eyes were on me, and I was escorted up to the large stage at the end of the big hall, and I see Mr O'Conner with a long bamboo cane in his hand. Fuck, this is going to be painful!

Then he goes into one – blah, blah, blah, girl, girl, blah, blah, girl – he was going into a long one. But no matter what I said, I didn't do nuffink, I might as well have been talking in Swahili. I was ten.

I was told to put my hand out, which I did, even though I say so myself, it took a huge amount of mental and physical discipline to put your hand out and keep it there and wait for that pain. Whoosh, whack! Fuck! The pain was incredible across my little outstretched hand. Pain. But I was not going to cry, no fucking way! So I bit the inside of my lip. Whoosh! More pain. Bite harder. Whoosh! I got six of the best; the fucking pain! After the punishment was carried out, I walked alone, along and off the stage, but I kept my dignity!

I made straight for the boys' toilet and spat a mouthful of my blood. My hands were on fire, and then I had a great idea: I would run cold water over them, to take the burning away. This was not a good plan! It felt as if my hands were on fire! The plan was bollocks! I locked myself in the toilet and cried alone, and in silence!

After a short time, I sorted myself out, and my mate Eddie shows up, looking like a puppy that has just pissed on a new carpet, and asked 'Did it hurt?' My response was in the form of 'FUCK DID IT!' and then from his pocket he gave me a gobstopper – a true mate. Behind every grey cloud is a silver lining, but in my case a gobstopper, which was like sucking a snooker ball!

When I got home I said nuffink to Mum and Dad, because if I did they would have said 'It's your own fault', so less said the better.

The next morning in the playground I was a celebrity. They all wanted to see my bruised hands. My misfortune had earned me a bit of a reputation as a hard nut, which was unexpected but kinda nice for a boy, and did my ego the world of good.

Then I saw her. She came over to see me, and she had bandages on her tiny hands, and she said, 'I told them it wasn't you,' with the biggest blue eyes you ever did see! And then she said, 'Did it hurt? Did you cry?' And I said 'no' on both accounts with a great deal of pride. OK, I lied! And then she said, 'You must be so brave.' I felt ten feet tall and a man. It was worth the pain!

She told them I didn't do it and it was an accident. Did I get an apology? Did I fuck!

It was summer once more and our holidays seemed to last for ever. We were always over the Wooden Bridge, all day long, and sometimes when we – I mean most of the kids – were flushed with dosh, we would get a Red Rover, which was an early form of a one-day travel card and cost the princely sum of two bob – in new money 10p! And we would spend the whole day hopping on and off Routemaster buses all over London, walking around the West End, looking in the posh shops and just having fun. The best day we had was one day my mate bought some stink bombs from a joke shop in Tottenham Court Road, and we set them off in the lift of Selfridges and for our trouble got chased out of the shop. Well, it was fun!

Eddie and I were great mates. After school we would go around the Archway and look in the toy departments of the Co-Op department store, and then head off to Woolworths, to look at the toys as you do. We never had a pot to piss in; in other words, we were financially embarrassed. So we would go on a bottle hunt and get the money back on the deposit – 3p – then head off to a shop called 'the British Tat', which was a junk shop situated off one of the roads of Dartmouth Park Hill, and go and buy some picture cards.

Nearly all the little boys of my age collected picture cards. They would come with a packet of tea. They had an illustration on one side and on the other was information about the illustrated side. They produced cards on various topics – British butterflies, flowers – and for the princely sum of one shilling you could send off to get the album to stick them in, if you so wished. At one time, cigarette companies did the same, and the cards are now very collectable today.

The other source of cards was bubblegum. You would buy your gum and get about four colour pictures of popular TV series such as *The Man From U.N.C.L.E.* and *Thunderbirds*, and one set was dedicated to the American Civil War.

We would play games with them at school, games called tippy-top and knock-you-down. The object of the game was to flick your card on the floor, and if your card touched your opponent's, you would win, and all the cards thrown would be yours. The other game we played was knock-you-down. This involved a few cards being leant against a wall, usually at a forty-five-degree angle, and you would try and knock them down by flicking your cards against them. The one who knocked the last card down won and scooped up all the cards that were thrown during the game. It was a very popular game played by little boys. Funny, I don't recall any girls ever playing that game. So off we would head to the British Tat with our loot, and for a penny you could buy a bundle, of ten cards held together with an elastic band, from how one might say this child of Abraham, a penny is a penny, my boy! We would bowl into the shop and stand at eye level at the counter and point and say, 'We wanna buy some cards, mister.' But what really, really interested me was not the cards but what he kept them in. It was a light-brown suitcase, which was absolutely covered in stickers of various sizes and colours and shapes, with exotic pictures of places like Zanzibar, Shanghai and Casablanca, and I recall quite clearly thinking to myself: I don't know where they are, but I am going there one day! Even just to buy the stickers!

Sometimes we would head off into London via the No. 14 bus and hit the museums all day long; no lunch, maybe a pocketful of sherbet lemons, and that was your lot, mate. I loved the science museum. I liked the gadgets, but most of all I loved the scale models that were on display. The detail was amazing!

I don't recall any of my mates in the flats going away on holiday; it just didn't happen. The most you could hope for was a family day out to Southend. One day I had a day out with my mum and dad, the only one I ever had, ever. We got the train to Southend from Crouch End, via Barking. It was a beautiful sunny day, and I was going to the seaside with Mum and Dad. It was one of the happiest days of my childhood.

When we got there, our first stop was to the Chamber of Horrors, which was housed in the replica of the *Golden Hind*, which was Sir Francis Drake's ship, and it was wonderful. But I was not too sure about the Chamber of Horrors, which showed various methods of torture. For a family day out? After that, we walked along the long pier, which seemed to go on for ever and ever, but I didn't care. I had a massive toffee apple to munch on as we strolled along the pier; the sun was hot and the breeze was cool, and the sea looked like someone had sprinkled it with shiny diamonds. At the end of the pier was an amusement arcade, full of machines that ate your money and made all sorts of noises when you won anything – that's if you did! After that we walked back to dry land, and fish and chips. This is the life! Then we went into the Cerson, which was a huge funfair that had a massive big dipper, which my dad took me on while Mum waved us off. It was very high and very scary, but I was with my Dad, and I knew I was safe because he had his big strong arms around me. And I fell asleep on the train home.

Then one day my dad took a day off work and took me to the Tower of London. It was here that I was bitten by the love of history. It was a castle in London and it was fantastic. I was so impressed with all the suits of armour, but my favourite place was the museum of the Royal Regiment of Fusiliers. It had guns, uniforms and model soldiers. It was the best! And I had a day with my dad, and that was priceless.

As kids we would do all sorts of things to occupy ourselves, like 'scrumping', which is a form of acceptable theft, from people's gardens. But we never ate what we nicked; it was the excitement of doing it. The only time I stayed indoors was when I was ill, and that was rare.

My mum would sleep most of the day, as night-workers do, and I was left to my own devices, safe in the knowledge that someone would look out for you. Well, that was the plan! But that was not always the case. On this particular day I was playing with a mate of mine called Peter, and we decided to do some wood carving, as you do, so, as necessity is the mother of invention, we used the kitchen drawer for our tool selection. Peter got the bread knife and I got a pair of scissors. So we got these lumps of wood and away we go. But soon after we started, I stuck the pair of scissors deep into my hand between my left index finger and thumb. It went straight into my hand. Fuck it hurt. It went straight in and was sticking out of my hand. So I am wailing like a gooden, blood running down my arm, supporting my elbow with my right hand as the blood dripped onto our new carpet. And the scissors were still sticking out of my little hand.

I ran out into the yard; I needed an adult and fast! As usual, my mate's mum was leaning over the balcony with a fag stuck in her gob. I cried 'Can you help *me*?' and her reply was 'You're not my kid.' Them words burned deep into my heart, like a branding iron. But good old Uncle Bill, the old boy I carried the ashes for, came to my aid and got Mable from next door to sort me out. She held my arm and very slowly pulled the scissors out of my tiny hand. It hurt sooo much! I was crying with the pain. Boy, that hurt. But once the scissors were out of my hand, the blood came with them. I was beginning to think was there any more blood left in me? So she wrapped a towel around my hand and was going to take me to the hospital, and as I was outside her front door ready to go, she looked up at Peter's mum, and I can still see the look on her face: it was utter and complete contempt. That did Peter's mum no favours whatsoever. She was then an outcast from our small close-knit community. Fucking right too!

And just as we were heading off to the hospital, my mum comes back from the shops with a look of horror on her face, and I was terrified that I had ruined the new carpet, but mum didn't give a shit about that: it was me who took priority. And we head off to the Whittington Hospital once more. I hated hospital. I hated the smell of them. They always had a real strong smell of some form of disinfection about them, and this time I was seen straight away, and for my trouble I was given two stitches and a tetanus injection. And for being such a brave soldier I got a box of Maltesers, which was very nice, thank you very much. I think the only thing more painful than that was going to see *The Sound of Music*. God, that was real pain: singing nuns.

So I spent my last year in primary school, and once more I was in Miss O'Conner's class, and I was selected with some other kids and put into small groups for slow readers – fucking slow: I hadn't got started! Summer soon turned to winter, and it was my birthday time, and I got an Action Man. Yes, I know it's a doll, but it was a doll for boys, and I had many a happy hour playing with it.

Christmas had a build-up to it. Mum would go out shopping all the time and I would spend my time trying to find my Christmas presents under their bed or on top of the wardrobes – all the usual hiding places – but I could never find them. Anyway, mum comes back from shopping one day with loads of brown carrier bags, full of stuff. And I helped her unpack on the kitchen table – you never knew, there might be sweets knocking about. Then she produces a dark bottle of some stuff, and I asked what it was and she said it was drink. Well, I could work that out; I couldn't read but it didn't mean I was that thick. However, I ask her could I have some, pretty please? And Mum poured me out a small glass, and I drank it – hello! This is all right! So I hatch a cunning plan, which was, when she goes out I will head straight for the cupboard and have myself a glass or two of what I found out later was Emva Cream sherry. So Mum goes back out and I go and pour myself a very large glass of this nectar, and I drink it like it was Tizer. Fucking hell, then it hit me! I was pissed! I got sick all over the place, and then I had the spinning ceiling, the full monty. I was wankered!

So Mum comes home and finds her little cherub, drunk as a lord, vomit down my V-neck jumper. And she could not stop laughing and said it was my own fault 'for being greedy'. Yep, that's a fair one! And I paid the price in full, as I always do! It was a memorable Christmas for that alone.

So the table was back in the front room and more big dead bird to eat, Mum sipping whisky, and Dad and I on the Tizer, as ever. That Christmas I got a Johnny Seven, which was the latest must-have toy for young boys. It was a machine gun and rocket launcher, combined with a grenade launcher. It was the dog's bollocks.

This was the year of Aberfan, when a coal slag heap slid down and engulfed the tiny community school, and 116 children lost their lives. I had a distant cousin who escaped, by being off sick that day. A whole generation was wiped out; it was a true disaster! It was also the year that Walt Disney died, which was very sad too. Would that be the end of the cartoon?

So it was 1967, the year of the *Torrey Canyon*, the oil tanker that ran aground. It was the year that the Hollywood legend Spencer Tracey died, and the year of the Six-Day War. And Francis Chichester sailed the world single-handed. What an adventure that must have been! And those long-haired layabouts, the Beatles, released the *Sgt Pepper* album. At that time of my life I had no interest in music whatsoever. The only time I would listen to the radio was when we came home from Mass on a Sunday. I would listen to *The Clitheroe Kid*, a radio comedy show of a little boy's adventures from some place north of Finchley. And then it would be *Family Favourites*, which was the armed forces radio service. It was then our services served all over the globe, and to tell you the truth I thought BFPO was a place and not British Forces Post Office. It was a bit like in 1982, when the Argentinean forces invaded the Falklands, and I was not the only one who thought they were in Scotland!

I was always shit at geography at school. It was stuff like what was the wheat production of Canada? But why? Who gives a fuck? But no one told me where Rutland was, or what a visa was. And how to get to Paris from Munich? No! It was so boring!

What I could never work out was this. If you're from Germany you speak German; if you're from Greece you speak Greek; and if you're from Poland you speak Polish. But why is it if you're from Holland you speak Dutch, and not Hollandish? Fucked if I know why!

Having said that, I had a mate at school called John. He lived with his auntie, who I thought was a bloke. She always wore a blue mac and a beret. I would often go to his house and play with him. He was an avid model-maker, and I might add a very good one. He had loads of them: models of the classic Hollywood horror characters like Frankenstein, Dracula and the Hunchback of Notre Dame. He was shit at reading, but he always had his head stuck in an atlas. He knew every capital of every country, mountain ranges and rivers; he was a walking atlas. But he never stopped licking his lips, and for years he had this bad rash around his mouth. I wonder why?

We ended up in secondary school together, but at the early stages he would bunk off school and would spend ages walking around Highgate Cemetery. He knew nearly all the graves' names and dates. He had a fantastic memory, but he was failed by the system. He just could not get to grips with the reading-and-writing stuff, and as for maths, don't even go there! But yet he could memorise places on the map! Odd, very odd. And he also collected bus tickets. Odd, very odd!

On Sunday afternoons there always seemed to be a black-and-white war movie. Well, considering we only had black-and-white TV, it was obvious! All the films seemed to have John Mills in the lead role; he was either in the navy or in the army, and it was good stiff-upper-lip stuff! If it wasn't a war movie, it was (or always seemed to be) a cowboy film with John Wayne doing his cowboy stuff.

Seven

At my school there was a huge emphasis on religious education all the time, and there were these major events in the Roman Catholic calendar of life. The first big one after your Baptism was your first confession. This was very important, because if you did not make your first confession you could not make your first Communion, which was a real biggie!

We had to practise for our first; we had to learn all the correct prayers and the correct procedure. It was rehearsed all the time as to what prayers to say and at what time.

So the big day came and we all marched up that enormous hill in a column of twos, all holding each others' hand, up to our church, which was St Joseph's. And we all entered the huge church in complete silence under the eagle eyes of our nun teachers. The church was enormous and it had a feel about the place; it was imposing, it was an important place, and it was God's House! I used to think to myself God had a lot of houses; I wonder where his bedroom was?

The church had a wonderful aroma about it; it had a smell of candles and the smell of wood floor polish, mixed with the aroma of fresh flowers which covered the altar, and which were strategically placed at the feet of the popular saint. But the final ingredient of this wonderful aroma was that of the strong scent of the incense burned at Benediction. It was one big overpowering smell, and I loved it! It was by far the biggest building I had been in to date. Well, it was God's Gaff! So we all entered and sat down on the great big long wooden pews in complete silence. The silence was almost deafening, and we all waited our turn to go into the confessional box and to tell God all our sins. And it was 'Bless me, Father, I have sinned.' I had loads: where do you start? So I came clean and spilt the beans, the lot! And I was given my penance. I had to say so many Hail Marys and loads of Our Fathers, and he told me not to sin any more – 'my son'. Well, that was me sorted with God! Clean slate. Well, at least for a while!

Next up was a real 'biggie': the First Holy Communion. This was a real whopper, I can tell you. This was the real 'biggie' in the Roman Catholic Church, and once more practise, practise; up the hill in a column of twos, all holding hands; practise where we would sit, when to stand, who would be to your left and to your right; what prayers to say at what time; practise, practise… I was beginning to think I would be married before I had my First Communion, but it was better than all that education shit! But this just had to go like clockwork, and God help anyone who fucked up. Well, that was the general feeling and we were all very nervous about it. Well, I was.

The big day came at last. I had my bath on the Saturday night, with a very generous helping of my favourite bath salts, Dettol. I stank of the stuff. Mum had bought me a complete set of new clothes and it was not even Christmas or my birthday; this was important. So, bright and early on that beautiful summer's sunny morning, I awoke and got dressed in my new Communion suit, which was grey and had short trousers. Well, I was not a man yet, so it was shorts. And I got a new shirt and a dickey bow. Yep, a fucking dickey bow. I hated it with a real passion: a fucking dickey bow! But hang on, that was not the worst of it, Oh no! I had to wear a pair of knee-length white socks! Oh no, not these! Please, pretty please, Mum; please don't make me wear these. Please! But I had no choice in the matter; that was the rig of the day and that was that, I was sooo pissed about it; these were what girls wore! I just hoped no one would see me. I would never live it down!

But even worse was to come. My mum put Brylcreem on my hair. I hated it. Why did I have to have that stuff on my hair?

My dad put a suit on. I had never seen him in a suit before, and he looked so big and so smart. He didn't have to wear white socks or even Brylcreem. He was a real man! And he was my dad. But I must say he did have a slight aroma of Old Spice. Well, it was not Dettol.

My mum bought a new hat for the big day, and this was a very special occasion and we all looked so very smart indeed and it was time to go. We had to wait for my aunties, Lilly Corbett and Lilly Brooks. Well, in fact they were not my real aunties: they were my mum's lifelong friends. They met during the war and became great mates. Lilly Corbett was from Ireland, and Lilly Brooks was from the East End of London. And every Saturday without fail, Lilly and her only child, Johnny, would come and visit Mum and me. Johnny was so very precious; he was kinda wrapped up in cotton wool. He was not allowed to get dirty, ride a bike, climb a tree. He was sooo very precious; in other words, a real mummy's boy! But on Saturday both Johnny and I would be dragged around all the shops in the world; well, at least all the shops in Nag's Head! But for some really strange reason we would always end up in a women's shoe shop. Why? What is it with women and shoes? I am fucked if I know. I am a bloke, OK? Now I have never, ever been out with the lads on the piss, and heard one of the lads say, 'Cooor, look at her shoes!' Never, ever, and that's no word of a lie! So after Johnny and I had been dragged around the shops we would be home just in time to watch the wrestling, and then Robin Hood and his merry men do their stuff; real boys' stuff!

At last we are all ready to go, and our chosen method of transport was the No. 210 bus, a single-decker bus that ran from Finsbury Park to Hampstead, via Hornsey Rise.

When we get to the church, the whole place was packed. The courtyard was full of people, and, to my sheer delight, I noticed that all the other boys were sporting white knee-length socks. What a relief! So we all looked fucking stupid! At least no one could take the piss! And we all had dickey bows. It must have been a compulsory dress code for the day.

All the girls wore a kind of, what you might say, wedding dress, and they all looked so very pretty. Well, for girls!

Well, it all went according to plan, as far as I could see. No one fainted or wet themselves and it went like clockwork, thank God! So we all gather outside in the church courtyard, and then the camera is out. My mum combed my hair and straightened my dickey bow, and 'Smile!' Click! The moment was kept for posterity.

It was then both of the Lillys gave me an envelope, which I opened with excitement. And to my joy and surprise, in each was a nice new ten-bob note. Ten shillings paper money; real paper money! I was a man of wealth and limited taste! I was loaded!

So I have the princely sum of a 'Nicker': one pound. But it's true what they say: no pain no gain. Well, it was worth the Brylcreem, but I am not so sure about the white knee-length socks; I would have rather not worn them for any amount of money! Dignity has no price. Well, that's the way I am!

After what seemed ages – all the grown-ups never stop talking, do they? Yap, yap… come on; I need to spend this money, I am thinking – we at last start to move. Thank God! The sweetshop will be closed soon! We walked down the hill from the church, Mum and my aunties walking arm in arm, talking and laughing. My Auntie Lilly Brooks had a wicked laugh; it was great when she laughed aloud, which she did often, and loud. It would always make me laugh, always! Dad and I followed up at the rear, me holding his large rough hand with my tiny sweaty little hand. He seemed so big and so strong; he was my Dad! And I loved him so very much; he was so very special to me! Now, as we walked down the hill, Mum crossed the road. I knew what this meant; it could only be for one reason, and that was the 'Catlic Shop'. I will elaborate. Going down Highgate Hill on your left was a small parade of shops, as is to this very day, but among those shops was the Catlic Shop. It was an old smelly shop that sold rosary beads, religious statues in every size you could think of, bibles, prayer books, hymn books; all the God Stuff. Well, to us it was God's Shop!

It was then that I realised God was Irish. Well, think about it: he lived with his mum, his mum was a virgin, he had twelve drinking mates, and he was a carpenter. I rest my case!

The Catlic Shop sold Irish newspapers, such as the *Cork Examiner*, and other Irish newspapers, and newspapers about the Church, and they also sold other items from Ireland, Galtee cheese and other stuff from the Emerald Isle. It only seemed to be opened on a Sunday, and Holy Days of Obligation. The shop was owned by two very strange men. They were brothers and were quite strange to me; they were so servile, ever so humble, real Uriah Heaps, and they talked like old women, and they always seemed to be wearing tweed jackets and V-neck jumpers, and hairy ties. I don't know if they wore white knee-length socks, but I bet they did! They seemed so very odd!

Mum bought me a nice new prayer book, just what I needed! After we had finished in the God Shop we walked across the road to the place I could not wait to get to. It was the sweetshop, but this was not just a sweetshop: it was a toyshop too! And I would stand and look in the window, which was eye level to me, and in that window was a massive selection of toy soldiers, and that will do me! So Mum and Dad and my aunties waited for me as I walked in with my loot. And it was first things first: I decided I would invest some of my dosh in a load of sweets. Where do you start? Yep, gotta be sherbet lemons, and then rhubarb and custard, and then some cola cubes, and must not forget black jacks. And for good measure, it was sherbet flying saucers. And last, but not least, a lucky bag! All these wonderful delights lived in large glass jars, in nice neat rows, and all were measured on a weighing scale, and then very neatly wrapped in nice white paper bags and placed on the counter, and exchanged for coin of the realm – in this case, paper of the realm. Once that was sorted, the rest of my loot was pissed up the wall on an assortment of toy soldiers, and I walked out of the shop skint but very happy.

We all walked home on that lovely hot summer day, and once more the table was put into the front room, just like Christmas, and we had some form of dead roast animal. Well, at least it was not fucking turkey! And loads of roast potatoes and all washed down with Tizer!

That evening I lay on the floor by the fire and played with my toy soldiers while watching Roger Moore doing his stuff as Simon Templar in the popular TV series *The Saint*. As I munched my way through my bags of sweets, for all the world doing my very best to look like a hamster! This was the life, and a day I would not forget, but, alas, a night I would not forget, either.

I don't know what time it was, but it was still dark, and I awoke with a pain in my mouth. I didn't know what it was, but it was real pain. I hoped the pain would go away, but it didn't; not a hope! I walked in to Mum and Dad's bedroom and woke my mum up. I was crying with the pain; I could feel the wet tears rolling down my face. When mum woke up, she seemed very concerned; I was in sooo much pain! The only medication we ever had in the house was a bottle of TCP and Aspro. My mum got out of bed and gave me a glass of hot milk with some Aspro, and laid my head on her lap as I lay on the sofa. I could not stop crying with the pain, but somehow I found sleep. Not for long. I don't know what the time was, but it was early, and there was a knock on the door. It was Millie Webber, Millie had come down to see Mum, and she saw me and gave me a big hug. I liked Millie; she was such a kind person. I was very fond of her. If you were in any trouble, and Mum and Dad were not about, Millie would always sort you out; that was Millie! So Millie has a look in my mouth and says to Mum, 'Ducks, you wanna take him to a dentist.' Millie called everyone 'Ducks'. But we did not have a dentist, so it was gonna have to be Eastman's Dental Hospital. Well, that was the plan! It was a real warm summer morning, and Mum's getting herself ready. Millie warmed a wool scarf by the two-bar electric fire and placed it on my cheek, and it was a great relief, I can tell you; the pain was awful. So Mum's good to go, and then she had a brainwave: she squeezed my school grey balaclava over my head and then placed a warm scarf inside. It eased my pain to a degree, but I hated that fucking balaclava. But on that day I was so glad I had it!

We catch the No. 14 bus to King's Cross and walk up to the hospital, which seemed miles away. At last we reach these imposing stone steps at the main entrance and walk in and head to reception. Then we are told to wait and wait and wait and wait. And then my name is called and I am taken into a room, a real strong-smelling room. All hospitals had a real strong disinfectant smell about them; it smelt clean, because it was! So this tall geezer with glasses looks into my mouth, and lots of humming and tutting. I just could not take my eyes off all the tools that were laid out in a nice neat row; they looked so painful! I am praying he does not put them in my mouth. They're sharp! I was terrified!

Then I had to wait again, and wait and wait, and once more my name is called, and I was led into a room and told to sit in the big chair. And then this geezer puts a mask over my mouth, and I was gone. It was gas!

The next thing I woke up and I was spitting blood and I was told I had had four teeth out. Four? Four! Have I got any left? But that pain had gone, and that's all that I could care about. As far as I was concerned, they could have taken the lot out! I still had pain but nothing like the pain I had before, but I felt so ill. So minus four teeth, we go home. I asked could I have my teeth back, but it was a no! OK, I only asked, for fuck sake! Well, that's gonna piss the tooth fairy right off!

When I left the hospital I vomited, and it was awful, but a lot less painful than that toothache, so we get the bus home at last.

At last I was at home, on the sofa, doing my wounded little soldier bit, as you do, with a blanket of course. I was the ideal patient. The things I do for Lucozade.

The only ray of sunlight that day was I received my first letter addressed to me! Yep me! Master David Edwards. It was my membership to the Tufty Club, which was a rather primitive road safety initiative, which was led by a squirrel who sported a blue coat, and had mates like Badger the Policeman, and I got a badge! Alas, this badge did not bring power or rank, but that was never on my agenda of life, thank God! So many years later I found myself sitting back in the dentist chair as a result of many years of opening bottles of beer with my teeth, as one does.

A funny thing happened to me. I was on the piss with some mates. It was a bit of a beano, a day trip to France for the day, and we all get wankered as you do, so on the coach coming back I find myself as chief bottle opener, with my teeth of course, and fuck knows how many bottles I opened employing this method. And we get back, and a mate meets us. I hand him a bottle of Vitamin K, (Kronenbourg) and he twisted the cap off! For fuck sake, it was a twist top, and I have opened at least two cases of beer with my teeth! Shit happens!

So of course this had nothing to do with me sitting in the dentist's chair. Yeah right! So the upshot is I ended up having a root canal filling, and the dentist has goggles, gloves and a face mask; he looked more like a welder than a dentist! So lots of whizzes, humming, prodding and pulling, and a fair bit of poking as well. So job done, and it was a lot less painful than I thought it would be – unlike the bill!

Well, that night it started. It started with a slight ache, then progressed to real fucking pain. I was almost climbing the wall with the pain; I just could not escape that pain. I took as many painkillers as I could from the twenty-four-hour chemist, but to no avail. The following day, I am down the dentist at first light, and I walked up to the receptionist, whose face was full of horror. My face had swollen. The whole side of my face was so swollen it had to be seen to be believed! And I said in a muffled tone, 'I need to get this sorted,' and point at the side of my face. Then the man himself appeared, and he took a look at me and told me I had an infected abscess, and there was nothing he could do until the swelling had come down, and as for the pain he would get me some antibiotics, but that was all he could do!

The pain was gripping me big style. I think if I had had a gun I would have shot myself. But after what seemed a lifetime, the swelling left my face and I had the tooth pulled. Thank fuck for that!

A couple of years after that I was in a boozer in Finchley with a mate of mine called Peter, just standing at the bar. And then I had this real sharp pain in my back; it felt as if I had been stabbed in the back with a red-hot poker! It made my eyes water, and I felt as if my knees were about to go; the pain was horrendous! My mind is racing: it can't be a heart attack; it's in my back. Then the pain hit my side, more pain, sharp pain. Is it my appendix? No, can't be; pain is too high? What the fuck is this? What's going on? Peter said, 'Fuck, you OK, mate?' The sweat was running down my face and my neck, and my knuckles were white. He could see that something was up. I was scared, I can tell you! I told Peter I was gonna go to the bog and try and sort this out. The pain was roaming around my abdomen. The only way I could ease it was get down on my knees and curl up, which I did in the bog trap; it eased off. I had to get this sorted and fast, so I got Peter to get me a cab and headed for Barnet General Hospital. I needed to see a doctor. I get to reception and ask to see a doctor, and I get all the usual questions: Who built the Brooklyn Bridge? What is the currency of Romania? The usual? Shit! I said, 'I need to see a doctor and quick; this is killing me.' So I took a seat and waited in pain, and waited, and then a doctor came and called my name, and then examined me and took a urine sample. Soon he came back to me and said, 'You have renal colic, which is very painful.' He's telling me! He gave me some very strong painkillers and said, 'You will pass the stone.' I said, 'How will I know?' He smiled and said, 'You will know when you pass it.' And do you know what – I did. And God, I knew it! It was like pissing a hot broken bottle. It had me on my knees, but at least the pain was over!

But the worst pain you will ever have is emotional pain; there is no pain like it. It's the worst pain you will ever have. It engulfs your whole being; it puts your heart in a vice and squeezes it so tight, and then it feels like a hot poker deep in your heart and soul!

There is no pain like it. It leaves no scar and no marks – only the one on your soul. There is no painkiller, no medication; just pain. I have had this pain in my life, and I would rather have an infected abscess or renal colic than suffer that absolute pain of the heart. It takes you down like nothing else will, and the only cure is time!

But yet with the passage of time, it only numbs that pain. You cope better, but the scar is still there deep in your soul!

For me I took refuge in the end of an empty bottle of vodka, but all that did was numb the pain and released that mental hurt by the comfort of sleep. But when you awake the pain is still with you. This is not the way!

The pain does go, and I was once told that that which does not kill you makes you stronger. Well, it did for me!

I hope I never have that pain in my heart ever again. The only thing I wish for in life – I don't desire wealth or crave fame, power, money or influence – is to part this mortal earth before my precious children do. If the higher power grants me that wish I will be a happy man. The really important things, you cannot buy with money; any amount of money!

Each year at school we had class projects on various topics, One year it was on Ireland. We learned about the counties, the provinces, the Irish legends and folklore and what Ireland produced – all this real boring stuff. But what really pissed me off was the way I was told what a bad man Oliver Cromwell was. Hang on: he was English.

Ah! But he was a real evil man, what he did to us as Catholics. Well, I did not subscribe to that. He was English; I was English;

England was my country, and I think Cromwell was a diamond geezer, but that's my opinion! I was in a tiny minority of one!

Then one year we did a project on Greece, which was fascinating. And the part I loved most of all were the stories from Greek mythology. I loved it. It was all bollocks, but it was kinda nice bollocks!

The bit I remember was the stories of the Trojan War, and the stories of Helen of Troy and the wooden horse, and the heroes of the war, such as Ajax and Agamemnon. It was great stuff!

But the year we did the Romans, that was the best! They were the dog's bollocks. We learned all about what the Romans did for us. The list was endless. I don't think they invented the car or the aeroplane, but I think they invented almost everything else!

There was a children's magazine called *Look and Learn*, which was great if you could read! But in one issue there was a centre-fold of a Roman battle, which showed all the different types of siege engines. I was so impressed; I loved the Romans. I wished I was a Roman. This education stuff was catching on!

When a war movie was released at the movies, it was advertised on billboards, strategically placed around the area. But the all-important factor in my case was the certificate the film was issued, and there were three categories: U, which was for all ages; A, which meant you had to be accompanied by an adult; and X, which was strictly for adults only. But for some reason or other, most war films were rated with an A certificate. This meant I would harass my dad to take me, and more often or not he would take me, but I think he wanted to see it too! And when we did go to the pictures, it was always on payday. Dad would get home early from work, change his clothes and shave, of course, and then off we went down to Holloway Road to either the Odeon or the ABC. In those days the cinemas operated a continuous performance, which meant you could go into the film at any time, and watch it, and then leave when the part you came in at came back on. Well, that was the plan.

The only film Dad and I watched twice in one sitting was *Zulu*. Other great movies of my childhood were *The Great Escape*, *The Longest Day*, *Von Ryan's Express* and *Operation Crossbow*: all great movies and true stories. Also at this time of my life was a series called the 'Carry Ons', which started in the 1950s with *Carry On Sergeant*, and the popular formula was repeated many times, such as *Carry On Cowboy*, *Carry On Camping*, *Carry On Abroad*, and so many others. They always seemed to have the same cast, with Sidney James, Barbara Windsor, Charles Hawtrey, Jim Dale, and the unforgettable Kenneth Williams, all supported by an endless list of other British actors, such as Terry Scott, and Hattie Jacques. It was the final years of the British film industry.

This was the year we had a big event at school. The school had a big TV, but it was never used. It was always locked up, and lived at the end of the hall, but today was an important day. All the school was led into the hall, and we all sat down cross-legged to watch the telly, to watch the launch of the *QE2*. It was an important day, and I felt so proud to be British, as I always am and always will be!

It was about this time that I found myself getting into fights at school. I don't know why, but I did. I always seemed to be in a scrap, and as a result I would find myself being caned, but nothing like those six of the best; nuffink! A fight would break out, and I'd be in it, and it would seem the whole school would gather around the combatants, shouting 'Fight! Fight! Fight!' And you would get shouts of encouragement such as, 'Kick him in the bollocks,' 'Poke his fucking eyes out!' Even though you were punching the living shit out of each other, you did not kick; it was the unwritten law.

In my teens and early twenties – and even at the ripe old age of fifty! – one would find oneself in a tear-up; and I have had a few, I am not proud to say, but I did; and what's done is done, and you can't change that! On occasion I would find myself in a brawl, and I nearly always landed the first blow, which was usually a headbutt, which tended to get the required reaction from my opponent. Then it would be followed by fists and boot, but never a weapon. In the culture I was brought up in, weapons were a coward's way out, and the only time a weapon was acceptable was when you were outnumbered, and then you could justify whatever was at hand. No one walked around 'tooled up', but on occasion in my teens, when our firm had a row with another firm, the only time you were tooled up was when you were out-numbered. They were the rules of engagement!

My days at St Joseph's were drawing to a close, and to tell you the truth I was quite sad about it. I was going to the big school, and I was quite apprehensive about it too. I was gonna be a very small fish in a big pond, rather than a big fish in a tiny pond, which I had got accustomed to. We had exams and stuff, which meant absolutely nothing to me whatsoever. To me exams were just for people with good memories. I had no idea how important they were until I was much older, and then it was too late for me anyway. To me, education is a one-bullet gun. If you don't get it right the first time, it's hard work doing it when you're older, as I know only too well!

Then, on Saturdays, a brand-new TV series hit our early morning TV. It was *Thunderbirds*, and that soon put paid to Saturday morning pictures. After *Thunderbirds* I would head off down Hornsey Road to Aladdin's Bookshop, which was not exactly a real bookshop; it was a comic shop, and it was the place you could exchange your comics. You would give them two of your old comics and that would entitle you to one comic, which was a fair deal! My favourite comics were the War Picture Library. These were small comics, not the normal A4 size, but they were great. They had a commando dagger on the glossy cover, and the stories were great. Well, to be honest, the illustrations were marvellous, and that's what mattered to me, as I could not read. I would kinda make up the story in my head. The hero was always British, had a square jaw and big biceps. And all German officers had monocles, and all RAF officers had big fuck-off moustaches and always seemed to be called Roger!

I would spend hours looking at them, and at night I would look at them under the bed covers with my torch – even more fun. As Mum worked at night I would be left to my own culinary devices during the day, and Mum would leave me two bob, 10p, to sort myself out with, so it would either be pie and chips or a pile of cakes from Scott's the bakers, or down the road to the pie-and-mash shop, which was handsome! I loved pie and mash with liquor, and a load of salt and vinegar, all washed down with a nice strong cup of tea. This was always a very popular meal. The place was always full and always had a queue, but alas, the pie-and-mash shops are gone, and now we have kebab shops. I suppose that's progress. But more often than not I would stuff my face with a banana-and-sugar sandwich, which I would make, and then piss my dinner money up the wall on a box of small toy soldiers. Much more fun!

On Friday, 'it's Friday and it's Crackerjack!' It was wonderful kids' TV. It was kids from different schools doing all sorts of stuff, and if you managed to take part in any of the competitions you would get a Crackerjack pencil, which I always wanted, but never did get one. I was forty-four when I got a Blue Peter badge, but at least I got one!

By far the most popular children's programme on a Saturday was *Dr Who*, who was a Time Lord who travelled time and space in an old Metropolitan police phone box, known as the TARDIS. And his arch-enemies were the Daleks, and soon Dalek-mania hit the shops, and all the kids would buy small toy Daleks to play with. But as for me, I thought it was a load of old bollocks. I don't do science fiction at all. The closest I get to reading science fiction is bus and train timetables, and I didn't reckon the Daleks were that dangerous because all you had to do was go upstairs, because Daleks don't do stairs; they were fucked when it came to stairs! Soon *Dr Who* the movie was out, and all the kids would be walking about with outstretched arms saying, 'Exterminate! Exterminate!'

It was birthday time once more, and I wanted a bike so much and begged Dad for one, and he said he would see what he could do. So Dad goes off down Club Row on a Sunday morning with Uncle Bill, as normal, and I wasn't allowed any more because I had to go to nine o'clock Mass, which, as far as my mum was concerned, was compulsory and that was that. And I would stand at the back of the church and look out of the window, hoping it would soon be over. Mass seemed to last for ever. And the trouble was, I could not *not* go in case I was asked any questions by Mum or by my teacher at school, so that was that!

So Dad returns home with a pair of fucking roller skates. I mean, there is a difference, but no, I got fucking roller skates. I was not best pleased, to say the least; the sense of disappointment was enormous! But I learned a very valuable lesson that day: always hope, but never expect! And that's the way I think even today!

Christmas was the same as any other Christmas, but this year I kept sober! And yet again we had more big dead bird with roast potatoes and all the trimmings. Mum seemed to be in the kitchen all the time, and Dad would fall asleep in front of the fire after eating a small mountain of mince pies and cream, as you do, and I would be lying on the floor in front of the fire with the latest *Valiant* comic album.

That Boxing Day we had visitors, which was an unexpected surprise. It was one of my dad's workmates called Don, who had a son called Keith, who was my age, whom he had brought with him. And they brought with them a gift; it was a game of Monopoly, which we all played, and Keith and I drank loads of Tizer, and Dad and Don drank brown ale and chatted for what seemed hours. This was the life! I never saw Don or Keith again. I don't know why, but they lived miles away, in a place called Borehamwood, which I think is still in England. I was always shit at Geography.

So ended 1967. The world said goodbye to Che Guevara, and the world had its first heart transplant in South Africa. Well, Mary Shelley wasn't that far off the mark, was she?

Eight

And so started 1968 and the year of flower power, which was a load of tree-hugging, long-haired layabouts who needed to get a proper job! Well, that's what Dad said! Who am I to argue! It was the year of 'I am backing Britain'. I don't quite know what all that was about; I think the concept was to do half an hour's work for free, which would support the country. Well, I think that was the plan, but I always backed Britain, because it was my country and always will be! It was also the year we had mass immigration from Asia, and the year that Dr Martin Luther King was gunned down, and there was a massive explosion in a towerblock of flats called Ronan Point, and the great British comedian Tony Hancock died alone in a hotel room in Australia, a tragic end to a comic genius!

Not long after Christmas I was taken to go and see my new school, which was called St William of York. It was just off the Caledonian Road and it seemed enormous to me. It seemed to have hundreds of kids, all boys, some enormous compared to me. It even looked as if some of them shaved. As regards to choice, I didn't have one: 'You're going to that school and that's that.' Well, to me a school was a school. As for league tables, they were as far off as Dr Who!

The day came at last. I was leaving St Joseph's for the last time. I was so sad. I had had happy times there, but that's life; and this new school was a new deal! Well, that was six weeks away, after the summer holidays. But as the holidays started, to my horror my mum and dad announced we were moving. Moving? Where? To Blythe Mansions. Fuck, not there! They were Leyden's sworn enemies, and I was gonna move there? NO! But as usual there was nothing I could do about it. And what was the reason for this move? We could have a balcony. Yep, our own private balcony. I was not a happy little bunny! But Mum was delighted; there was somewhere to sit out on a hot day. Yeah, OK, I'll give you that one, and I thought it would be an ideal place to keep a bike, if you had one! So we moved. This did not sit well with my mates. I was a turncoat, as far as they were concerned, but I could not help moving: it was my mum and dad! But with the passage of time we soon bridged that divide, so now there were loads of us out running about; even more fun!

As a matter of natural progression I became a Boy Scout. I was in the 59th Holly Park, Tiger Troop, and I joined the uniform-saving club, which we paid into each Friday night with our subs. It seemed an absolute lifetime to get the required amount for the purchase of a uniform, and the cost to me was quite substantial, because it gobbled up all my pocket money.

So the big day came. I and some of the other uniformless scouts made our way to Buckingham Palace Road, with a bloke called Kim. Now, I don't know if that was his real name or Scout name, but he was always called Kim. So I get the world's worst-fitting uniform ever. The trousers were, I am sure, owned by Coco the Clown. I must admit I was a bit pear-shaped, but for fuck sake not that shape! However I was not that bothered; all I wanted was the uniform, which meant I could go camping. That was the long-term plan that I had.

At last the day came for us, the 59th Holly Park, to go camping – yippee! So we are all waiting for the transport outside, which was late – by hours. And the transport was in the form of a removal lorry, which took us miles away to a place called Frylands Woods. To this day I don't know where it is; it's most probably now an Asda superstore. Anyway, we eventually arrived at the site, and it was absolutely pissing down. Well, it had to be; I was camping! In the rain we put up these tents and, as for trying to light a fire and keep it going, that was my task, and it was a real shit job. I was engulfed in a haze of thick smoke, coughing and spluttering. I stank of smoke, and was wet to the skin. Well, it couldn't get any worse.

So where was all the singalong stuff? It was bollocks! I was wet, cold and hungry. My blanket got wet – sleeping bags were an alien concept to me; besides, none of us had that type of money. It was a real miserable two days. I then decided if ever I had to do this outdoor crap again, next time I would be ready and I would know how to survive if need be! And I did! I attended several survival courses and became quite proficient in this art, long before Ray Mears found fame on our TV screens. And I love it. I have been in deserts and rainforest and jungle; and as I am putting this to paper, I am planning to go to the North Pole.

It was a long, hot summer. We would all be out playing, and then we heard that the Wooden Bridge was going to be turned into an adventure playground. That was great; it would even be more fun.

The most memorable event of the days of the adventure playground was the following incident. There were loads of things dumped off, like old railway-track sleepers, telegraph poles, old tyres, rope and rope nets and other stuff essential in the construction of an adventure playground.

So, among this stuff was a massive tyre; it was huge, it must have come off a monster truck or some form of monster tractor. So all of the kids dragged this massive tyre up this huge railway cutting. It was at a forty-degree angle, and about a hundred yards up a very steep railway cutting. It was high and long.

It was like something out of a Cecil B DeMille biblical epic – all the kids pulling and pushing – and at one stage of the game we even had ropes pulling on it. It took what seemed ages, but at last we got the fucker to the top of the cutting after shedding a pile of sweat. We were all knackered! So now we are at the top; what do we do now? I know: we sit in it and roll down the hill! Yeah! Yeah! But who? So I said fuck, it I'll do it. So we managed to stand the tyre upright, which was no simple task I might add. So I get in the tyre, and as tyres go it was a rather comfortable fit, if you ask me! But we have room for one more, so my mate Mickey gets in too. So I am facing Mickey; he's all nice and snug too. So it was thumbs up and bombs away! So the rest of the kids give it a massive heave-ho! And we were off!

Fucking hell! Fucking hell! I am sitting in this tyre, rolling down this steep hill at a serious rate of knots. Mickey looked absolutely terrified, and I must have looked the same! Spin, roll, roll... Well, we hit the bottom of the hill with a huge bump. It was like you see on telly when astronauts train in some form of flight simulator. But we had no safety factor whatsoever: no stop button, just gravity!

However, we did not, in the planning stage of this highly sophisticated scientific experiment, allow for the bounce factor, and didn't even consider the idea of a brake, and to say that was an error in our judgement was a slight understatement! It bounced and bounced and rotated like a spinning top and eventually stopped. We both climbed out and we just could not stand, as we were so dizzy. We were walking around with rubber legs just like Eddie Omo on a good Saturday night. We were met by rapturous applause and it was like hero status for at least five minutes, but none did it after us; I wonder why?

In the flats of Blythe Mansions we had a large playground, which was our football pitch, and in one corner we had some swings, and the playground was known to everyone as 'the Swings'. It was a big area and was surrounded by a very high fence, which had goalposts painted on the fence.

I recall a very sad incident. One day, loads of us kids were at the Swings playing football, and I was sitting on the swing, minding my own business, watching them kick the ball between two sticks, and someone kicks the ball right over the fence. And the person who kicked the ball over the fence had to go and get it; that was the rule. It was always easier to climb the fence than go via the gate and walk around. This was standard operational procedure.

So Ray, whose last name escapes me, kicked the ball over so he goes and gets the ball. He kicked the ball back into the Swings and then decides to climb back and join in the game via a small gap in the fence on the roof of the bike shed that made one side of the Swings. But as he was about to do so, he fell – head first. Now, I am watching this unfold in front of my eyes, and his head hit the concrete ground with such a crack. Fuck, that must have hurt, I recall thinking at the time.

But he manages to pull himself up and stagger. And then he fell again. He then got up again, and we all ran to his aid, but it was too late; his eyes were all over the place and he kinda mumbled 'I wanna go home', which was about a hundred yards way. So his best mate, Tony Partridge, took him home.

I think his dad took him to the hospital; I don't know how,

but no ambulance was called. We would have noticed it and very few had a phone anyway. So we all carried on as normal, as kids tend to do. The following morning we got the news: Ray had died. Fucking dead! He was fourteen. It had a massive impact on all of us. Dead? Fuck! He was only a kid!

The adventure playground was great. Someone, somewhere had got the funding and they employed three full-time play leaders: Lou, Nick, and some hippy-type bird from South America. All the kids came from all the flats – Blythe, Leyden, Hillrise, Coleman, Watersville and the Highland. Each block of flats housed about 150 families: work out the amount of kids. There were loads of us. And what a labour force! We built an aerial runway, which started at the very highest point and ended at the far end of the playground. It was a long rail runway; we had a large tyre, which you sat in – usually three of us – and then let go, and off we would go at a rate of knots. What fun! We dug tunnels and all that type of stuff. We dug one tunnel into the side of the cutting; it must have been twenty feet long at least, and not one form of support holding it up. Well, one night it rained and the whole tunnel collapsed. If anyone had been in it they would have been killed without a doubt!

Then one day we got given a massive squabble net, which reached from the top of the stone viaduct to the bottom, and that was great to play pirates on. I think the Health and Safety Executive would have had a fucking heart attack! But if you did get hurt, it was your own fault, and a simple don't-do-it-again attitude prevailed. We were masters of our own destiny, and the freedom was fantastic!

So the big day came and it was my first day at my new school, and I didn't have a clue what to expect, and I was very apprehensive to say the least. Hornsey Rise was a strategically good location for public transport. You had the No. 41 which took you from Archway to Tottenham; the No. 210, which was from Finsbury Park to Highgate; and then the No. 14 which went from Hornsey Rise to Putney, and this my chosen method of transport to my new school, which was St William of York Roman Catholic

School for boys, which was located in Brewery Road, just off the Caledonian Road. There was always a large queue at the No. 14 bus stop, which was situated outside the Favourite public house. So I was in my new school uniform: black blazer with school badge on the breast pocket; grey jumper; white shirt and school tie; and, most important, my first pair of long trousers, in which I kept my weekly dinner money and my bus fare. I was the only boy going to my new school on the bus. Most of my mates attended Tollington Park or Archway school, which were all in walking distance.

So as the bus turned up, I joined the scrum to get a seat, and it always seemed all the men sat upstairs. I think it was because you were allowed to smoke upstairs on buses then, and it always seemed to be thick with smoke from various brands of popular tobacco, such as No. 6, Sovereign, and not forgetting Woodbine. It was quite overpowering.

The journey took about half an hour. The most popular bus stop was always the Nag's Head. This was where everybody seemed to get off, and then it was on to my bus stop on the Caledonian Road – to be precise, right outside Pentonville Prison.

My new school was divided into two locations: the first- and second-year boys were at Brewery Road and the rest of the school was down the road in Gifford Street. In Brewery Road we occupied the top floors of the local primary school called Robert Blair, and our playground was situated on the roof, which was a novel concept.

So the bus stopped and I waded through a haze of tobacco smoke into the fresh air of the Caledonian Road. I recall looking around for a friendly face amidst the sea of new faces at this hallowed seat of education, but I didn't see one.

I entered the school and went up the flights of stone stairs leading to the roof playground, and I was so nervous I needed a piss, so I headed to the bog. Fucking hell, there were some rough-looking kids there, and they all seemed to be smoking, which I thought was real tough-guy stuff. So I emptied myself and left very sheepishly. Soon after that I met a boy from my primary school; great, I felt so much better; it was Martin! And then John the map bloke shows up. Now there are three of us. It was very reassuring and comfortable. We never had much to do with each other at St Joseph's, but now we had a common interest: survival! There must have been about 240 boys on that roof that morning, and all the eyes focused on one! He turned up wearing short trousers! Poor fucker! I would not have been in his shoes for all the money in the world. Did they take the piss out of him or what!

At nine o'clock a teacher appeared and rang out a hand bell, and we all had to form up in a big group, and then the other teachers emerged from the top of the staircase and formed a line. Then our names were called, and we had to form up in neat lines as the names were called alphabetically. It was about thirty to a class. Then the head teacher, a Mr O'Donovan, would announce 'You are 1A, and your teacher is Miss Magarry.' Then the class would descend the stairs to their new classroom. Then the formula would be repeated, until the last class of the first year was left, and that was 1D and that was my class, the lowest of the first year. They had put all the fuckwits together. Our names were called, and we lined up and were introduced to our new form teacher, and it was Mr O'Donovan. Then we were sent downstairs to our new classroom, while our form teacher carried out the class allocation of the second year. It was all very disciplined stuff – straight lines, no talking – and we were always called by our last name and I didn't like that, but there was fuck all I could do about it!

So as we go to our new classroom and are standing outside, a tall boy in my class called Jimmy, from Summers Town – looked a bit of a hard case – got himself in a fight with some geezer, a bloke called Docherty. Fuck, did they go at it! It was a real tear-up, fists flying. I recall thinking to myself this is gonna be a tough place, and these lads can 'have it', as one might say, a fucking good balls-out stand-up scrape, and very vicious to boot! I also made a mental note not to lock horns with Jimmy. We became good mates later.

The fight was brought to an abrupt halt by the sports master, a Mr Drabwell. He was a hard case, and he punished the fighter on the spot, with a well-placed slipper across the arse. But I remember thinking that must not have hurt as much as a punch in the mouth from Jimmy!

After the swift justice had been dispensed, we all filed in to our class and chose our desks. We were told to sit down. Then the register was called and once more just last names, a novel concept. So I was in 1D; so A, was for the brainy fuckers, B was for the average, C was for the not so thick, and D – well, that was for the really thick, and that was my class. Now, I know I am not the brightest colour in the box, but fuck me there were some really backward kids; I would go as far to say as almost in reverse. Some could not even write their name! We were all issued a cardboard box, into which we put our new-issue cartridge pen, a pencil, a ruler a compass, and our Bible, which I still have to this very day. Then we had to copy off the blackboard our timetable, which told you what time your designated lessons were. What I didn't get was that we had to go to other classrooms for our lessons and bring the correct books with you. All very new to me!

At 12.30 we had to line up and pay our school dinner money, either the weekly amount or on a daily basis. I was surprised how many kids got free school dinners. The food was not bad, but I fucking hate mashed potatoes and corned beef, which seemed to be a popular item on the menu. I never worried about food, as I was fed at home anyway, so it was no biggie, or I should say piggy!

I soon made new friends in my class and started to settle in, and at the bus stop I met a boy who lived in a house next to my flats. He lived in a house? Must be rich! But nothing could be further from the truth. He lived in the basement rooms of a large Victorian house, with his mum and dad, two brothers and a little sister – six living in three rooms – and had to share the toilet and bathroom with the rest of the residence. It must have been so tough on them, but a cleaner, tidier family you could not find.

Then there was Mickey. His nickname was Rawhide, because he only had one pair of trousers for school, and when he got home he had to take them off immediately and put his other trousers on, which always had the arse hanging out of them, hence Rawhide. Mickey had seven sisters, and his dad didn't go to work for some reason or other, but yet he was always on the piss. His mum was always doing washing, and not even the sign of a washing machine. Mickey and Steve, my other mate, were much brighter then me at school, but we didn't care: we were mates.

I soon settled into a routine of school and made more friends, but I hated Wednesday with a passion because it was sports day, which meant football or football; and when the session was over it was football, and when it rained it was football, and when it snowed it was football, and it was always football, fucking always football! We would get a coach to Hackney Marshes, and I would have to stand on the white touchline with the other non-conformists all afternoon, every Wednesday. I laughed!

But on Friday morning our class would meet outside the local swimming pool for our swimming lesson, which I loved. Anyway, we had a small ginger kid in our class, called Alex. Well, we all got changed as quick as possible to maximise our time in the water, so we had to line up at the side of the pool. The swimming instructor was just like a regimental Sergeant Major, and he shouts, 'You! Yes, you!' And pointed to little Alex. 'Don't you, dare get in my pool with those feet!'

Alex's feet were black – and I mean black –with dirt. Had he been down a coal mine? Well, the poor fucker just burst into a flood of tears, snot, the lot, and through his tears he sobbed, 'We got no soap.' So the RSM came round and made him wash his feet in a sink. God, I felt for Alex sooo much. The humiliation was unbelievable; no compassion whatsoever. The poor fucker. After that, he always bunked off school on Fridays. I wonder why?

He came from a very large family, and I think he lived in Camden Town, and they were very poor, and I was led to believe his old man would knock his mum about a bit. He was not the brightest colour in the box; in fact he was virtually illiterate in every sense of the word. He hardly attended school and was away for long periods at a time. And what we heard was that he committed a burglary and dropped his school bus pass (he might as well have dropped his passport) and was sent away, and I don't mean to Southend. The poor fucker never had a chance.

Not long after starting school, we realised you could go out at lunchtime, which was well handy. So it was fuck school dinners: now we had a choice. We could go to the penny cake shop and buy out-of-date cream cakes for a penny, or go down the chippy.

But what most of us did was buy a bag of chips, stick them down our fat necks, and then buy six cakes – a well-balanced nutritious diet. But some of the lads would buy only four cakes and blow the rest on fags, because you could buy singles then from the papershop across the road from the school.

As for education, it seemed non-existent. School was a place to go between nine and four, Monday to Friday. On reflection thirty-five years later, the conclusion I have arrived at is this: given the amount of illiterate children – and believe me, I am talking illiterate – wouldn't it have been easier to break them down into small groups of four and have a teacher for each group? But I don't think that was an option. With the limited resources it would not have been possible to accommodate such a simple system of that nature. Those that were illiterate were not stupid. We used to have a saying: 'I can't spell bus, but I can bunk the fare!'

I often wonder what happened to them all, and I wonder what would have happened if they did have that extra effort put into their education. Who knows? My saving grace was my love of history, and then one day the light came on for me! I was watching a popular TV programme called *Take Your Pick*. It was hosted by a tall man called Michael Miles, a very elegant chap. So the format was as follows. From the audience, a group of contestants would be picked, and the first part of the quiz show was, one at a time, they would be called to centre stage and the host would ask a simple question, like 'Is your name Fred?' And if you said yes, the small lady next to him called Monica would bang a gong and you're out. So the plan was you're not to say yes or no. If you went on to the next part you would have to answer questions on general knowledge, and if you passed that you went on to your chosen topic, and with this particular geezer, his chosen topic was military history. Now, knowing what little I still know on this subject, which is vast, it is a subject that covers all periods and all nations and is so diverse and interesting. So this geezer is asked loads of questions and he gets them all correct. And then comes the really hard question, and for this you are put in a sealed booth, and the questions are asked via a microphone and headset, and you were given a time in which to answer the questions. And if you got them all correct you won a large sum of money. Well, that was the object of the exercise. Well, he did and won a shitload of money. I was so impressed, and that was it for me! I was gonna study military history. Now, if he had been asked questions on British butterflies would it have had such an impact on me? Fuck knows? So that got me started in military history, which I still have an unquenchable thirst for to this very day!

During my life I have had the good fortune to meet some real experts on this subject, some very specialised, but the man I most admired in this field was a wonderful man called Alan Caton, and I will tell you more about him later. So my incentive to read was born, and in our small school library was only one book on this subject. It was a small book, called *Military Uniforms of the World*, by Blandford, which I always had out on loan. I would spend hours looking at the pictures of the uniforms. Well, it was a start. The very first book I bought was from a junk shop; it cost me a fortune – 2/- (10p) – and it was *Famous Regiments of the British Army*, and I devoured it. Well almost!

At school there were a few of us who didn't do football, and I didn't feel so alone any more. We never even had the opportunity to play rugby, or even cricket. It was football or nothing. And then a new game came out, called Subbuteo, which was like tabletop football. There was no getting away from fucking football!

But now that I had found what really interested me, I was off! I went to Woolworths, and bought myself a scrapbook, and started to collect pictures of soldiers wherever I could. It was fun and interesting too.

Some days Mum would get me in the kitchen at the table and get me to do the stamps. What a shit job that was. I would spend hours sticking Green Shield stamps in their books. What it was was when you bought stuff from certain shops, you would be given stamps, which you would collect and then put them in a book. And when you had enough books you could trade them in for luxury items like a toaster. But fucking hell! You needed about a million books to get anything! Hour after hour, licking stamps, to get a toaster. What was wrong with the cooker grill?

It was towards the end of the summer of 1968 that one Sunday afternoon we got a knock on the door. It was my Nanny Hilda! And my Auntie Mary and her little girl called Faye. They had come to visit us. How nice, to come all this way for the day! But that was not to be the case: they stayed with us for months. So it was Mum, Dad, Nanny, Mary, Faye and me, in a two-bedroom flat. So for at least six months my bed was the sofa in the front room, which I didn't mind because I got to stay up late at night. But it did put a great strain on Mum and Dad's relationship, what with Mum working nights and having people in the flat during the day. It was difficult. It was at this time my mum started to go to Bingo, in the hall in the flats.

It seemed nearly all the women in the flats played Bingo then; it seemed to be a national sport of women at that time! Mum would go to Bingo any chance she got. I don't blame her; her home was not hers any more. Well, that's the way it seemed.

My dad went fishing with a mate and that was it: he was, one might say, hooked on the sport. And whenever he was off on the weekend, he would take himself off to Southend Pier. Dad took me just the once, thank God! I was bored out of my tiny mind, just standing watching the fishing line, just in case it moved, which would indicate that he had caught something! Well, the only upside to this was at least I was not in Ireland! Soon after Dad had caught the fishing bug, he met a mate who was like-minded, and they decided to build a boat in Peter's back garden, which they did. It took seven years to complete. I wonder how long it took Noah.

My dad would spend every weekend down the boat, playing Noah, and when he was not down the boat he would be making something for the boat; he was a very gifted man with his hands. I was left pretty much to my own devices at that time. My nan seemed to do all the cooking, which was fine by me, as long as I was fed.

I always remember on Saturday night, this bloke would knock on the door and he would sell us meat, and we would always seem to buy a mountain of sausages. Why? I don't know why. But we always got a fucking great bag of sausages, and they were enormous, and we would sit down and munch our way through them while watching *Upstairs Downstairs*, as you do.

So summer ended, and winter was just around the corner, and then my birthday, which was followed by the usual festivities of Christmas and more big dead bird with roast potatoes, and mince pies, and so ended 1968.

Nine

1969 started, and this was the year John Lennon had a sleep-in, for world peace. What a load of complete bollocks that was! Yeah right, lads: put all your weapons down because John Lennon and that Japanese bird are having a sleep-in for world peace! What the fuck was he on? I don't know, but I wouldn't mind a pint of it!

It was the year of the Biafran War, and a load of students occupied 144 Piccadilly. Why? And it was the year of the Isle of Wight Festival, and the My Lai Massacre in Vietnam. Vietnam seemed to dominate the world news. Why? I didn't have a clue, but it was always on the news.

It was about this time that a new craze started in youth culture. It was the Skinheads, which took its name from the skinhead haircut, which was the fashion of the day. But this new cult seemed to endorse violence; it was a part of the culture of the day. I fell victim to this culture while waiting at a bus stop, where I was the victim of a well-placed headbutt, and a good 'filling-in' for no reason whatsoever. It was the first time, but I'm sorry to say not the last!

The skinheads had a particular dress code. The haircut was optional, not essential. You would wear a Ben Sherman or Brutus shirt, with a button-down collar. You would wear Levi jeans with a half-inch turn-up, or green docker trousers. But the real dog's bollocks was a pair of Levi Stay-Prest, white or cream of course. This was the ultimate fashion statement. And you had to wear braces, even if you didn't need them.

But the most important part of the dress code was the boots, and the favoured option was high-leg Dr Martens, where your trousers would come to the top of the boot. But the other optional footwear was cherry-red steel toecaps, and if you were the ultimate in cool you would cut the leather off the toecaps to expose the steel, which you would have polished. That was the real deal, the dog's bollocks! And as for top wear, it was a

Harrington jacket, or a Crombie overcoat three-quarter length, with a red silk handkerchief in the top pocket – and it had to be red. The formal dress code for the skinhead was a pair of shiny brogues with red socks; compulsory! And Prince of Wales check trousers and shirt. That was the fashion of the day. And I didn't even own a pair of red socks. I was different and therefore a target.

The fashion also coincided with the birth of football violence, which erupted in all the football stadiums across the country and in mainline train stations. It was exciting and dangerous and fun, as long as it was not you getting your head kicked in!

In my flats, there were three age groups. There was my age group, from twelve to fourteen; then you had the 'Little'uns', aged from four to eleven or so, and then there was the 'Big'uns', who were the much older lads and there was a lot of them. They were known as the 'Crew', or better known as the 'Firm'. Blythe Mansions' 'Firm' would fight other firms. It was a large part of the culture. And Blythe, in comparison to other firms was quite small, but they would take on other firms and win. The Archway was a mob; the Holloway was a firm, and so on. But the biggest firm by a long way was the Summers Town, by all accounts. So the 'Rise' i.e. Blythe, went down to Summers Town to 'take them', which meant to have a fight with them, or 'run them', to make them run away. Well, that was the way it was; I don't know why, but it was. So the Rise goes down to sort them out, and ran them. Fucking hell! This was unheard of, but they did, and the Rise's reputation of a hard firm was elevated to stardom! And on the rare occasion, some firm came up to sort our firm out. And as they came up the road they were met by three of the 'Big'uns': Brian, Peter and Steve. And like a bunch of raving lunatics they charged in these geezers and fucked them right off! So it was not about numbers: it was the quality. And a lot of bottle!

Blythe had a hard reputation as a hard area, due to the violence the firm dealt out, and was rather notorious for villains. And I knew some of these whose names are not important, but the area reputation went up in lights when a local villain was shot outside the flats and when a shotgun was used to sort out a row in the local boozer the Favourite. The advantage was, if you were out and got picked on by a crew, you would tell them you were from Blythe or Hungry Hill, as it was known – the collective term of the area, which included Hazelville Estate and all the other flats – and if you were filled in by anyone from another area, the retribution would be very fast in coming, and was quite reassuring. But the downside was, when someone else was filled in, you had to answer the muster. That's the way things were; it was very tribal.

There was a great emphasis on one's fighting capability; the better the fighter you were, the higher your social standing. Within the youth community, there was no esteem in one's educational achievements whatsoever. If you were a 'brainy bastard', life would be quite uncomfortable – so I was in no danger there then!

But the most important thing was if you ended up in a 'ruck' you did not run. This was the most important thing: you never ever, ever ran at a 'ruck', because you would be a social outcast, and one could never allow that to happen, no way!

It was about this time I found myself getting into fights at school, and in the flats. The reason why? I don't recall, but I always seemed to be getting into fights. The worst ones were the ones in the flats, for two reasons: one, no one would break the fight up, and it always ended in someone drawing blood, usually mine! And the other was, everybody seemed to have an older brother, who would come and give you a good dig in the mouth if you filled his younger brother in. And that was always the case with me. From a young age, I was no stranger to violence. I hate violence, believe me, but sometimes it's your only option and it's the only language some people understand. If that's the way it is, so be it! You must meet it head-on. It's the only way!

I remember one time there was this geezer called Tommy, and he always wore these massive hobnailed boots. This was not a fashion statement: it was what he always wore – as far back as I can remember. Anyway, he has a row with this little lad called Charlie, and Charlie gets a smack in the mouth and it's off!

Tommy was confident that he was on a winner, but Charlie got a cousin called Leslie, and he jumps on Tommy's back and grabs him around the neck, and Charlie steams into Tommy like a man possessed, and the pair of them give Tommy a real fucking good hiding – blood and snot all over the place. Well, it could not have happened to a nicer bloke! He'd had it coming to him for a long, long time, but there was fuck all Tommy could do about it, even though he had three bigger brothers, because so did Charlie and Leslie, so it was a well-balanced conclusion.

On one occasion, I had a tear up with a kid called Chrissy. Well, it was a balls-out fight, kicking, punching, biting, and gouging – the lot. So I gave him a bloody nose, and he whimpered off. It was a real hard fight, I might add, and I was nursing a bite mark on my thigh, which actually drew blood – fuck, it was so painful – and all of a sudden I get dragged backwards by the collar of my shirt. And as I turned around, all I can see is this huge clenched fist coming in what seemed like slow motion, and my brain is screaming 'NO', and it was bang wallop. I was decked in one, flat on my arse, and blood poured down my nose into my mouth. Nothing was said, just wallop bang. It was Chrissy's older and much bigger brother, Dave. Enough said. But he was at least five years older then me! And a lot bigger. WANKER!

The violence was also a big issue at the football. It was not about who won the match; it was about who ran each other's crews from their tribal location. The tribal location for our firm was the North Bank, at Arsenal. On the day of the match, all the local firms would meet up and go as one big crew. The arch-enemy was Spurs, whose tribal location was some end of the football stadium. I had no interest in football whatsoever, even now. So I was the odd one out. Some things never change!

This was the time when the Kray Twins were jailed for a very long time. It seemed to be a much talked-about event. I could not understand what it was all about, but it was important to some people, and an end of an era of organised crime in London's underworld history.

The biggest event of that year was man landing on the moon. Big fucking deal was my reaction. Who cares? And can you go there on holiday? No!

For me, the event of that year was when I took myself off to the Royal Tournament, which was a great day. It was a military tradition for many years, for the army, navy and the RAF. It was an ideal opportunity for the armed service to display its skills. For me it was the King's Troop Royal Artillery, and the display by the Royal Marines, and they had a massed band along with the Guards. And the highlight was the Field Gun Crew, which was the toughest race in the world, and I can believe that the race dates back to when the navy had to move cannons across country in South Africa. It was a sight to see: the sounds of men heaving guns, and pulling and dragging the guns and limber over the obstacles. It was very exciting stuff for boys!

Mum went to Ireland and left me and Dad. I was not going to Ireland and that was that. I was not going to carry one more bucket of water, watch cows in the field, and go on endless car journeys to obscure places to visit people I had never heard of, no way!

Dad was at work. I got dinner money and was left to my own devices, which was fine by me. So it was pie and chips and a bottle of Vimto – sorted! Then we got a phone, our own phone, which was great, but I didn't know anyone who had a phone, so who do you phone? It was not long after my mum came back from Ireland, and it was the day before I went back to school. Mum was out at Bingo and I was alone in the house, and the phone rings so I put my best telephone voice on and the conversation goes as follows:

Me:	Hello.
Caller:	Is that David?
Me:	Yes. Who's that?
Caller:	Anthony (who was my mum's lifelong friend). Is your mudder there? (In a strong Mayo accent.)
Me:	No, she's out.
Anthony:	OK. Well, tells your mudder when she gets in, tell her her mudder is dead.
Me:	OK, thank you.
Anthony:	OK, David. God bless.

I think this is the only chance to tell you about Anthony Connelly. He is a farmer and has been all his life, and he has never been to Dublin, his own country's capital. But when my dad died he came to England for his funeral, which was a huge mark of respect. He had never flown in his life; he had never been in a lift and had never been on an underground train. In fact, I don't think he had ever left Mayo, so when he got to Finsbury Park it was, one might say, a culture shock!

So here I am with this awful news to tell my mum. I just didn't know what to do. Who could I tell to tell? No one: it was down to me. I had to do it. I can't even begin to tell you that awful feeling I had deep inside me. I knew the impact would be devastating, but I had to do it. I did not really know my nan – only for a short time – but I recall thinking, what if that was my mum? So I was fucked! I had to tell her! It was not long before the key turned in the front door. God, I hoped it would be Dad! Nah, no such luck; it was Mum.

My mum walked in and said, 'Hello, my darling,' which was her usual form of welcome, but she looked at me, straight in my eyes, and she knew that something was up. My eyes always give me away; always! I said to my mum, 'Mum, come and sit down,' which she did, on the edge of the bed. And I think she was expecting me to confess to some heinous crime and wanted to get my side of the story first before it went loud! But alas, it was not going to be that simple. So I said, 'Anthony called and said Nanny has died.' My mum just burst into tears, uncontrollable sobbing. All I could do was put my little arms around her and hug her as tight as I could. It was an awful moment, but I had to do it; there was no way out. She seemed to cry for ever. I felt so useless, but what could I do? Fuck all! Dad came home and he was upset for Mum, as you would expect. Mum left for Ireland, without me. She flew this time, which was a degree of extravagance, but it was the only way to get there in a hurry.

I started my new school term, and it was my first day of the second year, and the formula was the same as the first year, but I am now in 2D, with the same lads, and my form teacher was a bespectacled, balding Scot called Mr Macintyre. He had a reputation as a strict disciplinarian and would take no shit! I fucking hated the Porridge-Gobbler, as he was affectionately known. He was on my case from day one. This was gonna be a shit year; I felt it in my blood, and that never lets me down.

On the second day of the new term, I witnessed one of the best fights I have ever seen, and I have seen a few, but this was a corker! In the morning, before the bell went, we were all on the roof playground, and there were two boys, one called Albert and the other a tall bloke called Raphael. They both had the reputation of being 'hard nuts' and it was only a matter of time before these two titans would clash. It was bound to happen sooner or later, and this was the day! I don't actually recall what kicked it off, but it started when Raphael was pushed by Albert; so it's off! The blue touchpaper has been lit: retire to a very safe distance!

So Raphael goes to take his jacket off. Both his arms are behind his back, constrained by his jacket, and Albert steams in like a wild bull. Blow after blow in Raphael's face; bang, bang as Raphael falls back. Albert did not let up for a second. Bang, bang! It was a flurry of blows to Raphael's face; you could hear the smack of Albert's bony knuckle crash into Raphael's face. Bang, bang! The whole school seemed to surround these two, but what was really strange was there was no one shouting encouragement, as was usual. Everyone was watching in stunned silence; not even the usual chant of Fight, Fight!

Raphael's face is covered in blood – nose, mouth. Albert is doing him big style. Raphael is now back against a wall, arms still pinned back, and I am thinking Raphael just can't take much more of this punishment; he just can't!

Then, from nowhere, Raphael's arms are free! He staggered to his feet and he was like a steam train, a fucking wild man. His face was covered in blood and snot, but his arms are like pistons. Bang, bang, into Albert. Now Albert's on the receiving end of Raphael's punches and starts to fall back. Raphael is in for the kill. There was a non-stop rain of hard blows. Albert fell to the ground, and his shaven head hit the stone floor with such a wallop, I heard it. God that must have hurt! He is now fucked! And Raphael goes mad! Bang, bang! More blows to Albert's face!

Then out of the blue came the deputy head, a big Irish man

called Hartnet. He was a fearsome bloke, I'll have you know. He always stank of booze. He wore a tweed jacket and carried his bamboo cane at all times and he was not bothered about using it – as he did that morning. He laid into the crowd of spectators with not an ounce of mercy – whack, whack – and made his way to the two boys at it. If you ask me, I think Albert had a very lucky escape, because I have no doubt that Raphael would have murdered him, and I mean dead, as in no more; deceased! So Hartnet drags Raphael by the hair. Hartnet goes fucking bonkers. Albert gets to his feet, with the help of Hartnet's huge hand on the back of his collar, and he then sends them down to wait outside his class. Hartnet shouts out at the top of his voice, 'Form up!' And you have never seen 238 boys form up so fast. And he's going down between the form, lashing out with his cane at thigh level, and I caught it on my arse; fuck that hurt! I think he lost the plot! So we are all told to go down to the hall, NOW, which we did in absolute silence. Not a word was said by anyone; not a word! And I am thinking he's going to cane us all; must be? But he can't cane all the school, can he? Oh yes, if anyone could, he could! Nah... So it's wait-and-see time. We all form up, and then the 'fighters' are brought to centre stage. Raphael's blazer was covered in snot and blood, and Albert's eyes were almost closed due to the blows he had received. He looked like a boxer after ten rounds in a fight, but this was bare knuckles.

So Hartnet goes into one big long one – blah, blah, blah – and told all of us we must write down 200 times *I must not watch fights at school*, and he wanted it in by the next morning. Fucking hell! If he's gonna do this to us for just watching, what the fuck is he gonna do to the 'boys'? Hang them? But what I did notice was that he had a real long cane with him this time, and I knew what was coming next; been there! So Hartnet, with his special-occasion cane, gives them six of his very best. Whoosh, whoosh... I could feel that pain. I actually saw the boys flinch as the cane hit its mark, but they took it like men; not a visible tear. And that pissed Hartnet off more!

Hartnet got his lines the following morning. He waited at the top of the stairs; there was no escape. I don't think anyone failed to produce – even Raphael and Albert!

School was pretty much the same, but Macintyre started to give us homework, which, in my class was unheard of. We had spelling tests and then we had to read aloud, which was all new to us and was very humiliating to most of us. And, to be honest, I don't think Mcintyre had a clue as to the level of our illiteracy whatsoever, and this I think he found very frustrating. How can you teach twelve-year-olds who have the reading age of a two-year-old? Sometimes he would just talk to us about history, which I loved, and he always seemed to carry his book, which was on Mary Queen of Scots. He always had it with him; always. He would sometimes just talk even for a whole double lesson, and I learnt a valuable lesson from him: it's not what you say, it's the way you say it! He would have a captive audience in us with his historical stories; I loved it. As for the rest of the subjects, I didn't give a shit! As we were a Roman Catholic school for boys, there was a huge emphasis on religious education, but only Catholicism, nothing about any other religion, which I think was a shame; it would have been nice to know something about other religions, but that was a taboo subject! But Jesus was a Jew, and Pontius Pilate was a Jock. Well, he was because his father was an officer in the Roman Army on Hadrian's Wall, so he was born a Jock. Not a lot of people know that, as Michael Caine would say! I hated Mondays because the teacher would ask you what the previous day's sermon was about, or he would point and ask you which priest said Mass. 'What Mass did you go to, Edwards?' 'St. Peter's, sir, noon Mass, and it was Father Bloggs, sir!' And so on.

Some years later we had some priest come to the school, and he asked would we consider becoming priests? ME? I was not even an altar boy! Me, a priest? Nah! Now a bishop, yes. Dave the Bish… it's got a ring about it. But I declined their very kind offer.

So school and home life was still the same; still on the fucking sofa, but what could I do? Nuffink. So summer turned to autumn and then it was my birthday once more. I so wanted a bike, I would walk down to Chamberlain's bike shop on Sundays just to look at the bikes on sale in the window, and hope I got one this year. All the kids in the flats seemed to have bikes, but not me. Then came the big day. YES! YES! I got a green racing bike! I was over the moon, I can tell you! A brand-new bike with three gears, and it was new! Most of my mates' bikes were made up from other bikes, type of thing, but this was brand new! And it was mine!

I was mobile at last, and we would all go off on our bikes for miles and spend all day out. We would take packed lunches and the world was our oyster – or our lobster!

Christmas was at the door once more, and the table was once more in the front room, and yes, even more dead bird, and roast potatoes, and a load of mince pies.

That Christmas I got a dynamo for my bike, and from my nanny and Mary and Faye, I got a saddlebag. I was all set for the Tour de France! Soon after Christmas, Nan got a job in a children's home by the sea, and she moved out, which just left Mary and Faye. One down, two to go! I was still on the sofa. The novelty had soon worn off and was now a real pisser.

Ten

So ended 1969, and in came 1970, a new decade. This was the year the jumbo jet made its first commercial flight; Edward Heath became the prime minister of a Conservative government; and Charles de Gaulle of France kicked the bucket.

I still hated school, and I hated it with a passion. Or I should say I hated my form master, Mr Fucking Porridge-Gobbler Macintyre. He was always on my case; fuck knows why. He was a real fucking bully, and if there is one thing I hate in life with a real passion, it's a bully. Bullying does not just take physical form, it can be emotional or psychological, but you can call it what you like – it's bullying, and I fucking hate it! I don't think he ever said a nice word to me, so fuck him was the attitude that prevailed. But then things started to look up. We had a newish art teacher; her name was Miss Marsh. She was a bit of a hippy, tree-hugger, vegetarian, OK yeah type of person, but she said to me one day, 'You have a flare for art.' ME? And she would spend a bit of time with me, and that extra input made all the difference to my confidence. I had always liked to draw, but she showed me how to shade and do composition. It was great to feel good at something at last! She then started a form of art club, during lunch hour, which was brilliant; I could do something with my time other then walk around the streets looking like a hamster with a mouth full of chips.

But sometimes me and my mate Martin would go off around the 'bombed' houses. Of course, they weren't bombed; they were in fact derelict houses, as the whole area was up for redevelopment. There was street after street of old houses, and we would go looking for stuff. Anyway, we go in this old house and we find a room locked. Hello? This looked most interesting... So with the help of a massive iron pole, we broke into it, and it was a room full of dirty books with pictures of naked men and women doing things that naked people do! My reaction was fucking hell!

We struck gold here! Martin's response was how? Well, he was never the brightest colour in the box, so to speak. 'We can flog these at school and make a fortune!' I said. Martin's response was, to say the least, was rather reserved; it was a flat no! Why? 'If we are caught with them in school we are well fucked.' Yep, he had a very good point; well, that's if we got caught. But he was not having anything to do with it; he was a good Catholic boy. So we decided to leave it, and we did. But that night I could not get the pound signs out of my greedy mind, so I decided that if Martin didn't want a piece of the action I would find another partner. Sorted. My mind was made up, and off I go to sleep planning on how I am gonna spend all my loot!

On the bus to school I meet my mate Mickey, who was always skint; that poor fucker had to save up to be poor, if you get my meaning. So I tell him the score and he's well up for it. So that was sorted: rendezvous at lunchtime and we will go and fill our boots.

So at the designated time we RV, and off we go; through a number of back gardens, and not to mention over various walls, to get to the loot. So we get to the house and we tiptoe in and enter the room. Mickey's response was fucking hell! Yep, exactly what I hoped for. So as we are looking at the merchandise, we hear voices outside, and we just froze on the spot and looked at each other in fear and panic. Fucking hell! What we gonna do? So we bestowed ourselves with speed and ran upstairs, which was a very stupid thing to do, as it was isolated cover; if it had gone tits up, we had nowhere to run! So we go into this room and it was ankle deep in opened envelopes, thousands of them, but all with different addresses on them. And it was not rocket science that this was a very dodgy set-up. But we froze in fear. We were absolutely terrified, hardly breathing in case they heard us. We could hear muffled voices, but we did not move. We waited and waited; these geezers had come for 'our merchandise'.

After what seemed a lifetime, the door downstairs banged shut, but we waited and waited. Then we heard a vehicle pull away and drive off. Mickey and I looked at each other and, without a word said, we ran down the stairs and ran for our lives as fast as we could to the safety of our school. And I think that was the only time I was ever glad to see my school. That was a close one!

It was about this time a real funny thing happened in the flats.

There used to be a bloke in our flats we all called Mad Frankie. He was as odd as a box of frogs. He was very tall and had these mad eyes and looked like Lurch out of *The Addams Family* on the telly. He had this jacket that was far too small and he had these really long arms, and he never spoke he just looked. He was not the full ticket, and everyone kept well away from Mad Frankie.

Well, one day I was in the Scouts and we did a thing called Bob-a-Job. This was to raise funds for the Scout movement. You would offer your labour, and you would be paid a bob (5p). Fair one. So I am paired up with this fellow Scout called Ian, who did not live in our flats. So we go along the balcony, which in this case was on the second floor, and as I am knocking on the door to offer our labour, Ian goes and knocks on Mad Frankie's door. No! It was too late. He's invited in by Mad Frankie's mum and he beckons me to follow him. Fuck, what could I do? He's gone in! Mad Frankie's mum was also not the full ticket. She would lean over the balcony and talk to herself for hours in her native tongue, whatever it was.

My bottle was going big style, but I just had to go in. So as I go in, Ian is in the front room, so I go in too, and what we see is a motorbike. Yep, a fucking motorbike, full size, in the front room. How on earth did he get it up the stairs? And what we could make out from her was she wanted us to get rid of the bike. Maybe she wasn't that mad. But what could we do? So we shrugged our shoulders and backed out very sheepish, and I am praying that Mad Frankie does not come back from the loony bin and find us.

So back to the main event. Well, me and my mates are in the yard just sitting about doin' nuffink. It was a really hot day. Anyway, out of the blue we hear this shouting and screaming, from Mad Frankie's gaff. It was really bad. You'd have thought someone was getting murdered, and by the sound of it it was Frankie's old woman. It went on and on, louder and louder. So by this time almost the entire population of the block are hanging out their front doors wondering what the fuck is going on. But no one would go near Mad Frankie's.

So after what seemed an age, a police car shows up, and two coppers emerge, and very casually get out of the Panda car and take a very leisurely stroll up to Frankie's gaff and walk up to the front door. And with even more shouting and hooting, the door opens slightly and they manage to get inside. And now the screams are cranked to the max! And within a couple of minutes the door bangs open with a big crash, and the two coppers are out of there in a flash and running up the balcony minus their hats and a ripped tunic. This was met with a great row and cheers of the resident spectators, wolf whistles and more cheers. The police beat a hasty retreat to the car, and are now on the radio! So everybody is waiting for the outcome, and now the word has spread like wildfire, and loads more people turn up to see the show. Then, soon after the call is made by the police, a meat wagon appears on the scene, and the back is opened and a load of coppers pile out. I think it was about six. So we have eight coppers to go and sort out our Frankie Well, my money was still on Frankie!

So all the coppers go up the stairs to Frankie's gaff, and the screaming has not abated whatsoever. What the fuck is going on in there? The coppers get to the door in one group, and they charge in; all that was missing was a bugle call for the charge! After what seemed ages, they all emerged, carrying Frankie. One had got him around the neck, one was on each arm and leg, and the others... well, they had hold of him around any part they could grab. But Frankie was not having any of this. Talk about restrain: it was like a rugby scrum, with Frankie as the ball. His fists were flying and he was kicking out. All the coppers' hats were off and their jackets torn, and a couple of them had bloody noses. This was full-on entertainment on a grand scale; nothing like it had been seen since Rome's Circus Maximus. Every one was shouting 'Go on, Frankie my son!' It was comical to see, but nice to know your neighbourhood took such an interest in one's welfare! It took ages to get him down the stairs. Frankie had massive feet and wore these boots, the sort of thing Frankenstein would wear, and he was kicking out. I don't know what wages the coppers were on, but those coppers earned their pay that day!

Eventually they get him down into the yard, and the back of the meat wagon is wide open, ready to cart Frankie off. So they managed to physically throw Frankie in the back of the van, and slam the doors behind him as fast as they could: bang, closed and locked. All the coppers seemed to breathe a collective sigh of relief. One was holding his nose as the blood dripped into a small puddle. Jacket epaulettes were ripped off, buttons missing. They looked in tatters. One of them went and collected their helmets, of which they were short of one as some kid run off with it. So they only take a few moments to sort themselves out, and then? The van starts to rock from side to side. It was rocking like you wouldn't believe, and all the coppers looked at each other. This man had massive strength to do that! But they can't drive off with the van like that. Frankie was going potty! The crowd started: 'Come on, Frankie; Come on, Frankie!'

So the coppers can't drive off like that, so the only alternative was to go inside and get them fucking boots off him! Then all the coppers stood by the back door of the van and we watched them brace themselves for the battle with our Frankie. At the given time, the doors were flung open, and they all steamed in at Frankie. All the people on the balcony, watching this new development unfold, gave one great cheer! The racket in the back of the van was unbelievable – shouts and hooting. Then all of a sudden we saw one boot come flying out, and then after that came the other boot! Then the coppers all piled out of the back of the van, and once more the van doors were slammed shut with a crash and locked. All the coppers took a couple of minutes to sort themselves out, and got in their car and van and drove off out of the flats with a great cheer!

Frankie's old woman was taken away in an ambulance, and we never saw either of them again. Frankie was a fucking nutter! But he was our nutter!

Eleven

So because of redevelopment to the block of flats where my mate Mickey lived, he had to move, which meant his large family of seven sisters, a new baby brother, himself and mum and dad. A total of eleven in the family. That's not a family: that was a tribe! And the house was situated near the Holloway Road. He attended the same school as me, and one day he announced that he had joined the Army Cadets. 'What are the Army Cadets?' was my response. He said it was like the Scouts but with the army, and you get a free uniform and get to play with guns. That sounded good to me!

So after school one day we made our way down to St James, to the Army Cadet Centre, which a was rather grandiose-looking building. I was impressed. This was no church hall set-up; this was the real deal!

Mickey took me up to the office and I was introduced to a member of the adult staff, and was then told to go and wait in the canteen, where we got a cup of tea, as we didn't have enough money to buy a bottle of Coke, and I waited until I was sent for. I spent my time looking at pictures on the wall of various men in various uniforms, holding regimental colours; all very military. As I waited, other boys came in and completely ignored me; not a friendly word of welcome from any of them. I am thinking to myself, maybe they're not allowed to talk to me.

Shortly after that, they had to form up for parade, and I'm back on my own. Then the chap I was introduced to came and collected me and took me to the office, and they took my details: name, address, that type of stuff. It that didn't take long, and I was told to go and join the others. It felt quite odd, no welcome to the Cadet force. It was all very official.

So I go downstairs and 'fall in' with the rest of the boys, and we do drill. Lots of marching about, stamping of feet, which was very important!

Then we had a tea break, and after that there was a lesson on the Bren gun, how it worked, how to strip it down. Our instructor was Sergeant Spanner; he really knew his stuff. Within a couple of seconds he had the weapon in bits, all lined up in a nice neat row of well-oiled and spotless parts, and then within a few seconds it was all back in one working piece, I was sooo impressed. I so wanted to be that good! And then we took it in turns to strip it down, and it seemed to take ages, as little hands fumbled around the cocking mechanism, and bumbled and dropped bits with a metallic clank on the highly polished parquet floor of the drill hall. Our instructor was patient and was an ideal tutor. He was always talking you through the motions and didn't seem to be bothered if you got it wrong. It was just a take-your-time, get-it-right sort of mindset. It was great! I had on my very first day marched up and down and held a real machine gun. This was the dog's bollocks!

My Cadet night was the highlight of the week, I just could not wait for drill night, as it was technically called, and I was so looking forward to getting issued my uniform, but in the meantime I would save up for my boots, which you had to buy yourself, and my school dinner money was put to one side. It would not take me long to get the money, and then I would get issued my uniform.

Each drill night we would do drill – lots of stamping about – and then a lecture on section attack, anti-ambush drill; all good stuff, and ideal for the future general I hoped to be! The other cadets were from various parts of London. Some of the cadets were rough because there was no one rougher than them. It was big fish in small pond, and I was a tiny fish! Just like school we were always referred to by our last name, which I disliked immensely, but hey, this was the army.

After about six weeks of attending regularly, me and two other lads were taken to another military-looking building to be issued our kit: our own uniform battledress; jumpers, heavy-wool-for-the-use-of, one; shirts, wool, two-for-the-use-of, two; and so on, until the kit bag that was issued to you was full and weighed a ton.

So the next drill night I am kitted out. My dad was impressed with my commitment and gave me a £1 towards my boots, which

I had got the day before from the local army surplus store in Hornsey Road. I stayed up late polishing my boots. I felt good in my uniform, and they say when you look good, you feel good, and I felt great. At least this uniform fitted, unlike my Scout uniform. Well, this was the army!

So on drill night, when we had drill, I could really bang my feet: left wheel, right wheel, about face; all the marching stuff. It was great. After we did our drill we would go and have a break in the mess – army-speak for canteen – and there you could get a hotdog, Wagon Wheel, Walnut Whip, and, of course, a Mars bar. I found it hard to make friends with some of the cadets. They somehow did not accept new people for some reason or other, which was very strange because they themselves must had been new boys once, but I did get quite chatty with some other new recruits. Maybe it was the fact we were all new boys and that gave us that common bond.

In the mess was a poster on the wall with all the badges of the British Army, and I said to my mate Mickey that it would be nice to collect them, as I already had one, which was my regiment, the Royal Green Jackets. Mickey told me of a shop that sold them in King's Cross, and if I wanted we would stop on the way home and have a look. So after the drill night was over, Mickey and I made our way to King's Cross, and under the large driveway that led to the mainline station was a small parade of shops, a coffee bar – which seemed to be full of railway men sipping tea, and smoking – a chemist, and the badge shop. The shop had loads of military badges, and sold useful stuff like camping kits, knives and binoculars and so on. I decided I would save my pocket money and collect army badges and one day I might just have them all. Well, that was the plan.

It was a couple of weeks before we were going away on week-end exercises. This is what I wanted; this was where we could put into practice what we had learned and play real soldiers. But there was a slight problem; it was bullying, and it was rife. The older and much larger cadets would walk up to you and stand as hard as possible on your highly polished toecaps. You'd be asked to lend money, which you never got back. The usual stuff.

Me and some of the newer recruits were a bit apprehensive

about going away for a weekend, which would leave us rather exposed to a higher degree of bullying. And it was then we heard about initiation, which was that when you were asleep, the other cadets – of course the older and bigger ones – would get you and cover your bollocks in boot polish. How very nice of them; how thoughtful. Nah! That's bollocks!

So off we go on the train to Aldershot, and then we walked to the camp. We were gonna be under canvas (i.e. in tents). Well we had a great time! Well, I did, map reading, patrolling, and even war stuff at night – and not a sign of anyone coming near me with a tin of boot polish! It was a wonderful weekend, even though I was knackered when I got home; it felt like I had been away for ages.

I was getting better at map reading, and my drill was coming on, and I knew all about the Lee Enfield .303 rifle, I could strip a Bren Gun and so on; it was fun. But there was this undercurrent of unease with some of the older and bigger cadets, who were real fuckers. I kept out of their way as much as possible.

It was soon camp time again, and off on the train once more and the long walk to our accommodation, which was an old cavalry barrack block, which I think was called Beaumont Barracks, a two-storey building. Downstairs was the kitchens and mess area, and via two very wide staircases was the very wide veranda, which led to the accommodation area, holding about twenty beds, and at the end, near the door, was a small room for the NCOs.

As we were getting sorted out and sorting out our kit, I was getting some strange looks from some of the older cadets. I just had a feeling in my blood, and that never, ever lets me down. I was on alert status. I felt tonight was the night I was gonna have a very shiny pair of bollocks before the dawn came, and I was not happy about the thought of it. So it's about 10 p.m. and it's lights out, and we are all in our bunks, and to my relief, and I dare say the other new lads' relief, one of the adult instructors decided to sleep in the end room. It was very comforting to know we had an adult to save us from the humiliation of the initiation.

The next day we were up early. We started with a large well-cooked breakfast, and then we were off in full kit to a place called the Long Valley, and it was here we practised section attacks, platoon defensive positions and all sorts of war stuff. At the end of what was a very long day we headed back to our billet, for some hot scoff, to sort out our kit, and go to our beds. I felt so uneasy; I don't know why, but I did. It was my blood telling me to be very careful. A few weeks previous I had bought a penknife from the local paper shop, just to have. It was not ever bought with any intention to use as a weapon; it's what boys carried; it was not unusual. But I just had it and carried it about. As I said, it was just a boy thing.

But as I lay in my bunk that night, I got my knife out and opened it and held it tightly in my clenched fist under my single pillow. I closed my eyes, but I did not want to find sleep, I was on full alert status; my ears were like a fucking bat's. I would listen to every sound, every creak, any sound heightened by my awareness. This would be the night it's gonna happen, as the NCO was not staying in the little room at the end of the barrack, and I was right!

It was very late that night when I heard some scuffled movements, then muffled frantic movements, just a couple of bunks down from me. Then I heard a muffled whimper. The BASTARDS! They were doing Dougie, a real small lad. I just kept silent, not a movement; I just gripped my penknife harder. Then I heard some sniggering and then silence; and then I heard a low, muffled crying.

In the morning I woke very early – I had barely slept at all – and looked down towards Dougie's bunk, which was empty. I got up and tiptoed down to the ablutions, and I saw little Dougie trying to wash the black polish from himself. He never said a word, but I could see he had been crying for a lifetime. I felt so bad, I could not say a word. I felt terrible inside that I had done nothing to help him. I felt a coward! And that's a terrible feeling to have; it made me feel sooo very low inside. Then I made a promise to myself that I would never stand by and let anything like that happen again to anyone; I would rather get a punch in the mouth than feel that bad inside. It was awful feeling! But I will give Dougie his due: he never said a word!

I then said fuck this, I don't need this. And after that weekend I handed my kit in and walked away from St James. I often wonder if the adult instructors knew what was going on. Was it 'character building'? Well my answer to that was bollocks; it was bullying to its highest degree. A man's character is better built with encouragement, not having his balls covered in boot polish!

Things at school were looking pretty much the same, but now we had exams, which to me was a new concept, as it was for the other boys, and I think the attitude that prevailed was that we had been crap so far, so why change now? And I can understand that.

To me at the time, exams were only to prove to others that you had a good memory and retained a certain amount of knowledge and were able to roll it out on the day of the race.

In my late teens I had some dealings with 'travellers' or 'pikeys'. They are not educated and had no formal education but were very sharp – at least the ones I had dealings with. They had to be sharp to survive!

I think this would be the only time I get to tell you about my dealings with the 'travellers' or 'pikeys' or 'diddycoys', whatever you wish to call them; take your pick. I used to use a boozer in Liverpool Road, called the White Horse, and I was there one Saturday lunchtime having a beer with a pal of mine called Kev. Now, Kev's story is an interesting story, which I will tell you about later. So we are having a beer, standing at the bar as you do, and it was the time almost every pub had a pool table, and pool was a very popular sport in the pubs, but as it involved the use of a ball and a long, sharp stick I had no interest whatsoever. So what used to happen if people wanted to play, they would place a 10p on the side of the table and wait their turn. Primitive but effective. There were quite a few geezers playing pool and watching the horse racing on TV between mouthfuls of lager. All very civilised stuff. But there were these three geezers playing pool. Anyway, there was a dispute as to whose 10p was on the table and who was going to play next. Well, these geezers are getting real cocky towards the smaller, slightly built geezer who was on his jacks (on his own). And this geezer had a type of 'Jackeen' accent, which is from Dublin, and the row was getting very heated and it looked like it would kick off any second. So Kev and I looked at each other, and it was like a form of telepathy; I could read his mind and he was thinking the same as me. Three on two! Nah!

So I said to this geezer, 'Look, pal, that's his 10p; I saw him put it down.' And his response was rather negative: 'It's got fuck all to do with you!' And then Kev said, 'It can be if you want it to be, pal!' And one of the three geezers decides now that there are three of us – me, Kev and the young pikey – the odds were not in their favour, so they decided to forget it. 'It's only a game, mate.' So it settled down and no one seemed to lose face. The game carried on and the young pikey just looked at me and Kev and nodded in thanks, so that was the end of that, so we thought.

About an hour later or so, more beer had been consumed and the pikey goes for a piss – well, you would do – but as he did, immediately two of the geezers follow him to the bog, so Kev and I decided to go as well. As we walked in, you could feel the tense atmosphere, but pikey had his piss, and so did the two geezers, and for that matter so did we. The pool players departed, and Kev and I are at the bar, and the pikey sends down a couple of beers and he came up to us and said, 'Cheers, lads. Thanks for watching my back,' in a very strong Dublin accent, so we said it was OK, we just didn't like the odds and that was the end of that.

A few weeks later I am back in the boozer on my jacks. It was a Sunday lunchtime, and the boozer was absolutely packed with pikeys. The place was rammed with them: men, women, the whole tribe was out! And they looked a real rough lot, I can tell you! So I am standing at the bar, waiting to get served, my tongue down to my knees, and then the governor's missus puts a pint in front of me, and as I go to pay she says, 'That chap bought it.' 'What chap?' I ask. 'That one.' And she points to a real big bloke at the far end of the bar. He looked a real fucking hard nut. You kinda get to know hard men. It's not their size; it's not what they wear; it's in the eyes. I can usually tell, and this man had the eyes. And what I did notice was the amount of Tom (jewellery) he was wearing. And he had enormous hands. And I had the feeling he was a pikey elder, if that's the right word. So I am thinking, Oh no! Is this the famous he-buys-me-a-drink-and-I-get-the-next round-in-and-there's-fucking-loads-of-them trick? Ah, fuck it, let's see what happens!

So I am minding my own business, watching the fat-knacker

band, which wasn't their name. It was a name given to the bands that play in the local pubs, usually Irish, middle-aged men wearing dickey bows, singing the hits of Don Williams or Tammy Wynette and other country-and-western songs, and I had the feeling that, under prolonged exposure, you would grow udders. I fucking hated it, but there was nothing you could do about it, so drink more beer! I don't get the point of the band playing music so loud you can't even talk or hear yourself think. You could not dance even if you wanted to, because they did not have a licence for it! Another of life's great mysteries; a bit like how do guide dogs know which road to turn up?

The object of the exercise was to get as much beer down one's fat neck in the required time of two hours, which was the Sunday opening hours, so speed drinking was the name of the game; that's the way it was. So I go back to the bar, and my eyes fall upon the pikey from the pool table a couple of weeks ago, and he sends me down a beer and comes over for a chat – well, it was more like a shout. His name was Tony and he was from Dublin. He had married into the travelling people, which was quite a rare thing to happen. He thanked me once more for standing up for him as a traveller. I said I didn't know he was a traveller, and the reason I helped him was because I didn't like the odds, but he really appreciated it, which was kinda nice. So he introduced me to various others and I felt so at ease with these people. The ones he introduced me to thanked me for helping their 'Little Tony'. They were rough people, but I liked them; not because of the fact they would not let me buy a beer, but because of the way they were. Then Tony introduced me to the 'hard nut' who sent me down the pint. His name was Sonny. He was a gypsy bare-knuckle fighter. I knew he was a fucking hard case!

Now let me tell you Kevin's story. I met Kevin in the local boozer. He was a tall man, about six foot with an athletic build. He had one eye, having lost the other in a car accident. He was divorced and had three sons, who were fine young lads. He lived in a nice flat above a shop in Upper Street, Islington. He was a second-hand car dealer, and he was going out with a nurse from the Whittington Hospital whose name was Sue. And we became firm mates; he was a good bloke.

So the second-hand car trade took a turn for the worse, and he got a job delivering meat for a wholesaler out of Smithfield, but that did not last long; he just didn't have the freedom, so he became a minicab driver to get a few nicker, as you do.

So we are having a light ale this night in the boozer and he says, 'This black geezer gets in his motor and asks me to take him to this shop near Finsbury Park, so I do. He goes in the shop and asks me to wait, so I do, but he leaves this bag in the motor. So I have a look inside and fuck me! It's full of money! Full of money; loads of it; all in bundles.' My reply was, 'Nah! You're pulling my pisser!' But he assured me it was the God's honest truth! Knowing him as I did, he didn't tell porkies, but what he did say was, 'If he does it again, I am having it away!' Fair one, I think to myself. And then the conversation moved on to more cultivated subjects, such as the index of the *Financial Times* and the price of beer!

A few weeks later I am at my mum's and I get a phone call from a pal of mine in Ireland, telling me the police are looking for Kevin Butler. He had done a bunk with a load of money and was on the Irish TV. Well, that was the first thing I knew about it; I hadn't seen Kev for a couple of days anyway. Mick was a mate, and he knew me and Kevin were good mates. You see, Kevin's mum and dad were Irish, and what had happened was the Old Bill had put two and two together and come up with forty-seven and a half! In case he did head to Ireland, good bit of forward planning on the Old Bill's side, but Kevin was a sharp bloke; he would have planned his exit down to the very last detail!

I knew nothing about it, but it made the newspaper the next day! I was surprised, to say the least. He had done it! I heard nothing from him whatsoever. But early one morning I get a visit from the Old Bill, and they wanted to ask me some questions about Kevin Butler, and I told them the truth; I knew nothing about it, and that was the God's honest truth!

I think the reason why they did not visit me sooner was I would imagine they had my phone tapped in case Kevin called me, and would trace the call or whatever. But I got all the 'Well, if he brings back the money, it won't be such a serious offence, etc, etc.' But they knew it was bollocks, and they knew that I knew it was bollocks!

I never heard from Kevin again, but many years later I am at a party and find myself talking to a retired ex-copper who had been on the case at the early stage of the investigation. And I don't know how we got talking about it, but this is what he told me: this bloke was a Nigerian businessman who gets a holdall full of cash – £250,000 in cash. So he calls a minicab and decides to go and purchase some pukka hi-fi kit from a shop in Tollington Way. So Kevin's the cab driver, and he tells moneybags he's going to park up the motor, and yep that's OK, and heads off to the shop, but leaves the bag of money in the car. So he gets his shopping and comes back to the car – but no car. And he waits and waits and waits. Soon an hour has gone by and no sign of Kevin or the money! Now he's flapping big time!

So he decides to call the police, and after a while the police turn up. So he tells the boys in blue, and they decide to go down the nick and get this sorted. So you have a Nigerian businessman trying to tell the Old Bill that he had £250,000 in cash in a holdall. Why? Which bank? So the police have to clarify where this money was from and for what? But by now the banks are closed, so they have to sort that one out. By the time they clarify that the money is legitimate, it's seven hours since anyone has seen Kevin or the money!

I knew Kevin as well as anyone, and what I do know, without any fear of contradiction, is that he was no fool by any stretch of the imagination, and if he did decide to have it away with the loot, he would have planned an exit strategy to the last detail, which he obviously did – ha ha! You can be a long way in seven hours with a holdall full of cash; anywhere in the world!

I never heard from Kevin again and have no idea what happened, but what did happen soon after was his youngest son was involved in an accident and was admitted to the Whittington Hospital. It was nothing serious, but the story was given to the press, who published it, and of course the police hoped he would break his cover, but he didn't. Kevin was too sharp for that. But I think he made a call to someone to ask how his boy was and was told the score, and that was the end of that strategy for flushing him out!

I never heard anyone say a bad word about Kevin; he was a

real nice geezer and was a good mate! So I do hope he got away with it. He never harmed anyone; he just took the money and ran. Good luck to him. And if ever you read this, Kev, be lucky and keep safe.

I have seen some very funny things in my life and, come to think of it, a lot of these have been in boozers, and one of the funniest things was in the boozer with Kevin, in the White Horse. It was a wet afternoon and we are standing at the bar with a beer, and this old West Indian bloke shuffles into the boozer. He's wearing an old trilby hat, and from the formation of his mouth I would suggest that he had no teeth. So he goes to the bar and asks, 'Can I have a bockle of Guinness, please?' And he's got this old mutt of a dog with him. Well, as he pours his 'bockle' of Guinness, the dog cocks his leg up the bar and pisses up the bar!

The barman, called Humy Mick, goes into one! And in a very strong Irish accent, 'Get der fuck off!' to the dog, and the dog whimpers off. And the old West Indian bloke says, in a very strong West Indian accent, 'You come kick me dog and call him fuck off, and you know him name is Bonzo!' We were in fits of hysterical laughter.

So the exams came around and I did my very best, and we waited for our results. These were not big important exams, but still exams, and some of them were not at all favourable and we had to take them home. And the attitude that prevailed with my classmates was 'no fucking way is my old man gonna see this' and they ended up in tiny pieces in the bus stop bin!

I took mine home unopened and waited for the 'fall out', but to my sheer surprise it was good! Fucking hell! This education stuff was starting to work! And I got an A in art; me, get an A! Fuck, an A! I was so proud of myself: an A!

A couple of weeks later I was given a letter to give to my mum and dad. Hello, this don't look good. Well, I did what I was told and handed over the brown envelope. I was quite concerned about it; what had I done wrong? And once more I was surprised. It was an invitation to the school prize-giving ceremony: I had won a prize for my art. I could not believe it! Me! A prize! I was ever so proud, but I did not share this news with all my class-mates, as I didn't think it would have been well received by many of them, so the less said the better was the order of the day.

My mum and dad were very pleased, and Mum said she would come along to the big event. The prize-giving was held in Islington town hall, and I was in my best school uniform. Well, I only had one, but it was spotless. I got a new pair of shoes and a new grey V-neck jumper for the prize-giving. The place was packed. The school had about 500 boys and of course only the selected few were awarded a prize, but the place was packed. My name was called and I walked along up the stairs to the centre of the stage and was given a box from the headmaster and a round of applause. Much different from the last time I took centre stage and a darn lot less painful, I might add! I returned to my desig-nated seat and opened the box. It was a fuck-off box of paints and brushes. I was over the moon. It was mine and I had earned it. My joy knew no bounds.

In the long summer evenings I would run around with my mates in the flats. My mum would take little Faye out on the No. 14 bus to Green Park, and they would walk along Piccadilly, and look at the posh shops and then along to Shaftsbury Avenue, and then get the bus home. It was a nice way to spend a summer evening, but me, I was happy playing out.

One evening Mum and Faye came home and said they had seen a shop that was full of soldiers and army stuff. Well, that captured my imagination straight away, and I asked Mum all about it, and she said if it was a nice evening next week she would take me and show me, and that was a promise. And that was a promise I would not let her forget or break, no way! True to her word, the next summer evening she was not at work, we hopped on the No. 14 and headed to Green Park and walked along Piccadilly and passed some very posh shops. And there it was: the soldier shop. It had regimental drums and swords and uniforms and, most of all, model soldiers. I cupped my hands around my eyes and looked inside. It was incredible! Loads of glass cases with model soldiers in uniforms and all sorts of headdresses. It looked fantastic, but was it a museum and not a shop? But I saw price

*'Oddball', me and 'The Neff' on our way to a fancy-dress party,
1975*

Me at the age of four. 'Almost a man!'

The Favourite!

Front of Leyden Mansions

Leyden Mansions.
I lived on the ground floor

Blythe Mansions.
Image courtesy of the Islington Local History Centre

Traditions staff: a league of real gentlemen!
Bob, Mr Caton, Mr Griffiths and the one and only Brian Sheppard.

tags on some of the items, and then I was sure it was a shop.

I recall this moment in my life as if it was only yesterday: I turned to my mum and said, 'One day I am gonna work there.' And Mum's response to that was, 'Yes, dear, of course you are.' But I knew deep down in my heart I would; I just knew it in my blood. I would one day!

School was much the same: usual shit, different day. But two things happened about the same time. Mr Porridge-Gobbler Macintyre decided he would take those of them who wanted to go to the cinema, to see the latest Hollywood blockbuster *Butch Cassidy and the Sundance Kid*, starring Robert Redford and Paul Newman. This was a certificate A, which meant you needed an adult to be with you if you were under eighteen. Well, that's the way it was. So all the lads wanted to go and had to bring in 2/- (10p); but me, I would not go anywhere with that man, only to the fucker's funeral! The boys had a great time and by all accounts Macintyre behaved himself.

The other memorable event was at the height of the skinhead cult, and the school would not tolerate any of this in any way. They banned the wearing of boots and imposed a strict uniform policy to ensure it did not proliferate within the school, but that was easier said than done! Well, my mate Mickey got himself a crew cut haircut, and it suited him. It was short, but it kinda fitted his head, if you get my meaning. So my other good mate, called Steve Tannet, decided he wants a crew cut too. Fair one, nothing wrong with that. So he gets the loot off his dad to get a haircut on the way home from school. So he goes to the same barber shop as Mickey did. Well, I don't know what happened; I think there was what one might call a language barrier, and Steve asks for a crew cut, and fuck me did he get one! He was like an egg; they cut it almost to the fucking bone! He was bald! I mean bald; fucking bald! You could see the veins on his scalp. Steve's dad goes fucking berserk! And he is grounded except for school. Well, when I saw him at the bus stop in the morning, it looked worse. Everybody was looking at him; he looked like a new recruit in the French Foreign Legion. So he goes to school, and the form master goes fucking bonkers and poor old Steve could do fuck all about it. They gave him a letter to take home to his mum and dad. What could they say? 'Dear Mr Tannet, please buy your son a wig!'

As I said, the school had a real dim view on the skinhead thing, and boots were not allowed, no fucking way; that was the law! But some kids, that's all they had. These were not a fashion statement but all they had. Only if you brought a note in from your mum were they allowed; the only reason.

So it was a Monday afternoon and it was the last lesson. It was hymn practice and we all had to attend; it was a no-way-out option as they took a register, so that was that. So all 240 boys sat in nice neat rows in the main hall, and the sun came through the large windows, and it was a beautiful day. And we are about to give it large with 'Onward Christian Soldiers' and the other usual hymns. But sitting in the front row straight in front of me was a geezer called Patterson, and he was a bit of a lad; not a real villain, just one of the boys. Well, he's sitting down with his legs stretched out, at the end of which was a big shiny pair of Dr Marten boots. This was asking for trouble, and it was just around the corner and closing in at a rapid rate of knots in the form of Mr Fucking Porridge-Gobbler Macintyre.

He walks in the hall with a bundle of sheet music under his arm and his glasses at the end of his snotter (nose), plonks his arse down at the piano, ready to give it whompo! And, like a radar, his eyes fell upon Patterson's boots. Light the blue touch paper and retire to a safe distance! Didn't it just! Macintyre has got the instant camel (not a very happy bunny). 'What are you wearing, boy?' in a real loud Scottish accent. Patterson's response was 'Boots.' Not 'Boots, sir'; just 'Boots'. And now Macintyre goes fucking bonkers! 'Boots? Boots! You know the rules boy! Why are you wearing boots?'

Patterson's response was someone had thrown his shoes on the roof of the art class. Macintyre goes into a large one, strides over to Patterson and grabs him by the scruff of his neck and frogmarches him over to the window, which, in fact, overlooked the art class roof. Which was lucky for Patterson, for there was a pair of shoes on the roof, to our amazement. But somehow this made Macintyre even worse; he lost the plot and started to whack Patterson about the head with his open hand. Patterson makes a dash for the door. It bangs open with a loud crash, and he legs it down the corridor. And by now Macintyre is chasing him, and Patterson is shouting at the top of his voice. Fuck knows what was going on out there! Probably murder!

So while this is going on, the rest of us are really playing up, throwing hymn books at each other, shouting, fighting; mayhem! Mayhem? It was almost a riot!

So after a short time the deputy head shows up and restores some order to the mayhem, but we can all still hear Patterson screaming his head off. No one knew what was happening, so the deputy head heads off to investigate the screams of Patterson, and he has a concerned look on his face as to what the fuck is going on down the corridor. So as soon as he's out of the door, it goes mental again: shouting, screaming, more bedlam! He must have been halfway down the corridor and comes back to maintain order, which he did, but he still needs to find out what's going on down the corridor. So he bites the bullet and leaves us once more and goes off. He's gone a short time and he returns with this real wimpy-looking bloke who was a supply teacher for the first year: long trendy hair, velvet jacket, and a flower-power-type shirt. A bit of a girlie, if you ask me. And what I had noticed was he didn't walk: he minced.

So order has been restored, and we all settle down, and the deputy head leaves us once more. Well, he must have been gone all of two minutes and this wimpy teacher says the one thing he never should have said: 'Does anyone have a spare hymn book?' For fuck sake, what a stupid thing to say! Well I was sitting in the second row from the front, and the air was full of flying hymn books. Everyone lobbed their book at him; he was bombarded with 239 hymn books at the same time! It was so funny to see! Well, the deputy head returned and restored order, and was really pissed with our behaviour. I wonder why?

I don't know what happened to Patterson; he never came back to the school and nothing more was said about it. But Macintyre did quieten down after that. Fuck knows why, he just did. I still hated that man.

Home life was much the same. Mum got a new job as a cleaner for an airline coach terminal at the back of Tottenham

Court Road. And at long last Mary and Faye left us, and I got my bed back. At last!

When I was not out playing in the flats with my mates, I would be watching TV, and popular TV was *On the Buses*, starring Reg Varney, *The Fenn Street Gang*, and *The Saint*, starring Roger Moore. By far the most popular programme was *The Avengers*, which I thought was a complete load of old bollocks. You had this aristocrat-type English gentleman who drove a convertible vintage Bentley, and his name was John Steed; and his accomplice was Emma Peel, who wore tight leather jumpsuits and was an expert in unarmed combat. And they would go off, solving crimes committed by some lunatic professor, who had invented a race of robotic men, called Cybernauts. What a complete load of old bollocks! But the nation loved it.

We broke up for the summer holiday, and it was the usual: Mum and Dad at work, and me left to my own devices, which was great. I was the master of my own destiny. But for some reason I found myself getting into more fights and on a regular basis, and more often than not I would be the recipient of a fucking good hiding, but I was not going to be bullied any more.

There was one bloke in particular, called Danny. He was a lump of a bloke; he was always on my case. Any chance he had, he would have a go at me. He would spit on me and all sorts of stuff, and of course I had no brothers to back me up or go and sort him out. It was down to me! One day he just walked up to me and punched me in the mouth for no reason at all, but he never did it to anyone who, for want of better word, had back-up. In the flats where we lived I had loads of mates, but if they got stuck in they would get it from him too, when they were on their own; and then they would get their older brothers, and it was like that. I think they call it politics!

Anyway, one day the cunt has a real go at me, and bangs me right in the mouth, and fuck it hurt! It cut deep into my lip. It was so painful. Well, that was it! Now I am gonna fight back; this was the time. My blood was at boiling point; I had such a rage in my heart, I was fit to kill! So after I had sorted my lip out with TCP, I had made up my mind I was gonna do him! So I watched him and waited for him as he strolled across the yard. I ran upstairs of one of the blocks, and I had a big old army web belt in my hand. It was a 1938 pattern type, which had a big fuck-off brass buckle on it. This was my weapon; that was gonna balance it out. So I ran up the stairs to the third floor and shout out to him, 'Danny, you fat wanker! And you are one lazy fat bastard too!' He goes bonkers. 'Wait till I get my hands on you!' 'Yeah right, fatty!' So he's heading straight for me, and he's worked it out: that the block I was shouting from had only one staircase, which meant I was trapped: no way out! Well, that's exactly what I wanted him to think. For your information this was the tactic employed by Hannibal at the Battle of Cannae in 216 BC, when he fought Lucius Paullus and Gaius Varro and won! But though the Battle of Cannae was not fought in the stairwell of a block of flats in Hornsey Rise, the outcome would be the same if my plan failed: it would be a massacre!

Danny Boy heads to the staircase, and I run down from the third floor to the second floor, and hide behind the corner of the balcony and wait for him to pass me. My heart was beating like a drum, my mouth was so dry, and I was shaking with fear; and I am thinking if this goes lumpy, I am fucking dead! But as fate would have it, my luck held, and, as planned, in his anger he comes up the stairs. And I am thinking should I go now, and have the advantage of the elevated height, or stick to the plan? This is all happening in milliseconds, but I keep to the plan. And as he turns his back on me, I lash out with the belt buckle across the back of his head, whack! And again, whack! He lets out a shriek of pain and holds his head. I don't stop; I just keep going; whack, whack! I had a tiger by the tail; I had to keep going! I remember shouting at him, 'How does that feel?', over and over. He started to cry and cower away, in tears.

I could not believe what I had done! I was shaking with fear, but I had done him; I got him! The feeling of utter exhilaration was magnificent. I don't think I had ever felt that good in my life before; I had won! The scent of victory in my nostrils was almost intoxicating! I had fought back!

But I knew I had to keep well clear of him in case he started on me again, but at least I fought back. Yes, I used a weapon, but he was much older then me, and was much bigger too. My mates were well impressed with what I had done, but warned me to take great care in case he got me. I was careful, but I never had any more run-ins with him.

It was another bright sunny Sunday afternoon, and my mate Rob and I decided to go for a walk over the Hill, which was Crouch End. And in those days nothing was open on a Sunday, except the odd papershop which usually closed at noon, and there was nuffink open at all, not many cars, and it was a bit like a small provincial town; on a Sunday it was dead. All that was missing was the tumbleweed blowing down the road. So we would go window-shopping just to kill time before we went back to my place to listen to the charts on Radio One. Well, that was the plan. We get as far as Cecil Park Road, and we are met with the sight of about seven or eight 'young'uns' from the flats. Their ages ranged from five to ten, and they were walking up the hill wearing these jumpers, big fuck-off jumpers, real chunky ones which were the height of fashion at the time. So they got these jumpers on, which were about twenty times their size, and to add to this they were all wearing short trousers with snake belts and the arse out of their trousers. Some had plimsolls; some had sandals. And they were just normal kids out of the flats, well worn I would say, but not ragged – that's a bit much. But none were from well-off stock, if you get my meaning. But they got these fuck-off jumpers. So I said to little Freddy, who was from a large, poor family, and he had fuck all, 'Where did you get those from?' His response was 'We nicked them' – with a great degree of pride, I might add. 'Well, I fucking know that,' I said, 'but from where? All the shops are closed.' And Freddy and Paul said, 'Simple. We will show you.' So we all head off down the road, the lads still wearing their swag, complete with price tag.

So we come to a trendy men's clothes shop, which had a mock-Georgian bow window and was called Barnaby Rudge, which, of course, was a character of Charles Dickens, and its name suited the shop's character. Rob then says, 'How the fuck did you nick the stuff, then?' And little Freddy produces a folded-down car aerial from the inside of his trousers, and it had a hook on the end, which they had made by bending it double; sorted! But Rob and I look at each other and still can't work it out. And then the light goes on! Then Freddy kneels down, puts the aerial through the letter box, and hooks a jumper off the rail and pulls it through the letter box! So fucking simple! Rob and I just laughed. And then we got some for ourselves. Well, we just couldn't not, could we? I often wonder what the shop keeper thought when he opened his shop on that Monday morning. As for the 'young'uns'... well, you got to give them 11 out of 10 for ingenuity! I am still shit at maths!

Another memorable incident comes to mind, which also happened about that time. In Blythe Mansions was a hall. I suppose you could call it a 'community hall', but the word 'community' was not a common word then. It became a 'buzz word' much later. It's like so many words have changed; if a geezer was a homosexual he was a poof, and the word 'gay' was never used in that context. And the word 'paedophile'... it sounds like you would find in it the tool cabinet at metal work at school. Anyone who was a kiddie-fiddler – not that we ever heard of anyone – was a 'nonce', and that's being kind about it. I would rather call them 'dirty sick bastards'. And there were other words, like counselling; never heard that one either, but that's the way it was. But many years later, I was working in a museum and found myself being a co-ordinator of a weekend event, and I was summoned to a meeting in the marketing department. And we have this meeting, and this was the final statement from the chap in charge; so stand by: 'OK, then. We've thought out of the box, and this is what we got, so now we have an overview, we will touch base next week!' Now try it in English! But that's marketing speak.

For me to translate this episode I will have to give you the layout of the flat. The flats were built on a hill and the main entrance to the hall was via Watersville Road, and access to the hall itself was up a long flight of stone stairs, which brought you to the doors. Once past the door, on your immediate right was a pair of double doors that led you into the hall itself, which was quite large, and at the far end was a purpose-built stage. If you walked straight ahead, you came to a single door which led into a kitchen area, and on the right was a serving hatch, where drinks were served at Bingo night or the occasional wedding. And if you looked straight ahead, you had a staircase, leading to the roof, where there was a tennis court, which was never, ever used for its original intention but was an ideal place to store our wood for Bonfire Night! If you went down the stairs, you came to the health clinic, and on that level was the ground floor of the flats and the most common access to the health clinic. Got it? Good.

So Barry, Rob, and Paul and I were sitting about doing nuffink, in the porch, and there was a wedding going on in the hall, loads of people all dancing to the sounds of Alvin Stardust, the Rubettes and the Bay City Rollers. And as we are just listening to the groovy sounds, the kitchen window is flung open, with a metallic clatter, and we look up. Hello? we all think collectively. So we all leg it up the stairs of the block directly opposite the kitchen window, and we see loads of booze on the windowsill. That looks interesting. So we decide, one might say, to liberate the booze. So as Paul was the youngest, and was by far the best climber – and well he did have the right kit on, in the way of plimsolls – he was volunteered to climb up the cast-iron drain-pipe leading up to the window. So he shins up the pipe in no time, hangs on for dear life with his right hand, and then reaches out with his left hand and grabs a bottle and drops it. And with the aid of Barry's parka coat we catch it. Rob has one end and I have the other end, and the bottle plummets down into the coat with a thud. Sorted. What did occur to me was if we got it wrong, the bottle would hit me or Rob on the head; then we would be fucked!

So it goes according to plan and Barry shouts up 'Next!' And then thud. 'Next!' Thud. We managed to get three bottles of booze; not bad. So what do we do with them? Yeah, I know, we will drink them. Good plan! So the three of us drink two bottles of Stone's Ginger Mac – whatever that was – and a big bottle of vodka. We drank the lot! I was drunk, pissed out of my tree, monged, wankered, inebriated, plastered, all the above! And I can safely say the same for the others. Paul chucked up, and that was it: we were all off. We got sick all over the gaff. I had rubber legs; all I wanted to do was lie down, but somehow I made it to my front door eventually, and I remembered praying that my mum was at Bingo, and Dad would have his head stuck in a book, or be asleep in front of the telly. In those days we never carried keys; you just didn't, but what you did was get the front door key, and tie it to some string, and put a small nail in the door, and hang the key string down past the letter box, so all you had to do was put your hand through the letter box and pull the string, and you would get the key. Not rocket science but it worked.

So I let myself in and headed straight to the bathroom, which was next to the front door, thank God! Washed my face and then bumbled into my room and collapsed on my bed in a heap, and I struggled to get my vomit-stained clothes off and pushed them under the bed, and lay on the bed and watched the ceiling spin and spin. And next to my bed was a box full of comics, my prized collection of the War Picture Library comics. Well, then it came up; more vomit. Fuck, there can't be any left! But there was and it all landed in my comic box! I just didn't care I just wanted to die! And even more came up! At last I found sleep and awoke with such a thirst! I felt I had gone to bed sucking a postman's old sock! But I had to clean away the evidence. As soon as I could, I tiptoed into the kitchen and dumped my clothes in the washing bucket, after I got them as clean as possible. Then I sprayed the room with fly killer – it was the only spray that we had – and then I said farewell to my comics down the chute. That was a real pisser I can tell you. Well, that was the price I paid, and I was sooo rough too, but I always pay the price in full, always! Well, that was the second time I got pissed, and it would not be the last!

Later that Sunday morning I go and knock for my mate Barry, and his mum comes to the door. 'Hello, Mrs Stanley, is Barry coming out today?' And she said, 'No. I am sorry, he's not at all well; he's been sick all night. I doubt if he'll go to school even!' Oh! Thank you. So I go and knock for Rob, and his mum said the same, but if he didn't get any better they would get the doctor! Oh! said I. And then she said, 'It's a nasty bug about. Be careful you don't get it!

And I recall thinking to myself, yeah right, it's called Gingermac-vodkaitus; Eddie Omo suffers from it a lot!

Well, you will be pleased to know they made a speedy

recovery, just in time for school, and for years after we laughed about it. Just the smell of that stuff and my guts heave.

It was the last week of my school summer holidays, and that one day would have such an influence in my life, and it was at the ABC in cinema Holloway Road.

I went to see a film called *Zulu*. I had first seen the movie some years earlier with my dad in 1964, and due to its popularity it was re-released at the cinema. This was light years away from the video, and the cinema was the only place you could go and see a movie, other than your standard black-and-white TV. The cinema operated a continuous performance. It would be a support movie – usually a Hollywood B-movie, generally a western; then a series of Pearl and Dean adverts, which was the local car dealer and larger local businesses; then an intermission. This was the time when a lady would stand by the stage and sell you a choc ice, or an ice-cream tub, and not forgetting Kiora orange juice, which you would suck dry with your straw and make a rude noise!

Then it would be the main feature, and this film was brilliant, amazing, and for the benefit of those who are unfortunate enough not to have seen this movie, it is the true story of a small detachment of British troops in the Zulu war, who were held up in a small mission station called Rorke's Drift, surrounded by thousands of Zulus, yet managed to win the battle. The film starred Stanley Baker, supported by Michael Caine, and this was the movie that made him a star. But I needed to find out if it actually happened that way. Was it really true? How many troops took part? So many questions but no answers. Where do you start? I did not have a clue. But I was determined to find out, somehow. The concept of using a library was alien to me. Besides, the only library was at school.

There was no point asking Mum and Dad; they had no interest in that sort of stuff. So I had to wait until I got back to school, and this was the only time I ever looked forward to school! The new school term started, as always, on a Monday morning; no change there then! So back on the No. 14 bus, but this time I was going to the 'big school'. This was a completely new ball game altogether; this was the big boys' school. It was like being a first year all over again, but this time I knew loads of boys, which was quite comforting. It was the usual: form up and call the register to make up the new forms. Three of the boys in my class were promoted to 3C, which was nice for them, and we got three new boys, one from Portugal and two from the West Indies to make our numbers up. The school had lots of boys from various nations. Lots of lads were from Irish stock, a fair few from Italy, some Poles, and a fair few from the West Indies. That was the formula of St William of York, Roman Catholic school for boys.

I was in 3D; some things never change. Our form teacher was a chap called Mr Buckley, who was from Grenada. He was the school's woodwork teacher. He also spoke with a slight lisp, which was a constant source of taking the piss. All he ever did was take the register and teach woodwork, which I fucking hated, making fucking teapot stands and three-legged stools. It did nothing for me or any of my classmates. But the real downside of having him as your form teacher was you could not bunk off his lesson because he took the register and would know if you were absent, which was a real pisser!

I found myself getting into more fights; I don't know why, but I did. I always seemed to be in a brawl, the result of which was I would be caned, but I was kinda used to it. They say you can get used to anything, and after that day I was caned in primary school, nothing would ever hurt me as much again! But I had a teacher called Mr Singh, and he gave me a letter to give to Mum and Dad, which I did, and it resulted in my mum coming up to the school to try to sort it out. Ha! Fat chance! But she came to the school to see him, which resulted in the promise of a good hiding if I got into any more trouble. Then a strange thing happened: Mr Singh said to my mum, 'Why don't you get him to do karate?' I could not see the sense of it, but that would make me a better fighter; that would do me! James Bond! Yep, that will do me!

But of course, looking back at the bigger picture, it was the perfect vehicle for self-discipline, self-control and opportunity to vent aggression. My mum agreed with him, but not me. I was busy looking out of the classroom window, and as usual not paying the slightest attention whatsoever. Martial arts would only make me a better fighter; that was the concept I had in my tiny, empty head. I paid no more attention to his suggestion and carried on with my happy lot!

As for my thirst for knowledge about the Zulus, it was unquenchable. Now, at the big school, we had a real library, not just a book trolley; and, most importantly, there was someone you could ask if you had any problems, which was great. So the first chance I got I asked the school librarian if she had any books on Zulus. 'What Zulus? Zulus what?' It was rather an incredulous response; anybody would think I had asked her to get her kit off! Zulus; yes, Zulus. I assured her I was genuine, and it was Zulus. She looked at me, very perplexed, and asked me to follow her, which I did, and she pointed out a large set of books that all looked the same; they were a set of encyclopaedias. Nah, that's not what I wanted. And then she said had I tried the public library? What? Yes, the public library, the one in Offord Road.

After school I decided to walk up to Offord Road and see what the score was. I entered the library in complete silence, in my school uniform, and proceeded to ask the bearded geezer at the desk the big question, and he ignored me. And then eventually he looked at me as if I had crawled out from under a stone at the bottom of his garden, and said, 'Yes?' in a very condescending tone. 'Do you have any books on Zulus, sir?'

He liked the sir bit, I think.

'Zulus?'

'Yes, Zulus.'

'Zulus?'

Now I am beginning to think is it a swear word. Well, if it was, I hadn't heard that one before!

So he looks at me and says, 'This way.' So I played follow the leader and followed him through the endless bookcases; sooo many books! I loved books, even though I could hardly read. So he comes to a big bookcase and points to a row of books and says, 'Down there,' and walked away. Cheers, mate! The section had a label with big black letters written on it: South Africa. So I cast my eyes down the rows of books and there it was! *The Washing of the Spears: The Rise and fall of the Zulu Nation*, I pulled the enormous book out and it was like a fucking house-brick! I am never gonna read this in one lifetime!

So I joined the library and took this brick of a book home and started to try to read it. I did not know where to start. Yes, I know page one would be a good place to start, but this was a serious fuck-off book! I would spend hours casting over each page until I came to the words Rorke's Drift. I had found it! My joy knew no bounds, but I just could not read it; my reading age was that of an eight-year-old! And how many eight-year-olds read books on Zulus? So what I would do was write down the words I could not read, and then take them to school and ask my English teacher Mr Singh; my English teacher Mr Singh! And I would ask him what the word was. What was great about him was at lunchtime he would sit at his desk and read a really big newspaper that covered all of his desk. So I would take out my neatly folded piece of paper with the word I didn't know, and he would tell me, and after a few days he asked me what I was reading? And I told him and why. He seemed to be quite surprised and said I should bring it in so he could see the book, which I did, and he was surprised to say the least, because it was such a complex and specialised subject! But it interested me, and that's what mattered. I was starting to read for pleasure. And it started to fall into place, slowly but surely. His help was wonderful. I read the account of the action of the defence of Rorke's Drift, which was even more exciting than the film. I loved it. I was hooked and the light was truly on, and I was off!

It was about this time the nation was going decimal; what a pisser! I was shit at maths at the best of times, and I had just got my head around the old pounds, shilling and pence – half-a-crown, ten-shilling notes, and the good old sixpence. I just get it sorted i.e. twenty shillings to the pound, and twelve pennies to the shilling, and the fuckers go and change it and go decimal. Why? What was wrong with proper money? But there was nothing I could do about it; it's called progress, and I had to adjust like everybody else in the kingdom. But I got to grips with it; had no choice.

My birthday was just around the corner, and I was trying to decide what I wanted for my present.

Well, what I wanted was a pair of Dr Marten boots, which was the ultimate must-have fashion accessory, and they must be high-leg of course! But they cost a small fortune to me: 66/- in old money. In new money it was £3.12, but it still a lot of money. To my surprise and horror, I was told in no uncertain terms I would not be getting them. Why? And then Mum said she was gonna send me to a karate club. What me? Nah!

But Mum and Dad were resolute in this matter; I was going to karate, and that was that. What I thought in later life was for fuck sake why didn't they send me for private reading tuition? It would have made my life so different. But that was not going to be the case, so it was karate for me, like it or lump it, and as usual I had to lump it. Some things never change!

Where my mum worked, for the airline company, her head boss was a chap called Mr Desousa, and he was a black belt in karate, and my mum had talked to him about it, which I think coloured her vision to a huge degree. So it was karate for me; my fate was sealed. I think this is the best time to mention Mr Desousa. So years later, I was talking to him, and he mentioned he was a black belt. OK, yeah... so's my Auntie Mable. Anyway, as the conversation developed, I mentioned a specific karate move, and as we were in the rear of the building without the viewing eyes of anyone else, he did this specific move, which was a side kick, but this was well above my head; and he held it there for a good few seconds. It was perfect: posture, balance, perfect! I was so impressed. I have only seen that done a few times and then only by experts in the art. He *was* a black belt!

So one winter evening after school, my mum takes me off to a karate club. How she found out about it, God only knows, this was light years away from the world of the Internet. But she did, and off we go, back on the No. 14 bus to King's Cross, and up along Judd Street to a place called the Tonbridge Club. We enter the building and climb the stone staircase to the gym and the office; and we stood and watched a karate class in action. Given the time of the class and the day of the week, I didn't realise it but was an advanced class. I was so impressed. This looked the bollocks. If I could do that I would be well handy. That would do me!

Soon after watching the class, a well-dressed man came out and said 'Mrs Edwards?' and Mum said yes. And he invited us into the office and started to tell us all about karate, and that it was a very serious sport, and that I was to take it seriously; and with a smile he said that I was not to use it in fights at school, Me? Never! But I am thinking, Oh yeah, I can't wait! I was mentally composing a list of all the fuckers I was gonna sort out straight away!

So I am trying to look as angelic as possible, saying, 'Never, not me'. I could feel my nose growing longer as we spoke. Then it got down to money, the serious business, and he said membership would be ten pounds. Ten pounds? That's a fucking fortune! Ten pounds! Anyway, to my utter surprise, my mum said OK and did not bat an eyelid. Then he went for the jugular and said I would need a karate suit, and that was £3.00. Oh, and that was compulsory. I am thinking he's taking the piss. But once more Mum handed over the money. I was gobsmacked! Mum produced three nice new £5 notes out of her purse and placed them on the desk. I had never seen that much cash in one go in my life; it was a fortune! And then came the final blow: he said the lessons are £1 a week, for two lessons. And once more Mum dug into her purse and handed over the money.

I was given a start date, which was such-and-such a date in January. This was the date the all-new beginners' course started. The plan was to get all the beginners together, and the maximum number in a class was thirty. If you were the thirty-first you had to wait for the next intake. Well, that was the plan.

I could not believe someone would spend that much money on me! But that's love! However, I was told in no uncertain terms that I would go, and that was that; not open for debate.

When I awoke on the day of my birthday, I bimbled into the kitchen half-asleep, and on the kitchen table was a large carrier bag from Direct, the shoe shop in Seven Sisters Road. I opened the bag and box, and it was a brand-new pair of high-leg Dr Marten boots. I was over the moon; I was full of joy. They were the dog's bollocks!

Then it was Christmas again, and the table was in the front room, and even more large dead bird with roast potatoes, and all the other seasonal grub. And that year I got a radio and £10. That was great. I could get what I wanted, which was a real change. We all had our dinner and sat down to watch Steve McQueen escape from Stalag Luft III. In other words we watched *The Great Escape*, which I think was the first time it was on the telly, and it was great. Even mum watched it! And even today Christmas is not Christmas without it!

So ended 1971. This was the year of the Ibrox Park incident, where sixty-six people were crushed to death at a football match. The world said goodbye to Satchmo, Louis Armstrong, the great trumpet player. Students rioted in Tokyo. Fishermen protested about the EEC policy, two American astronauts drove on the moon and Idi Amin took power in Uganda.

Twelve

And 1972 started. I was fourteen, and life was beginning to change for me. At school, me and my mates were thinking about our job prospects, and how very limited they were due to the high level of illiteracy. This calls to mind my mate Twink. When the careers bloke came around to ask him what he wanted to be, he said, 'I wanna be a coalman or a clown.' Well, at least he was honest! I would have paid to see the careers bloke's face when Twink said that, but he didn't become a clown or a coalman; his life was destroyed by drugs and alcohol. But after a long, dark journey, he found his way back to a normal life. He's one of the nicest people you could wish to meet, and I am so happy that he found that light at the end of the tunnel, and with the help of a higher power survived. So many didn't!

As for me, I had no idea what I wanted to be whatsoever. It was a wait-and-see-what-turns-up attitude. But many years later, when my daughters were at school, the head teacher gave a speech, and these words rang in my ears: 'Education is the key to the manacles of poverty.' How very true. I wish I had known that then, or even have someone sit me down and say, 'Do you have any idea what you want to do?' 'I wanna do this...' Well, you need to learn that or this, and you need to get it sorted. But they never did, and I didn't know any better, but that's the way it is. I can't change it and there's no point honking about it!

All I was interested in was military history. I loved it. And one Saturday afternoon on BBC2 was the film *The 300 Spartans*, starring Richard Egan. It was the story of the battle of Thermopylae, and once more my thirst was unquenchable. I needed to know more about this and I found myself thumbing through books on the Ancient Greeks, and becoming fascinated by the Spartans. And once more there was limited reading material, but I read what I could find, so I found myself reading books on the ancient wars with Persia, and Xerxes and his father Darius, and the story of the

Persian Army, under the command of Xerxes, building a massive pontoon bridge across the Hellespont, which was two miles in width! It was a long way from Janet and John books at school, and the *Beano* and *Dandy*! I was very slow, but at least I was reading it, and what I did read stayed in; well, most of it!

So it was January 1972, and I take myself off to my first karate lesson. I was rearing to go. Our class was held in the basement of the building, which, when not being used by the karate club, was a basketball court and dormitory for youth hostellers.

Our instructor was a small Japanese man called Tatso Suzukie, and he was 7th dan, which is some serious rank in the world of martial arts. He started when he was fourteen years old and had dedicated his whole life to the art. So, under the eagle eyes of our instructor, we were were shown basic exercises, stretching and pulling, all of course to warm up. OK, so when do we start chopping house-bricks in half with our bare hands? But that was gonna be a long, long, long time away. In fact, it was gonna be light years away! So we are shown how to make a fist, and it was then I noticed I was the only boy in the class, and, as a point of fact, I was the youngest in the whole club. I may have been a bit on the large side, but I was still a boy. But what did surprise me was the amount of adults who didn't know even how to make a proper fist – where did they live?

I think the reason I was the only boy at the club was most probably down to the cost. Anyway, karate was a little-known sport at that time. The only people that did it were James Bond and the secret agents of the *Man from U.N.C.L.E.*, which gave the sport an elevated exposure to this ancient Japanese art of unarmed combat. But that was not going to last much longer!

After we had done the basic warm-up stuff, we were paired up, and I was put with a geezer called David. He was eighteen years old and was a pupil from Eton no less! He was a nice bloke, but he did not have a clue. I am the new boy too, but he did not have a clue. I think the best way to describe him is the Harry Enfield character Tim Nice-But-Dim, but he was from fucking Eton! I remember thinking to myself, Fuck me, if your mum and dad are paying for your education, they wanna get their money back! He binned it after a few weeks.

I kept going three times a week, twice for tuition and Satur-days, where there was a form of optional opportunity to practise – and this is quite funny. I don't wish to offend anyone, but this is no word of a lie. We had an instructor who, at the time, was a brown belt and was only inches away from obtaining his coveted black belt. Well, this person had a slight speech impediment, a stutter. Well, all the commands of the movements in karate were in Japanese; even the counting was in Japanese. So we are all lined up and the commands are in Japanese. Well, Japanese with a stutter! Fuck, that was hard work, I can tell you! So I still had to go, no matter what, so I did. But I kept my karate lessons a secret; this was gonna be my secret weapon!

School had changed, or I had – probably the latter. I was starting to grasp the concept of education, but I was so far behind it was untrue. I had started to grasp its importance, which was more than some of the lads in my class, but now exams began to loom on the horizon, and, of course, exams dictate your future job prospects. Like the other lads, I had limited prospects, but some had far fewer than me, and that's saying something!

As we were in the big school, I did not have the facility of the use of the art room at lunchtime, which was a real pisser. But at least I could go to the library when it was open, after I had stuffed my face with cream cakes and chips, a well-balanced diet for a fat git! I still loved to paint and draw, but I would do this at home in the winter evenings, and it was an escape from watching *Crossroads* and *Coronation Street*. I could never get my head around the idea of people watching programmes about a fictitious northern commu-nity; it just did not make sense to me. But as Bertie Bassett would say, 'It takes all sorts.'

It was about this time the local church near the flats opened a Saturday night youth club, so we had a place to go on a Saturday night, which was great. It was run by the vicar, who was a real tall geezer with blonde hair and spoke with a real posh accent, and his assistant was a Mr Greenaway, and he was a real nice bloke too. It made all the difference for us to have somewhere to go, other then the porchways of our flats, or the Wooden Bridge. You paid your subs, which was 5p, and for that you got a cup of squash and two biscuits. Not bad, if you ask me. But the downside was halfway through the evening, while we were drinking our squash and munching our biscuits, the vicar would give a small sermon on something or other. Hey, that's the price we paid to use the club. That was a fair one!

We could play table tennis and snooker, neither of which did anything for me. At one end of the hall, all the girls would sit around the record player and listen to the records they had bought, and the main players were Alvin Stardust, the Glitter Band and, of course, the Osmonds; and last, but not least, was David Cassidy. And no doubt they would go home and sing into their hairbrush, in front of the mirror. And I have been reliably informed on this matter, as my mate's sisters all did it. Odd! But that's girls.

I was beginning to like music and would religiously listen to the Top Twenty on a Sunday evening, just like everyone else did, but the highlight of the music week was *Top of the Pops* on a Thursday evening. It was almost an institution for British pop, and I loved it.

Soon after St Mary's opened its doors to the local youth, my local Catholic church did the same on a Wednesday evening, which was kinda good as we had another place to go. It was the same formula, and it was nice to meet other kids too. And then the local YMCA joined in, but on a Friday night. So what with my karate and youth club, my social diary was rather full. Well, it was better then just hanging around the flats, which would usually end up with us getting into some form of mischief. The clubs were great for youths of a difficult age, because you don't want to be indoors and you're too young for the pub; the odds of you ever being served in a pub were very remote, as we were kinda policed by our own community. If you walked into any of the local boozers you were bound to be seen by someone and they would know your age. There would be someone's dad or uncle or older brother or just a neighbour, so you had no chance. Even buying booze was much the same; the only place you could buy drink was an off-licence and that was that.

Just down the road from our flats was an off-licence, and it was commonly known as the Fat Bird's, or Smelly's. The reason for this was it was owned by this real big fat woman, hence the Fat Bird's, and she had loads of cats and the place stank to high heaven of cat piss, and fuck did it stink! Hence Smelly's. Well, my mate's older brother had a real sweet tooth, and we were dispatched to the Fat Bird's to get a load of sweets. It was a Sunday night and nothing was open, only the Fat Bird's. She sold a limited assortment of sweets – Toblerone, Mars bars, Walnut Whips and Wagon Wheels – but she also sold Harvey's Bristol Cream Liqueurs, and she would not even sell us them! So no chance of getting a bottle of brown ale! But yet you could buy cigarettes. I didn't start to smoke until later in life. Late starter. Some things never change.

What was great about the youth clubs was it broadened our social circles and we could meet other kids, even girls. The girls in the flats we grew up with were mates, and treated the same as any other mates, and romance was never an issue. They were just girls and some were very tough, but we were very protective of our girls and the young'uns, and if we got into real trouble we would get the big'uns. It was rather tribal, but reassuring.

Due to my karate commitment I was given £2 a week: £1 for my karate lesson and the other for my bus fares. What was left I pissed up the wall on whatever. On Saturday I would go to my karate lesson, and afterwards I would walk down to King's Cross to the badge shop, to buy an army badge to add to my ever-increasing collection. And to fund this I would save my school dinner money, as the food was shit anyway, and I was fed at home, so it was not an issue. After what seemed an age, karate was beginning to fall into shape. The beginners' class got smaller as people dropped out, but I stuck with it, and I was beginning to actually enjoy it. I would bunk off school to go to the gym (dojo) and practise, and I would sit and watch the private lesson, which was one-on-one. These lessons were very, very expensive, but what started was I would be asked to do combination. This was when I would kick at my opponent and he would block the kick, and then he would kick at me, and I would try and block him. Of course, this was all for the benefit of the person paying for the private lesson, and I got to practise for nothing. Lovely jubley! I would watch the instructor in awe of these masters of the art; they were fantastic. The muscle control was incredible – it was a sight to see. They would do a high round-house kick, which is quite difficult to do, but it was like watching poetry.

The one instructor that I watched all the time, his name was Majie. His skill and power were incredible; his knuckles were massive. What he would do was, there was a wide plank of wood about an inch thick, and about two feet long, and had some rough hemp rope wrapped around it and secured to a vaulting horse. And he would spend hours just punching it, hour after hour, bang, bang, bang. And each time he punched the board, the whole thing would rock with the impact of each blow; he was a very powerful man. Sometimes he would hold a heavy weight in his fist and punch. He was so fast. He would get a student to try to block him, but no chance; he was too fast. I would think to myself, if he got in a street fight, he would kill a man with those fists no problem. He was a very hard man indeed. I admired him greatly; he was my role model. I wanted to be that good. Well, we all have dreams.

But one Saturday after my karate class I decided to go down to that soldier shop in Piccadilly and go and have a look inside. So back on the No. 14 bus, down to Piccadilly, walk up past Cogswell & Harrison, the gun shop, and past Fortnum & Mason, and I found myself standing outside 188 Piccadilly, Tradition. It had an amazing shop window; it was full of military helmets, swords and model soldiers. I just stood there and stared at it all, and after a while I decided to pluck up the courage to go inside.

I opened the glass door and walked in and was awestruck. The shop had cabinets full of swords, medals and decorations, and cabinets full of highly detailed model soldiers, all different types and nationality. But what really caught my eye was a large model of the farmhouse at Hougoumont, which was in the Battle of Waterloo. It was brilliant! It had figures with ladders and even a battering ram; it was a real work of art! I was gobsmacked; it must have taken a lifetime to make. I spent ages just looking at it, every detail; it was the dog's bollocks!

Once I had absorbed all that, I walked down to the end of the shop, and on each side was a cabinet from floor to ceiling, full of pre-WWI headdresses. I had never seen so many in one place in my life. I then plucked up the courage to ask the gentleman who was sitting down by the staircase, in my very best polite accent, 'Excuse me, sir, how much do the soldiers cost?' I can still see him now. He rose to his feet and said, with a nice smile, 'They are £6.50, sonny.' My mental reaction was £6.50! Fucking hell! That was a complete fortune! £6.50, £6.50, fucking hell!

He must have read my reaction, and told me that they were all hand-painted and that there was an unpainted department upstairs. I thanked him and then asked would it be OK to go upstairs, and his reply was, with a nice smile, 'Please do.'

The whole place had a museum feeling about it; to me it was a place of worship! I made my way up the narrow, green-carpeted staircase to the unpainted section. The whole room was ceiling-to-floor full of unpainted soldiers, all in nice neat rows. There must have been thousands of them, every nationality and period you could think of. They were the traditional scale of a model soldier, which is 54 mm, like the Britain and Timpo figures you could buy in Woolworths; but these were special, hand-painted and in lead. They were all neatly priced at £1.80; that was a fortune to me. £1.80. And then you had to buy the paint too. Not a chance. But I knew one day I would; one day!

In the corner of the shop was a cabinet that had plastic figures, made by a company called Helmet, and all the figures were of mounted French Napoleonic cavalry, but these were 50p each. Now you're talking! I made my way round all the shop, just taking it in. I then said thank you to the rather elderly gentleman who was sitting at his desk, and was in engrossed in an old hardback book while munching on a biscuit that left a trail of crumbs all down his well-worn yellow waistcoat. As I left the main shop I thanked the chap of whom I had asked the price of the soldiers; he had been so helpful. So I made my way home on the bus, thinking of ways to get money and buy some soldiers. When I got home I told my mum all about it and she was pleased for me.

All week I was scheming how to generate more money to buy soldiers, so that was that: it would be no more school dinners for me. And the chips and cake shop could go and fuck themselves. I just needed to get as much money as I could, so I then decided to walk to karate from school and save the bus fare, and see how much money I could save till the next Saturday. Well, that was the plan! On Friday night I had a count-up of my money, and I had managed to save a £1, a princely sum I'll have you know! On Saturday afternoon I made my way to Tradition once more, but this time I was loaded, I purchased a Helmet kit, of a French Imperial Guard horse grenadier. The figure was plastic, and it came with a colour print of the figure, which showed you the correct colour to paint it, but I had a slight problem: I didn't have any paint to paint it with, so I resorted to the Royal Bank of Mum and Dad, and to my surprise I was given a ten-bob note; I was over the moon. So I bestowed myself with haste to the local model shop Tunny's in Turnpike Lane and I purchased the paint I needed to paint my soldier. I was a very happy little bunny!

The result of my labours was shit. It looked so very easy, but it was shit. But I did my best, and I was proud of my work. Now I had the figure I would try and find out about it, what they did, which battles they fought in. I wanted to know all about them, but my research material was very limited. In point of fact, I had nothing to go on, but I would find out somehow!

The following weeks the pilgrimage was the same; I became a familiar face. I would walk in and be acknowledged by the staff. I would spend ages looking at the figures, and I even took a notepad with me to write down the uniform details of the painted figures. I could only afford the Helmet kits, but the uniform detail of the painted figure was a valuable source of painting guides.

I did this week after week. I had abandoned my badge collecting and had focused on my model soldier collection; not toys – that used to piss me off so much. They are not toys; you don't play with them. I admired them, the detail that goes into something so small. I rest my case if you ever see the work of Bill Horan, one of the world's greatest model soldier artists. His work is breathtaking; his eye for detail and skill is incredible, and his skill in anatomy is wonderful.

The day I will never forget was, for some reason or other, I was delayed at karate, and I was late going to Tradition. A German philosopher, called Jung, talks of a thing called synchronicity, which means right place, right time; and this was the right time and place for me, and would not be the last time synchronicity would touch my life! I walked into the shop as usual, along the highly polished floor, and spent an age looking at the stuff in the cabinets as I usually did. At the end of the shop was a group of men, about four or five in number. I said hello and was acknowledged by two of the group with a knowing smile. I made my way upstairs as usual and said good afternoon to the immaculately dressed chap, who was sitting at his desk, munching on a digestive biscuit, and he even offered me one, which I accepted, and had a munch too. I made my compulsory purchase and descended the narrow staircase, clasping my small white bag with the word 'Tradition' emblazed on its side, and made myself as small as possible to get past the group of men chatting at the bottom of the stairs. I walked to a glass case and started to make notes of the model of an Empress Dragoon. As you may be aware, they were the Empress Josephine's favourite regiment and were not allowed to grow moustaches – but you probably knew that. And this very tall man with glasses, in a blue pinstripe suit, came over to me and said, 'What have you bought, my boy?' The man was immaculate – suit, tie, shiny shoes. He was obviously made of wealth and taste. So why is he talking to me? My response to his question was, 'I bought this, sir,' and showed him my purchase with a degree of pride; and then he said why didn't I buy a lead one? And I said, 'I can't afford it; they are a lot of money.' And he just stopped and looked at me for a few seconds, and said come with me. So I did, and he went and opened a glass case, picked a figure up very gently between his thumb and index finger, and said, 'You have this. Paint it and bring it back to me next week and show me.' I was lost for words. He placed the figure in my outstretched hand, and I just looked at him. He smiled, and then said to one of the other men looking at me, 'Alan could you please wrap this up for…?' And he looked at me. 'David, sir. David.' 'Yes, wrap this up for young David.' And the man took it and wrapped it in a funny type of paper, and then handed it to me. I thanked him and said my goodbye, and I would be back next week, for sure!

What I did notice was these gentlemen had the same aroma my mum had when she was cooking Christmas dinner; it was whisky. But as I was about to leave, the man I had first spoken to said, 'Hang on, son; do you know what figure it is?' I said no. He then asked if he could have my notepad? I handed it over, and in very neat, small writing he wrote the following: 'British Foot Guard 1815; red tunic, white lace, black pack, grey greatcoat, grey trousers, etc, etc.' he handed over my note pad, and once more I thanked him and made my way home. I could not wait to tell Mum and Dad.

I really took my time painting the figure; I did my very best. I could not wait till Saturday to show that nice man my figure; it seemed an eternity away, but the big day came.

I walked into the shop and the man that was called Alan was standing there, and I walked up to him and said, 'I brought the figure back, sir.' His response was, 'OK, sonny, let's have a look then.' I produced the neatly wrapped figure and very slowly unwrapped it and handed it over; and once more he held the figure between his thumb and index finger and examined it. He looked at me and said it was very nice. Well, in actual fact it was shit, but he was being kind; he was that type of man. Then the man who gave me the figure came down the stairs and said, 'Hello, my boy, let's have a look at the figure.' And Alan handed him the figure, and he too held it between his thumb and index finger. I held my breath, and then he said, 'Very good, my boy; very good.' I was sooo proud of myself; my joy knew no bounds. It was like someone had turned an electric fire on in my nervous tummy! Then he looked over the top of his glasses and said 'Would you like to work here?' I just could not believe my ears! Me work here? I just could not contain my excitement. I sort of blurted out 'YES!' with a massive nod. He said, 'Good.' Then he said to Alan, 'Alan, is Alec about?' and Alan said, 'Yes, I'll go and get him.' So he headed down the stairs and a couple of moments later returned with a chap who I presumed was Alec. He was one of the chaps from last week. He said to Alec, 'This is David, and he's going to start work with us next Saturday.'

'Hello, young man. I am Mr Griffiths, and this is Mr Caton, and this is Mr Maitland – he owns the shop, and is the boss.'

Mr Maitland said, 'OK, my boy, I look forward to seeing you next week.' He then left us and returned upstairs. Mr Griffiths then said, 'We open at nine o'clock and we'll see you then.'

Once more I could not wait to tell Mum and Dad my great news. I was lost for words to express my joy! And what I did say to my mum was, 'I told you I would work there one day!'

The following Friday, Mum took me off to a shop at the Archway called Jameson's, and got me a complete set of clothes on HP, which seemed odd to me. It was only me, and Mum and Dad both worked, so why the HP? The only downside was you could only have a limited choice in Jameson's, but I didn't care: it was new clothes and it wasn't even Christmas or my birthday. But I was told I could only wear them at work.

Saturday morning came along at last; I was up at the crack of dawn. I had hardly slept a wink with nerves and excitement. But I was also very worried: what if I had to read or do adding up? I was fucking useless at that stuff. But I had no choice: I had to bite the bullet. And I then adopted the attitude of let's see what happens and just do your best; that's all I could do! So I put my new clothes on – I even smelt new! I got the bus to Piccadilly and made my way to my new job, and my first job!

I stood outside the shop before nine o'clock and just looked in the window, and then Mr Griffiths arrived and said, 'Good morning, David.' He proceeded to unlock the shop door and I followed him in and was asked to wait, which I did, while he went around turning various switches on. And then he said I had one of the most important jobs to do. I just looked at him and he said, 'Go and make the tea!' Mr Caton arrived at that moment and showed me the kitchen, and I made the tea, which was gonna be one of many occasions in the time to come.

By 9.15 everybody had a brew, and I addressed them as Mr Griffiths and Mr Caton, and I was introduced to the Biscuit Man. He was Mr John Edgecombe. I always called them Mister.

My next job was to polish all the glass cabinets in the shop. I would polish the cases until they shone, I would use vinegar and water, and as the result of my labours I would have a gleaming glass cabinet. I would then use a floor buffer to maintain the highly polished floor, which was always shiny, and I took great pride in my work, no matter how menial it was. My other job was to cut up wrapping paper, which was stored under the counter of the shop.

At the end of this very long shop was a staircase that led down to the basement. The basement was as long as the actual shop itself, and it was here all the stock was kept, and there was the post room, and the packaging area, and of course the kitchen, where we had our kettle. That kettle never seemed to be off; there was always a brew going to fill the array of various mugs with varying amounts chips out of them. Our seats were upturned old tea chests, covered in a thick red felt. Well, this was Piccadilly! And then we had the toilet area, which had a sink next to it, and then the rear of the cellar. This was a dark hole of a place; you could hear the people walking on the street above.

It was here that the Tradition magazine was stored prior to its dispatch to its subscribers across the world, The magazine was called *Tradition*, and was without doubt one of the best military magazines ever published, for its day; and its quality was by far the best. It had such a broad spectrum of articles, as diverse as you can get, from Panamanian Light Infantry to Polish Artillery of World War Two!

I think this is the best time to tell you about the people I worked with at Tradition, and I will start at the top. The man who owned the company was a gentleman called Roy Belmont Maitland. To the best of my limited knowledge he was a German Jew, who managed to escape Nazi Germany. He came to England and joined the army, and was in the intelligence corps. After the war he started Tradition, I believe from a market stall, and now he had a place in Piccadilly and the finest military shop in London. What a great achievement!

Next in the chain of command was Mr Alec Griffiths. His mum and dad were from Scotland and had moved to London, to be precise the Caledonian Road, and he knew my school from a kid. How strange was that? He joined the regular army before the outbreak of war and became a very early member of the SAS. He saw active service in North Africa, and in later life – well, my later life – over a glass of beer he told me some of his experiences, which I will now pass on to you.

When he was with the SAS in North Africa, his squadron were attacking a German airfield, miles behind enemy lines. So they sneaked in and laid explosive charges on the aircraft, which all went bang at the designated time, and, to coin a phrase, it had 'gone loud' to say the least. There was aircraft blowing up all over the place and, under the command of the SAS legend Paddy Main, they drove up and down spraying everything in sight with twin Vickers machine guns. It was straight out of the *Valiant* comic stuff. So they did what damage they could and then head off into the 'Blueie' desert. However, a good few miles away, as they are driving on this road-cum-track, they saw headlights coming towards them and it was obviously an enemy convoy. So what did they do? This convoy felt safe, being that far behind the lines; we are talking hundreds of miles. So they swing their twin Vickers machine guns around and, as they draw parallel with the convoy, everyone opened fire, machine guns blazing away, hand grenades thrown. It was a balls-out full-on contact. The convoy was Italians; they did not know what hit them. The SAS did not take one casualty, but alas that was not the case for the Italian convoy! Then they turned off and headed over the horizon.

When the Allies invaded Italy, Alec was a part of it and was actually captured, which was not a good thing, especially if you were in the SAS, the reason being that Hitler said of the SAS. 'These men are dangerous and are not to be taken prisoner, and are to be shot if captured!' Well, Alec was captured by some German paratroopers, but by some miracle managed to escape after being captured. He went for a shit and made a dash for it, and managed to survive a hail of machine-gun fire. He ran for his life; he dared and won.

So, Alec finds himself in an old outbuilding of a farm, and was discovered by some Italian peasants – his words, not mine! They take pity on him and feed him and sort him out. He was in a bad way, as he said.

Then after that he said, 'I don't remember much; I was pissed most of the time!' What actually happened was it was kind of harvest time, and all the farmers would go and help each other, and the farmer whose land who had just had the crops in would lay on a big party. As Alec was an Allied soldier on the run, he would stay in the barn, and at night the vino would come out and, as Alec was never afraid of strong drink, he got stuck in as you do, and before you knew it, it was 'Knees up Mother Brown, under the table you must go!' And the next day was another farm and he would sleep it off in the barn, and then it was 'Knees up Mother Brown, under the table you must go!' What a life!

One story he told me made me laugh. The people that looked after him said that he needed to get some civilian clothes. He headed off to the local shop and got kitted out. He was given a hat, which was compulsory for all Italian farm workers. But the shop, for some reason or another, had no mirror, so he steps outside to adjust his new set of clothing in the reflection of the shop window, and as he is doing so, to his horror a German motorcyclist turns up. FUCK! The German asked him in very bad Italian, of course with a German accent, where such-and-such is? And Alec said, in a very poor Italian, with a real Cockney accent, 'Longo faro wayo downo roado.' And to his amazement the German thanked him and headed a longo faro away downo roado!

After the war he got a job as a van driver for the *Evening News* paper and then met Mr Maitland, who offered him a job and he was the manager of Tradition for many years. Alec was, one might say, an expert on the British Army. He was a complete mine of information; he even knew of every regiment that took part in the Battle of Waterloo. And apart from that he was a real nice person; I had sooo much respect for that man. He was kind, considerate and generous. It was one of life's great pleasures having known such a nice man. The last time I saw him was at an SAS reunion in 1999, and we chatted for hours and, both of us not being frightened by strong drink, had a good piss-up! Alec passed away in 2005. I will miss him. I am so glad our paths crossed.

Then there was Mr Caton. He was second in command after Alec. He was in the RAF Regiment and was one of the best model soldier makers of his day. He could paint and make master figures, and he was a truly gifted man. Like Mr Griffiths he was a mine of information, but his real passion was yeomanry, which is British volunteer cavalry. His knowledge on this topic was truly amazing. But Alan was special to me because I spent a lot of time with him. He was a great influence on me, with the study of military history, but he could talk about anything. He was the man who showed me how to paint. He was very patient and he took time with me. And as for Mr Griffiths, he is one of life's nice people, and I am honoured to have known such a person. I will never forget these people, ever!

Then there was Mr Edgecombe; he was a real English gentleman. His dress was immaculate, except for the occasional trail of biscuit crumbs down his waistcoat. He was by far the most punctual man I have ever met. You could set your watch by him, providing you had a watch – and I didn't. During the war, he started out life as a private, and by the war's end he had made captain, which was quite an achievement, and he had served in the Guards Armoured. His specialised subject was artillery, and it was his passion, and once more he was an expert in this field.

Tradition employed a few part-time staff as well as me. I, of course, was at the very bottom of the food chain, but I didn't care: I was very happy. Peter Beaton was a part-timer who was also an actor. He had quite a few parts in some TV shows but nothing big (well, that was why he was at Tradition). He had served in the Royal Navy, and I don't know what rank he had. His passion was for the German Army pre-World War One, as Germany was all separate principalities such as Saxony, Westphalia and so on: a very specialised subject. I bet he didn't find many books on that subject in Smith's the bookshop, but his other interest was the history of Napoleon's Army of the Imperial Guard, which was Napoleon's elite force. He did know his stuff on that topic. Again, a nice man who always treated me well and never took the piss.

Then there was another 'actor'; his name was Charles Rea. His claim to fame was that he was in the opening part of a Michael Caine film called *The Ipcress File*. But his passion was not what one might expect: it was the Marx Brothers, the Hollywood comedians of the 1930s. He knew every word of every script: *Duck Soup, A Day at the Races*, etc, etc. Well, whatever makes you happy! But to have worked there he must have had some knowledge of military history; it stands to reason.

Then there was Nicholas Courtney. He too was an 'actor', but he was quite successful, as he was the Brigadier in the hit TV series *Dr Who*. Not quite Mel Gibson, but he was a firm member of the TV cult series for a good few years. He was also a very nice man, and he would talk to me about acting and all sorts of things – a real nice geezer!

On the full-time staff was a geezer called Terry Hooker. He was a small bloke in his early twenties. He was engaged to a young lady called Roselyn and was on a big-time 'Jews' course'. In other words, he was saving every penny for the deposit on a house and a wedding. But he was a generous man, his kindness knew no bounds, and we got on like a house on fire; it must be an age thing. I always called him Terry, and before I turned up he was at the bottom of the food chain. But Terry was Mr Fashion; he always wore a blue pinstripe suit and a colourful shirt, with big fuck-off collars and a kipper tie, again with a big fuck-off knot. And he was in command of the post room, a very important position I'll have you know! He had not served in any branch of the service due to a small heart defect; like a hole in it. Wimp!

His specialised subject was armies of South America, such as Venezuela and Brazil. Once more it was a very specialised subject, but he loved it with a passion. He was a real nice bloke.

The only stick in the mud was a small bloke called Peter. He worked on a Saturday upstairs with Mr Edgecombe, and he was a complete cunt to me. He was a short-arse fucker and wore glasses and had a club foot, and he was training for some job in the legal profession, but he gave me a hell of a time, I can tell you! What he would do – of course when no one was about – was stand hard on my toe with his club foot, and it would real fucking hurt. And then he would pinch me and have a sneering grin, and any chance he could he would make me look stupid, especially in front of the customers. Why? Fuck knows. I could not say a word, because I was the new boy; but he soon left, thank God! But he will never know how close he was to getting a punch in the mouth! It looked like the self-discipline of karate was beginning to work!

Then we had the upstairs staff. There was 'the Colonel'. This was Colonel Nicholson; he was the editor of *Tradition* magazine. He was a really tall bloke, bald and wore glasses, and was of a very athletic build. His domain was the top floor of the building; it had six floors and he was at the very top. What I remember about him was he was the most forgetful person ever. He would finish working at five, come all the way down the stairs, bid us all good night and leave the shop; and within a few minutes he would walk back to collect something he had forgotten. And as he would walk out the chaps would say 'Is he or isn't he?' And sure enough he would come back! And the chaps would have a nice grin on their faces. I never had much to do with him, but he was always courteous to me, and that's what matters.

He worked with a geezer called David Schinaman, who I think was related to Mr Maitland. He was a real tall bloke and skinny, was in his early twenties and was a very trendy dresser, but he had a condescending tone about him towards me. Maybe he thought it was funny – weird sense of humour. His chosen specialised interest was the American Civil War, and he was very clued-up on that.

Then we had the Major; his name was Major Roach-Kelly. He was a major in one of the jock regiments and was Tradition resident expert on Britain's toy soldiers. He always reminded me of Winnie the Pooh. He had this fixed grin on his face, always wore a brown duffel coat with mittens, and had the most highly polished shoes you ever saw. I remember one day I was working with him upstairs and it was raining, and he said it reminded him of the rainy season in India, the Monsoon. And one thing led to another and the word 'discipline' came up and then he starts, 'I was in Pune, or was it Sholapur? No, it was 1937, or was it 1938? No it was Pune, or it could have been Sholapur, but that was in 1937, but it must have been Sholapur…' This went on for ages, and I am standing looking at him like a guppy, mouth open in bewilderment. So I am thinking, cut to the chase, for fuck sake; and he said when he was upcountry on a hunt, when he got back a whole column of soldier ants had marched in and eaten their way through his accommodation, but fortunately did not eat through his gramophone records, 'Which was jolly fortunate, you know, as getting gramophone records in Pune was jolly difficult! Or was it Sholapur, or Pune, 1937? Or was it 1938?' I think he had lost the plot! But that was the Major!

Then there was a chap called George Banko, who had been in the Polish cavalry during World War Two, and took part in the last cavalry charge on German tanks. He was wounded and was a prisoner of war for six years, and that was a true test of survival and a great feat in itself. He was of slight build and was always immaculately dressed, but he had a really bad back. He could not lift anything heavier than a cup of tea. He also suffered from a disease called Narcolepsy, which is a form of sleeping sickness, and he would just nod off in the middle of a conversation. He'd just nod off and snore! He always referred to me as 'my dear boy'. A real gent!

Then there was Mrs Heathield, who was the boss' secretary. She was a large woman with red hair and she kinda dressed like a hippy, with long dresses, and she always wore beads around her neck. She was, I would imagine, in her fifties, and she was affectionately known as 'The Kraut'. This was never meant in a nasty way – they were not that type of people – and she always called me 'my darling' in a very strong German accent.

Soon after I joined the firm, a young school leaver joined us; his name was Les. He had just left school, and what had happened was the school careers' bloke said, 'Well, what do you wanna do?' And Les's response was 'Don't know, mate?' 'OK what do you like?' came the reply. Les said model soldiers, and the upshot was the career's bloke phoned Tradition and Les got a job; sorted! He was about my height and slim, and had blond hair, and was from East London. His real passion was music, and he loved to play the drums. We got on like a house on fire; the most important thing in life is a great sense of humour. But the best part about it was I didn't have to call him Mister; he was just Les. And we became really good mates.

Les was at the end of the food chain, Monday to Friday, until Saturday, when I took up this most coveted, which was fine by me! Then, soon after I started, came the one and only Brian Sheppard! He was as mad as a box of frogs but in a funny way. He had served in the army and in the King's Troop Royal Artillery, and was by far the smartest man I had ever seen. I was sure you could shave with the sharp crease in his trousers, and as for his shoes – they were like glass they shone so much! If you got too close he would say 'Mind the toe caps!' He used to kill me and Les with his tales of gargantuan piss-ups in far-flung corners of the Empire during his service for Queen and Country. He was also a real nice bloke, a real Beer Monster! And he said I was to call him 'Brian', which was kinda nice too!

I will never forget on Christmas when they had all popped next door to the pub, the Yorker, and came back all rather jolly. Terry and Les had been left holding the fort, so to speak. So they all bimble back after the boozer closed, and then someone had the great idea to do some drill practice, as you do when you have a belly full of beer. So the Brown Bess muskets were taken off the wall, and the three of them commenced to drill – by the right left turn, present arms! Shoulder arms, by the left! – and marched up and down the shop, about turn! Feet crashed into the floor as if it was the parade ground. Left, right, left, right, about turn! More feet crashing into the very highly polished floor; my floor.

Terry decides it would be a very good idea if I go downstairs and make some coffee; good plan. So Les and I descend to the bowels of the earth to the kitchen. Kettle on! And Les and I can still hear the marching – it was really loud: crash, crash, about turn! It sounded as if the Brigade of Guards had turned up! So I am sorting out the brews with Les, and then we hear another about turn! And then a shriek from the toilet, and me and Les looked at each other. Then the toilet door is flung open and Mrs Heathield bimbles out holding her head. What with all the stamping and banging, the light fitting in the toilet had come loose, and the light bulb fell on her head, while she was having 'a sit down', so she emerged from the toilet holding her head. We just could not stop laughing! And the more we laughed the more angry she got! But we just could not stop. And after she had found the funny side of it, she walked away, and Les said, 'Can you imagine her looking through her knickers for broken glass?' Well, the mental image of her rummaging through her knickers for broken glass was… well, don't even go there!

Tradition had one more character to add: his name was Nap Harris. He was a small man and he always wore this massive old overcoat, which was filthy. He wore fingerless gloves and an old brown trilby hat, and he always had his pipe stuck in his gob. And to add to this he always had a dewdrop on the end of his nose which, when he had a mind to, he would wipe off with, without doubt, the world's dirtiest handkerchief. And as soon as he had wiped it off, another would appear just like magic. And he spoke with a squeaky accent and was, what one might say, a child of

Abraham. The story was that for generations his family were in, one might say, the military rag-and-bone business, and he had a warehouse in a secret location, where he had loads and loads of stuff – and good stuff, I might add. He would park up his Rolls-Royce, unscrew the silver lady and walk into the shop with an old box tied up with string and say, 'Give this to Roy' (Mr Maitland), and chat. But in that box would be very rare and valuable items.

The story goes his family acquired a whole regiment's uniforms from the Army Pay Corps in the 1900s and cut all the leather pockets out and melted them; and from each pocket came a small amount of gold. So multiply that by a regiment, and that's a fair lump of gold. Well, that's what I was told and I have no reason to disbelieve it. Some years later he had to move his warehouse and decided not to hire a lorry – cost too much money – so what does he do? He buys one, and once the move was over he sold it! And yep, he made a profit! Once the move had taken place, Tradition found itself full of militaria, and I was tasked to move some of the stuff, and in a crate was a load of old Kilner jars. And I asked Mr Harris 'What's this, Mr Harris?' And his reply was 'Mud, boy; mud!' And I looked at him very inquisitively. 'Mud?' 'Yes, boy, mud. It's Waterloo mud! It's for the experts.' I did not have a clue, but what I found out was he would get a piece of militaria from the time of Waterloo and put this mud on it to give it more authenticity! This was light years away from the TV series *CSI*.

Well, they were the people I worked with.

At the end of my first day, Mr Griffiths called me to one side and said 'David, about your wages.' I had not even given it a thought, to tell the truth, and that's no word of a lie! And he said, 'What about £1.50 for a Saturday and a £1 in the week?' I said yes, of course, and thanked him. I was over the moon! I had earned my first pay: a whole £1.50. I was loaded. And with my wage I went upstairs to buy a lead figure; I was 30p short, but I had saved my dinner money and I bought a figure off Mr Edgecombe, and then he said, 'David, you get a staff discount.' That's a new one on me. Discount? So instead of paying the full £1.80, I paid only £1.00. This was wonderful – change from my wages! Life was looking good!

Of course, this meant no more karate on Saturdays, but I had a job and I was earning money. My mum and dad were so pleased for me, as one would expect, and I was happy I was working in Tradition! My dream had come true. I said I would and I did! I was kinda living two lives, if you get my meaning. I lived in the flats and had my mates who swore, and smoked and that stuff. (I didn't smoke – I started late, so some things never change!) But on Saturday I was 'Little Davy'. Names are a funny thing. My name is David, but I was always called Dave or Davy; but if I was ever in the shit, I was David! Strange. On Saturday I was the tea boy, cleaner, errand runner, or whatever else had to be done, but I felt very privileged to work there. I really felt honoured!

During my school holidays I would work in the shop each morning. I would clean the glass cabinets, restock the *Tradition* magazines, and buff the floor, but the most important thing was to make the brews. I was shown how to wrap a figure and it had to be done in a certain way; and when you think the price of a painted model was £25, which was a lot of money, you can appreciate why it had to be packed in a certain way. Fair one!

But my big job at the start of each holiday was to clean the edged weapons, swords and bayonets. Terry was my tutor in this field. He showed me how to handle them and clean them, with great care and in meticulous detail, and he would tell me about the weapon and where it was from, and all he knew about them, such as the maker's name and the date of issue. This experience was priceless; no one had such access to items such as these, to handle them and get a real feel for them. It was priceless experience and I loved every minute of it! Every minute!

But what I wanted to do was get my hands on the military headdresses. I wanted to get a feel for them and have a really good look at them, take them apart and see how they were made. But that would be a long time away, a whole year. These helmets started at about £250 each, which was an absolute fortune, considering the average wage. But the day soon came, and my tutor was Mr Caton. He showed me with great care how to handle these valuable items. I got the feel of the genuine article, which was again a priceless experience.

Time was beginning to fly by. My education was getting a lot better, and I started to work at it; I wanted to know about things. I had to get better at reading; I needed to, but my spelling was still shit. Christmas was the same: more big dead bird and roast potatoes and *Ben Hur* on the telly, the usual stuff. Christmas at Tradition was a wonderful time. The atmosphere was great, and I got £1 for Christmas from Mr Maitland. What a very nice, generous man.

Thirteen

So ended 1971 and began 1972. The memorable events of the year were the Munich Massacre; the Watergate scandal, which rocked America; the death of J Edgar Hoover, founder of the FBI; and the troubles in Northern Ireland took a turn for the worse. It was the year of Bloody Sunday. This was when British paratroopers opened fire and killed a number of people, and the bombing in mainland Britain was stepped up. Any resolution was light years away.

It was about this time that exams were being thought about and I decided to do my best. A lot of the lads didn't give a fuck; it was too late to worry. So a lot of the lads left school and entered the big wide world and I never heard from any of them again.

The only claim to fame my school had was that it was the school where John Lydon went. He became better known as Johnny Rotten, the leader of the punk rock band The Sex Pistols. He is now a part of British rock history, and good luck to him. I didn't know him personally but his younger brother was in my year and was a nice bloke.

That summer I worked every day I could at Tradition and was paid the princely sum of £6.50 a week, which to me was a lot of money. I could buy my own clothes, the ones that I wanted, and I started to buy books; me, buying books! I still do, even ones without pictures! When I returned to school I was put in another class, and the reason was it was the topic I had chosen to take exams for, rather then my ability. Well, that's the way it goes. But I was palled up with a mate from St Joseph's primary school, and he was, and still is, my lifelong close friend, Tony Sarno.

We hit it off at once. We shared the same interests, and we were inseparable. I am blessed with his friendship. I have been blessed in friendship; I have six really great mates, ones that I can turn to at any time, no matter what. And I am safe in the knowledge that they would help me, no matter what shit I was in! I am blessed; may God keep them safe ALWAYS.

To be totally honest I don't remember what subjects I took in my exams and that's no word of a lie, and I don't know whether I got a GCE or CSE. Who gives a fuck? But I wish I had at the time. It's funny how your life turns out. I wonder what I would have become if I had a good education... But I didn't and I am happy, and I have had a great life. I would not change a thing; it's moulded me into the person I am, and I would not change that for all the gold in the world!

I was never really motivated by money – only once, and that was a mistake, and a person who does not learn by his mistakes is a real fool! I have never been motivated by power or influence; it does nothing for me. I just wanna be happy with myself!

Karate was my chosen sport and I was beginning to get good at it. I was told to take a grading, which I was not best pleased with, but I did and passed, and became a green belt. But in those days, before you were allowed to wear a green belt, you had to earn points in free fighting; I will elaborate. When you grade you have to demonstrate a set of movements which, of course, are in Japanese. Once these movements are carried out correctly, you pass. Well, that's the plan. But when you grade for your green belt you have to demonstrate a sequence of certain movements, of course in Japanese; and then you have to fight and win three points, either in half a point or in a full point, and these had to be won in a contest, and it was not just a case of hitting someone: it had to be a good contact, a well-executed blow. I have known people to take ages to get their points, and you could not move on to your next grade until you had earned your points. It was a theory and practical.

It was then that I learned that you can't make a lion out of a lamb! But what really put me off the martial arts was a new TV series called *Kung Fu*. It was the story of a Shaolin monk crossing the Midwest in the 1880s, and during each episode he would get flashbacks to his time at the Shaolin temple, when he was called 'Grasshopper' by his master. It starred David Carradine, and the nation went Kung Fu mad, and clubs sprang up everywhere, with real sinister names like 'the style of the black mustang'! Yep. That's no word of a lie. It was a complete load of bollocks to the trained eye, but it did elevate the martial arts, which was good. It

160

did not give the public a true insight into the art, but a lot of people made a lot of money.

Then Bruce Lee hit the silver screen, and he was the real deal, and it was such a great shame that his young life ended so soon, but that's life. Tony and I would bunk off school, when the lessons had no direct influence on the chosen subjects. Well, you know it makes sense.

I could not go to work if I bunked off, due to the fact I was in my school uniform, but Tony and I would walk around the West End for hours looking in shop windows, and we would spend a lot of time in Chapel Street market in Islington; anywhere but school. The big upside was we had a teacher, a history teacher; his name was Mr O'Brian and he was a great teacher. His passion was medieval history, and what he did was great. He had us collecting matchboxes, which we filled with clay from the art department, and then dried them out on the big fuck-off radiators, and the result was a small brick. And with some sand and cement we built a massive medieval castle on a sheet of plywood in the corner of his class. It was brilliant; I was very impressed. It was the dog's bollocks!

My social diary was a rather busy one, what with youth clubs and karate and working in Tradition. I was a real busy bee. With the youth club on a Saturday, our social circles expanded, and our 'firm' was getting bigger, and I made new friends. Some are still close mates, even though our paths separated. Many years later they crossed once more, which was really nice.

It was about this time a new craze was born. It was glue sniff-ing, and to this very day I can remember who brought this craze to our community. His name is not important, but what he brought had such a huge impact on sooo many lives. We had no idea at the time, but it did. The procedure was you would purchase a tube of a very well known glue, a packet of crisps and a packet of Polos. You would throw away the crisps and squeeze the tube of glue into the empty crisp bag and hold the bag in a fist and inhale through your mouth, and it would get you high as a kite. Oh – the Polos were to disguise the smell of glue on your breath. Now some of my mates, Twink, Larry, and Alan, really developed a taste for this stuff. I would not go as far to say they were addicted, but they used the stuff a lot! But without a doubt Alan was the one who really excelled. He could no longer get the 'buzz' on a tube, but needed a tin of the stuff to get to the required level of buzz that he craved. It got to the stage he would pour the contents of the tin into a fucking carrier bag and inhale. This was a daily occurrence. Alan had a job in a printer factory. He would get paid and work out how many tins he needed a week, and put that money away to one side for the glue. He was hooked!

I did not find myself drawn to this. I don't know why; it just did not appeal to me at that time. But I am sorry to say I did cave in and became a 'sniffer'. What happened was we were all up Waterloo Park, and all the lads were sniffing, and Alan's bag had gone flat. This was a term used for when you can't get a buzz. So after he had bought another tonne of gear and got his new carrier bag, he gave me his old bag, and I started, and I was high as a kite; it was a real buzz. I tried it a few times, but I had a very close miss one night and Alan saved my life. It was on a Friday night and we had been to the YMCA youth club, and then we all bought a load of 'stuff' and started sniffing in this old bike shed, which is now a part of the local museum in Crouch End. So I am sniffing my head off, like the rest of the boys, and by all accounts I collapsed and was out for the count. And to add to this I started to vomit and was choking, but I was unconscious. And some of the lads panicked and ran away. By the way, they were not from our firm but kinda hangers-on is the best way to describe them. But Alan stayed and shouted to Rob, my mate, to give a hand. They got me on my side, cleared my airways and slapped me into consciousness. I was so ill, but Alan didn't leave me nor did Rob; they sorted me out. I was very lucky, and never touched any form of drug ever again. Not for me! But I am sorry to say, some of my mates did, and it took their lives, and for some it ruined their lives. If it was not drugs, it was alcohol. Joe died in jail; Dodger died in jail, Johnny burned to death when he was pissed. Sammy died of a drug overdose. Steve was stabbed to death over a drug deal. Chalky drank himself to death at a young age. Steve was 'lifed-off' for murder; Barry was 'lifed-off' for murder; Tony was 'lifed-off' for murder. Johnny went down for armed robbery;

Derek, armed robbery; Andy, armed robbery; Eddie, armed robbery; Larry, armed robbery. Tony Mac was shot in a gang fight, and Twink did a lot of bird, as did Ricky, but with the help of a higher power they found themselves and lived to tell the tale.

Larry is a good pal of mine and he done a lot of bird; last count was twenty-eight years! Many years ago Larry told me this and it kinda stuck in my head. How true it is I don't know, but on a 1 to 10 I would say 9, and this is what he told me, When he was young he was off the rails big style and was fast heading for a stretch in the boob (prison). Anyway, he is sent to see a couple of psychiatrists, and they ask him loads of questions. It was a real beanbag session type of thing, and one of the shrinks says to Larry, 'What would you do if you saw a battleship coming down the M1?' And Larry's reply was, 'I would get in my submarine and sink it!' And the shrink said, 'Where did you get the submarine from?' And Larry's response was, 'The same fucking place you got the battleship from, mate!' Larry was and is sharp, but the Sweeney were a lot sharper; hence he spent twenty-eight years in nick!

I don't know why but things started to change. Some of my mates started to go 'creeping' – burglary. I think it was due to the fact they were skint, and it was an easy way to get money. Due to the lack of education, their job prospects were, one might say, very limited. On the education front I was in the same boat, but I had a job. Besides, to steal anything was not in my blood.

It's common sense that no education equals shit job; that's the way it goes. As for further education, well, that was a completely alien concept. The plan was leave school as soon as humanly possible and bring some money into the home. Everyone was paid in cash on a Friday – it was the normal thing to get paid on a weekly basis, and everyone knew where they stood. As for the idea of a credit card, that was light years away, and if you wanted to get anything of a high value you got hire purchase and paid it off weekly. If you wanted to save a few quid it was the post office. Banks were for rich people!

It was only a matter of time before some of the lads got their 'collar felt' (arrested) and what narrow chance you had of employment due to the lack of education was made even smaller when you have a criminal record. Some of them ended up becoming full-time criminals, and prison was an occupational hazard!

It was about this time I saw her!

I had made friends with a lad in my flats called Charlie; his dad was the caretaker of the flats. Charlie was at my school and was a really nice bloke, so one summer evening I go and knock for him and his sister opened the door. She was like an oil painting. Her name was Cathy, and she had long blonde hair and brown eyes. Charlie had mentioned he had sisters but I never paid any attention. I didn't even recall noticing them about. But that was gonna change.

Cathy worked in the local butcher's on a Saturday, and when I finished work and would walk up to the flats we would bump into each other and walk home together. We talked for England! So before long we would sit next to each other on the bus going to school. She went to the local Catholic girl's school in Holloway. It was called Mount Carmel.

So I decided I would ask her out for the day. So I plucked up the courage and asked her out, and to my surprise and great joy her response was yes! The day was set. I would have a bath on Sunday before I went to Mass. A bath in the day! It must be love! I met her after Mass and we got the bus to Green Park and walked along Piccadilly, looking in the posh shops. She had never been uptown before and she loved it. I showed her where I worked, and she was very impressed. We talked for ages as we walked around the West End. She had mentioned she wanted to see the latest Hollywood blockbuster, *The Godfather* and her wish was my command! The major problem was I was underage; in fact, we both were. So I adopted the 'let's go for it' option. So... I walked into the cinema and in my deepest voice asked for two tickets please, and bingo! The machine at the ticket office spat out two tickets! Sorted!

After watching one of the best movies ever made, we headed up towards Shaftsbury Avenue to the posh Wimpy. Well, it had velvet seats and to us it was posh, but it still had the little plastic tomato ketchup dispenser, which made a rude noise when you squeezed it! We talked and walked for ages, and it was time to go home. I walked her to her door and bade her goodnight. I had spent £6.50! A week's wages, but she was worth every penny!

I never actually asked her out official-like; it was a natural progression. Whenever I had the money, we would go into the West End and watch a movie and, of course, a posh Wimpy. No pie and mash for her; it was nothing but the best for her! We would see each other at the Saturday youth club, and she would sit with other girls, listening to the records they had brought, but at the end of the evening I would walk her home. I was hooked!

But I could never bring myself to ask her out officially, and I think it was in case I got a knock-back, and so I decided to let it find its own level. In other words, I didn't have the bottle to ask her out – I was a coward!

Then one day – it was 25 November – there was a knock on my front door and I answered it and it was her! She was standing there rather sheepishly and said to me 'Happy Birthday!' And she gave me a neatly wrapped box. I invited her in. I was so surprised I was lost for words. I opened the nicely wrapped box; it was a Timex watch! And then she kissed me! Fuck the watch! My heart was beating like a fucking train! I was in love!

Someone once said, 'Love is a misunderstanding between two fools.'

Soon after that I got an invite to a party. It was gonna be a real sophisticated do: glasses, nibbles and all that. I asked her would she like to come with me and she said she would love to! We had a wonderful time; I even danced. Some evenings she would come up to my place and we would play records and talk for ages about all sorts of things, but nothing serious. She was so unhappy at home. It seemed her mum and dad were always having a go at her and did not like her going out. They were OK with me because I was a good catholic boy! me!

But then came a night I would never forget. I had asked her would she like to come out to the movies, and she said that she couldn't: she was washing her hair. OK, fair one; that was that. But that evening I popped down to see my mate Rob, who happened to live in the same block as her. So it was about 11 p.m. and I was just leaving Rob's and walking up to my block. I don't know why, but I stopped and turned around and saw her with another person. I was quite puzzled – she was washing her hair! I stopped and looked. She was with geezer called Tommy. I knew him. He was a lot older then me, and was a real Jack the lad! And they stopped and kissed; they snogged just outside her front door. I could not believe my eyes. I was so hurt; she had lied to me! I had trusted her, and she had lied to me!

I can't even begin to tell you how I felt, but I made a promise to myself I would never trust anyone again! Ever! I saw her the following day and made out nothing had happened, but I never took her out again. She looked at me and, as usual, my eyes gave it away. She could not hold eye contact with me. The eyes are the windows to a person's soul, and I believe that!

Fourteen

So started 1973. On 1 April VAT (Value Added Tax) came in. It seemed the right date for a new tax – April 1st! Makarios was re-elected as president of Cyprus, and President Nixon handed in his notice at the White House due to the Watergate scandal. And Paul Newman, and Robert Redford made a great movie called *The Sting*. And the world said bye-bye to J R R Tolkien. He gave the world *The Lord of the Rings*.

I got on with life at school and at work, and the day of the exams came and I did my best. As soon as the results came through my letter box, I saw that I had not done as well as I thought I might have. And then I noticed the name: it said Daniel Edwards. I was not my name and the results were shit, so I didn't even bother getting my certificates.

It was time for me to leave school, which I did. I was glad those days were over, and it was time to join the real world! I started to work for Tradition full-time, and as a result of my going full-time I was now working in the factory in Islington, where we actually made the castings of lead soldiers. In a nutshell it was factory work and it was real boring stuff, but at least I was working with my mate Les, who was an endless source of humour. And to make a dull life even better was the one and only Brian Sheppard, who came down to the factory three times a week. He made all the difference; he was an endless source of fun! You can have a real shit job, but the people you work with make all the difference; well, that has been my experience of life.

My full-time pay was £12 a week after tax, and I was not best pleased, but I had no choice. Some of my mates that had jobs seemed to earn a lot more then me, and that was a real pisser, but that's the way it goes!

I had decided to become a fireman, and at one stage it had even entered my mind to become a copper, but nah! Not me. My chance of becoming a fireman soon flew out of the window. I had got myself a criminal record and this is how:

For some reason or other I was just sitting on the wall outside my flats watching the world go by, as you do, and this car pulls up and two of my mates, Kenny and Barry, pull up in a motor, and the geezer that was driving was called Tony. I didn't know him but I had seen him about; but if he was with Barry and Kenny, he's gotta be all right. Well, that was the train of thought. Barry was a thief and quite a good one. He had a lot of bottle and was real cool in tight situations. Kenny was a bit of trouble but not a thief so to speak; Kenny had fallen foul of the law a few times but nothing real big. He was on what we called a 'bender', which was a suspended sentence, which means any more trouble with the law, he's going away this time for sure. So the boys say do I fancy a lift? Yeah, why not? It didn't occur to me the car might be nicked! So off we go!

So we are driving about in this motor, and I say to Tony 'Nice motor', and he just smiles. And I am looking out of the window, and as we are driving down Ashley Road, a police car drives up and passes us, and then it turned and started to follow us; and then the sirens go and they are after us! 'FUCK' was Tony's response, and his foot hit the floor with a rate of knots and we are off! The car was nicked!

Now the Old Bill are chasing us and we are going flat out; it was a full balls-out police chase. I was terrified about getting nicked more than crashing into a lamp post. The tyres were screeching as we took corners and I was shitting myself! Barry and Kenny were yelling directions and the plan was hit the Wooden Bridge and leg it! But with all the confusion, Tony took a wrong turn and we are heading away from the Bridge. Fuck, fuck! The boys are yelling 'Stop the motor! Stop the fucking motor!' The plan was to stop and leg it! Good plan; at least once out of the car we were masters of our own destiny. There were two coppers in the car and four of us, so we had a good chance of getting away, as long as we got out of the fucking car!

So we hit this bend and the car screams to a halt and we are off, all of us running like lunatics up the road, legs pumping like pistons; my heart was pumping like a train. I didn't even look back. It looked like our plan was working, but the plan had one flaw in it: the two Old Bill had radios, which meant they had communications that equalled more Old Bill. So I am running like a lunatic and to my sheer horror I hear more police car sirens, and a police car pulls up in front of me! Fuck, fuck! So I turn up this road and I got a copper chasing me. Now I am slowing down; I am fucked, but he's fresh out of the car and he's gaining on me. So I run into these flats and I see this wall, which was about four feet high, so I jump it, and fuck, it was about ten foot down the other side, and I land with a crash. I am fucked. I can't move; I had damaged my ankle. I managed to get to my feet and tried to run, but it was no good: I was fucked. I made it to a wire fence and was doing my best to climb it, but just as I was at the top I felt this hand grab me and he said the immortal words 'You're fucking nicked!'

I was totally exhausted and I was wet, in pain and well and truly nicked. Well, at least I was not pregnant! I was bundled into the panda car and taken to the local nick in Hornsey. Within minutes I was looking at the four walls of a cell. The cell door banged shut behind me, and I did not like it!

What was my mum gonna say? Fuck, what will Dad do? Fuck. So I am sitting in the cell thinking to myself, what am I gonna say? Did they catch any of the others?

After what seemed an age I was taken out to the interview room and asked to make a statement. What do I say? I couldn't say what happened. I could no way tell them who I was with; that's being a grass, and I could never do that, no matter what! So, I am sitting there feeling very sorry for myself, as you can well imagine, and this copper said to me, 'Here's your mate's state-ment.' They had got Kenny, and his statement said that he had asked me to come for a drive, and that I didn't know the car was nicked. Well, that was true, but he said he was the driver. Why? I knew why later, but Kenny put himself up for it. I was charged with being a passenger in a stolen car. I was charged and bailed to appear at Highgate Magistrates' Court, and after what seemed an age I was released.

Kenny's mum came down and got him bailed. Kenny never said a word about the others; not a word. Nor did I. Well, you just don't; it was the golden rule, which you never broke, ever! When I got home I told my mum, and she was really upset about the whole thing and she told my dad, and he was not best pleased about it and said I was stupid!

A week later I found myself sitting in the Magistrates' Court, waiting for my case to come up, and my fate. I was given a £10 fine, and for some reason Kenny walked away with a fine too. He was sure he was going down this time, but he didn't and never did. He took the path of the very straight and narrow, and so did I. But it would not be the last time I would find myself in front of a judge, I am sorry to say!

But the real pisser was that I had got myself a criminal record, which did not help my career prospects. I was now one of the lads; I had a record.

It was about this time other things started to change. Some of the lads had developed contacts with other geezers from North London and became a part of the 'Hornsey firm', but these geezers elevated the level of violence to a much higher level, and I found it quite unnerving, to tell the truth. The incident I will remember started rather innocently and got completely out of hand. It started with an egg fight. These geezers drove past and threw a load of rotten eggs at some of the lads, and I would have thought the response to that would be to retaliate in kind later. Well, that's what I would have done.

I don't know why, but the whole thing got way out of proportion. Some of the lads decided to go down to this particular geezer's place and sort him out, but the main players were a group of blokes from Islington, and they were going down to sort this geezer out. The geezer's name was Mickey. So me and Rob decide to go along and watch the 'straightener', which we thought would be a one-on-one, no tools, man-to-man, but it did not quite turn out like that!

A gang of us bowl down to the flat in Crouch End, and Rob and me are standing back, waiting to see what was gonna happen. Well, they knock on this geezer's door and I think his mum came to the front door. Then Mickey comes to the door, and he had just got out of the bath. He just had a pair of jeans on and was still wet, and he came outside to get it sorted, and I think it's gonna be resolved by negotiations. But I did not like the way it was going; it was in the air, and I felt it in my blood, which never lets me down!

Voices got raised and I heard Mickey say, 'Just give me five minutes and I will get some of my mates and then we can have a sort out.' Now any thoughts we had of this being a straightener were fast disappearing! He wanted to get his mates? Well, that's a fair one! But it was gonna go lumpy very quick. He goes to get in his car, and as he's about to, one of the 'Angel firm' smash the back nearside window in with an iron bar. As he turns to sort that out, another one of them hit him on the back of the head with an iron bar. It was all done with precise timing. And then another caves the windscreen in, and then they rain blows down on him like a pack of wild animals, blow after blow. There was blood all over the place. This all happened in just a few seconds, but somehow he managed to keep on his feet. Fuck – he was taking a real hiding, and I think I know his mindset: 'If I go down I am dead!' So he managed to keep on his feet and by some miracle he managed to break through the hail of blows and run for it. He was running for his very life!

Rob and I were gobsmacked. Fucking hell, what was all that about? I felt horrified and disgusted. This was bang out of order; this was not the way things are done! I have known some right fucking hard cases in my life, but they would have never done that. This was not on!

The main perpetrator of this savage attack was from the Angel. As we were walking back to our flats I remember saying to Rob, 'There's gonna be some serious comebacks over this, and these fuckers are gonna piss off and leave us in the shit.' He agreed, and I was right – there was gonna be a comeback and soon. You can't do that and get away with it, not in Hornsey Rise!

I was always very careful. I was always on edge, but I felt safe in the flats. I knew they would not dare to try anything on us in the flats; it would be suicide. But we had to be careful when out and about, and I was right! And then a couple of weeks later, the geezers from Islington had a run-in with a Greek firm from the end of Hornsey Road. They were a big firm. They never bothered us, and we never bothered them, which was fine by all of us! I don't know what the cause of the trouble was, but it resulted in the Greeks arranging a 'straightener' with the geezers from the Angel firm, who, for want of a better word, were our allies. And the venue of this clash of the titans was the Wooden Bridge.

So we are all up the Bridge waiting with the Angel firm. There were about twenty of us, and no one was tooled up, as it was gonna be a straightener – well, that was the general consensus. So the Greeks turned up, but only about six of them, which reinforced our thoughts that it was gonna be a straightener, as we knew the Greeks could field a big firm. They had a reputation for being well handy and could have it, meaning they were good scrappers.

Now this is what happened. One of the Greeks says, 'OK, who wants it?' and looks at one of the Islington firm. And one of them said, 'I don't wanna fight; I will get my trousers dirty.' I think to myself, that's not the response I was expecting, but that's what he said, and one of the Greeks said, 'Well, take them off then.' Then one of the Islington firm said, 'Cut the mouth out!' The Greek just tutted. And fuck me, out of nowhere this geezer pulls out a fucking great bread knife from the back of his trousers and slashed him right across his face between his top lip and nose. Fucking hell, was the collective reaction! And we all moved back, and blood was all over the place. And then a few seconds later he slashed out again down across his face, right down his cheek. It was a deep gash. He grabbed his face and stumbled away, covered in blood; there was loads of blood. And then we all fucked off.

What the fuck was all that about then? This was heavy shit. I didn't need this; I couldn't get my head around this. This firm was a bunch of fucking nutters. They were gonna kill someone one day! The general vibe was keep away from these geezers; they are bad news and someone's gonna get 'lifed-off'.

Now the Greek firm had no idea this was gonna happen, but they knew it was not us. Their beef was with the Angel firm. There was gonna be a comeback. I just hoped I would not be around!

Most of us knew we had to keep a low profile with the Old Bill – but that was the least of our worries. We were more worried about being done by a team of geezers with iron bars!

Not long after the attack on Mickey, Alan and I were walking down to Crouch End on a Saturday afternoon and Alan goes into W H Smith and I go down the road for a piss in the public toilets. As I am walking up the road to meet Alan, there's a commotion outside the shop. It was Alan; he was the centre of attention. He had been beaten up in the shop by a team of geezers. This was midday on a Saturday! They had given him a real 'filling in', blood and snot – the works, the bastards! Alan was like me; we had nothing to do with what happened to Mickey. So that's the way they are gonna play it; get us one at a time! I was on full alert status, and after what happened to Alan I had every reason to be! I was not going down without a fight, no fucking way, not me!

A few weeks later, I was in Crouch End. As one might say, I was eyes about; I had eyes like fucking saucers. As I came out of the record shop, I notice this van drive past me, and I see these faces looking at me. I did not recognise any of the faces and I felt very uneasy about it. So I walk down the road, past Smith's and I see the van again, and they are definitely looking at me. So this is it; it's my turn, is it?

So I walked into Woolworths and bought an axe! That will do me. I am thinking if this goes lumpy and the Old Bill are involved, my cover story would be, 'I just bought the axe, Gov'nor, and these blokes attacked me, and I used it as self-defence.' Well, that was the plan!

In those days Woolworths had a side exit that led into Coleridge Road (I think that was the name of the road), and, as I came out, three blokes jump out of the van and come charging at me! I ripped the bag off the axe with some well-chosen words, like 'Come on, you cunts!' and ran at them with the axe, and – surprise, surprise – they ran away. I wonder why? One jumped in the van and drove off at a rate of knots and left his two mates. Good mate. Yeah right!

I chased one, and the other one legged it off in a different direction completely. So I am chasing this geezer down the Crouch End Broadway on a Saturday afternoon with an axe in my hand shouting 'Come on, you cunt!' I chased him down the middle of the road, dodging the oncoming traffic. Cars were hooting and people stopped and just gawked at this raving axe lunatic! Which was me!

I lost him down by the Queen's pub, and it was then I heard the wail of the police sirens. Fuck! I dumped the axe in a convenient front garden and tried to walk in the pub as calm as possible. The sweat was pouring out of me. I walked into the pub toilet and locked myself in. My heart was pumping, I just could not stop sweating, I was out of breath, and I was fucked! What if I got caught and nicked? It would be serious shit; attempted murder, carrying an offensive weapon? All this was racing though my mind! Every time the bog door opened, my heart stopped. After what seemed a complete age, I composed myself and walked out after washing my face. As I walked out a No. 41 bus stopped at the crossing, and as it was a Routemaster I jumped on it and headed over the hill to Hornsey Rise and safety.

Once I got back to the flats I told my mates what had happened, and the plan was to get this shit sorted one way or another! The upshot was one of 'the Big'uns' – I think it was Peter – went down to the Holly Park firm's boozer, which was the Stapleton, and spoke to them. Peter is not, and never has been, short on bottle. If you ask me, he's got more than his fair share. Well, one thing is for sure; if they had 'done' Peter they would have been well and truly fucked. That would mean the 'Big Boys' would come out to play, and believe me you didn't want them on your case, no fucking way! Peter, I believe, told them the score and that we had no idea it was gonna go lumpy like it did. We were spectators and the people they needed to see were the geezers from the Angel firm. He got it sorted, and we all sighed with relief and that was the end of that. But I always kept my guard up when about!

But, alas, it was not the end of the violence; it just seemed to go on and on. One night I was with a couple of mates and Alan says to this complete stranger, 'Who the fuck are you looking at?' as you do! The bloke never said a word, and I said to Alan, 'What the fuck was that about?' Alan just laughed and that was the end of that. But was it fuck! This bloke turns up mob-handed and it kicked off big style. It was a real tear-up, people hit over the head with pool cues and all sorts. And one of the fuckers tried to throw acid in Alan's face, but just by sheer luck Alan got out of the way. He was pinned down on the pool table as they were about to do him with the acid, but just in the nick of time Rob steamed into them with the fat end of the pool cue. Alan was sooo lucky! It was a full-on balls-out gang fight! But somehow we managed to beat them off. I have no idea where they came from, but that was one night I won't forget in a hurry. By the grace of God, I came out without a scratch, Fuck, I was lucky; but I was beginning to think my luck would soon run out!

On the work front, at Tradition, I was spending more and more time at the factory, making model soldiers, but it was just factory work to me, and I began to hate it. The money was shit too, compared to my mates'. I was not a happy bunny!

I had reached a level of model-soldier painting that was good enough to be sold in the shop, even though I say so myself. Each week I would bring my work into the shop and get paid for it, but they had to pass the eagle eye of Alan Caton, who was a real hard taskmaster. If my work was not up to standard I would not get paid, and have to do it again, and that often happened. So I had to be happy with them, and it was better to paint four figures well than chance your arm with Mr Caton.

I then made a decision to get another job, and my dad said I could work with him in the building trade, so I finally plucked up the courage to leave Tradition and tell Mr Griffiths I was gonna leave. He was very sad about it, and to tell the truth so was I, but money is money, my boy! I was not destined to be a factory worker on shit money!

Mr Caton had a long talk with me and I felt so bad about it. They all treated me so well; it was like working with your uncles and Les was like an older brother. I loved military history with a passion, but the money was shit. The day I left, they all clubbed together and bought me a book. They all signed it, and I still have that book, as do I my school Bible, and Mr Griffiths said if I ever wanted to come back there would always be a job for me, which was very comforting to know. How kind that was; I was gonna miss them!

So I started work with my dad, on a very cold winter morning. We were working on a conversion job, making a large house into various flats. It was hard physical work, knocking down walls, shovelling up, filling skips, pulling down ceilings, carrying bricks and mixing up plaster. It was hard work but it was £25 a week, a whole tenner more and not a penny paid in tax. That will do me!

It took a bit of getting used to, but after a few weeks I was OK. I began to enjoy the physical side of the work, and it was productive. We did all the work except the 'sparks and plumbing', which was done by the appropriate tradesman. We worked for a small bloke called Joe, who had a contract to do work for a local housing association. We had loads of work, and we only worked Monday to Friday. We had just one break a day, and that was a well-balanced nutritious healthy meal: egg, chips, beans and sausages, and a fried slice and a mug of tea at the local greasy-spoon cafe.

People did not have any concept of healthy eating: it was chips with every thing. And all the cafes had endless menus written in chalk on a blackboard. There was no McDonald's, no Burger King, or any other form of fast food, other then a local fish-and-chip shop, and that's the way it was. Well, there was the Wimpy, but that was a bit on the posh side of life for us!

My Dad had a partner in work; his name was Arthur and he was from Hull. He shared my dad's passion for boats and fishing, and they were great mates. Arthur was a carpenter by trade, and a very good one. He and Dad could do anything. I don't think Arthur ever read a book in his life, but he was great with his hands. Arthur loved country-and-western music. Well, to be precise, his favourite was Marty Robbins, who was very big in the late 1950s and early 1960s. Arthur played his tapes all the time and it would send me mental! I was a Led Zeppelin man, but at least it was not Cliff Richard, thank fuck!

His real hobby was knife throwing and sometimes, when we had nothing to do, which was not often I must say, he would practise his knife-throwing skills. He would stand a scaffold board up at the end of the garden of the house we were working at and throw his knives. He was shit hot. I think if he had been younger he would have been on the stage for sure, and he could even throw an axe, which takes some doing, and it was always on the target. I put it down to that North-East Viking blood in him!

Arthur was a confirmed bachelor, and he shared a flat with his Uncle Norman. I think Arthur's ideal woman would have been a woman who owned a boat, liked fishing, and in her spare time did a bit of axe throwing as a hobby. I wonder why he never got married?

It always reminds me of what Oliver Reed once said when he was asked what his ideal woman would be, and he said, 'My ideal woman would be a mute nymphomaniac who owned a pub!' Well, I can't add to that!

After a while I was beginning to pick up stuff, like rendering, first fixing, and other basic stuff. It was nice to see the end product and what you'd achieved for your money. It was hard manual work and I loved it.

I still kept up my karate, and due to politics there was a bust-up in the federation, and Majie went his own way and started his own style of karate. Well, these things happen in life.

I read an article in one of the martial arts magazines about him. He was known as the 'heretic' because he had developed his own style of karate, which I must say, knowing Majie, would be a no-frills form of style and a very effective form of hand-to-hand combat; very effective.

But one night that was all gonna change. I was waiting for the No. 14, as usual, and some of my mates showed up and said do you fancy a beer? Why not and I did, and I liked it, The Beer Monster was born! 'And mine's a lager and lime, cheers mate!' So I never got the next bus after all. I liked the beer and I decided to go on the beer, and I even started to smoke. Well, I was always a later starter, and I had a lot of making up to do!

So Friday night it was pay day and down the boozer. This was new to me. I had not done the pub bit before, but I liked it and I developed a taste for it, which was great. So Friday night was on-the-piss night, and when young people drink a lot there is usually trouble, and it was usually a fight in one pub or another, but you could almost guarantee a punch-up in the Favourite, always.

It was then I decided to go over the hill to drink in Crouch End, and my pub of choice was the King's Head. It was a beautiful pub; it had flock wallpaper, velvet seats, flowers in vases placed around the pub, and was a different place altogether. I felt comfortable and at ease here. It was only over the hill, but there was no fat-knacker band pumping out a load of country-and-western music, and no load of pissed-up Paddys, no mad pissed jocks called Jima who wanted to fight everyone, no public bars full of groundwork builders covered in mud as if they had just got out of the back of Murphy's van, no gang of old West Indians slamming down their dominos while drinking their 'bockle' of Guinness. It seemed a different world, and I liked it.

It was New Year's Eve, and me and some of the chaps decided to go for a light ale up in Highgate, for a civilised, cultured and, of course, sophisticated evening, as one does. But I just didn't want to be over 'the Rise' because you could bet your life there was gonna be a fight; there always was.

So this the beginning of 1974, the year India tested its nuclear bomb. Why? For fuck sake, the country has immense poverty and they spend a load of dosh on a fucking bomb that they are never ever gonna use? Why? It was the year Gerald Ford got the job in the White House, and the Labour government wins its second election, and the world said farewell to jazz legend Duke Ellington.

And me and the chaps are in the Rose and Crown in Highgate, having a few light ales as you do on New Year's Eve. So I walk in the boozer and I see a couple of real old dears sitting in the corner, and I said, 'Hello, Darling, how's it going?' I just talk to people as I do. So I am at the bar and it's my shout, and I ask these old dears, who must have been at least in their seventies, 'What do you want to drink, gorgeous?'

These old dears were straight out of a black-and-white episode of *Coronation Street*. They had hats and bags, the full Monty. Well, their response was 'Yes please, young man.' So I said, 'OK, sexy, what's your tipple?' and it was a collective 'Barley wine, please.' So barman, three bottles of your finest Barley wine, my man! The barman's response was 'Of course, sir' with a sarcastic smile. All this was done in high humour; well, it was New Year's Eve. So he serves up the drinks and I hand over the booze to the 'girls'. Sorted. So me and the chaps are having a nice drink, talking politics and economics – the usual topics of conversation of an intellectual nature, along the lines of 'I got mad-pissed last Saturday night and got a tattoo on my arse' type of thing. The usual banter.

So more bunny (talk) and even more beer. When Barry goes to get the beer in, he sends over a round of drinks to the two girls. Now maybe they are thinking are we on the tug, trying to pull them? No fucking way! They were old dears and we are a few lads out on the piss on New Year's Eve and being generous to a few old dears.

Then the sound of Big Ben – Ding, Dong – and everyone cheers and start shaking hands with everybody in the pub. I get a peck on the cheek from a woman; all very good-natured stuff, and very festive goodwill. And then I made a big mistake! I go over to one of the old dears and go to peck her on the cheek and wish her a Happy New Year. Well, that was the plan and it seemed a good idea at the time. As I go near her face, she grabs both my ears and locks on to me and sticks her tongue down my throat! Fucking hell, she is full on! Do you think I could pull away? She had such a grip on my ears, it hurt! I shudder even now. I could feel her false teeth clacking away, and the smell of Barley wine, it was awful. I managed to pull myself away, but I was mindful not to hurt her. I was gasping for breath. The look on my face by all accounts was that of sheer horror. I was stunned! My ears were glowing with the lack of circulation; they even had nail marks on them! I wiped my mouth with the back of my hand to get rid of the bright-red lipstick. It looked like I had snogged Coco the Clown. Come to think of it, I wish I had! The old bird had such a smile on her face; she was beaming like a Cheshire cat!

Well, my mates just could not stop laughing. They were in hysterics, snot the lot; the whole pub was laughing, but what could I do? Fuck all! I felt such a fool. Hey, it's New Year, get over it! Even the words Barley wine still make my blood turn to ice.

A few days before that it was Christmas – well it would be! And as I am a Catholic I decided to attend midnight Mass at my local church – after the pub was closed of course. So I am standing at the back of the church with the rest of the other Catholic drunks, as you do. Well, there was this big old boy standing in front of me, and he was swaying back and forward and kept standing on my toes and it hurt, so I had two options: 1) to tell him, or 2) just

179

go and stand outside and freeze. I took the latter. Well, it was Christmas.

So I am outside and I see this young lady, and I just started to talk to her, and she said, 'Well, what did Father Christmas get you for Christmas?' with a real nice smile. And I said, 'A train set, but what I really wanted was Pan's People.' (They were an all-girl dance team on *Top of the Pops*.) She started to laugh. I was fucking freezing, and I don't mind the cold, but that night I was freezing! All I had on was a shirt, a pair of jeans and a moccasin; I had left my coat in the pub. We were talking and she noticed I was freezing, and she said, 'Do you want to put my scarf on for a while?' and I said 'Yep, but only if I can walk you home.' And she said, 'OK!'

Her name was Bernie, and she lived in Crouch End with her mum and dad, and we talked all the way back to her home. She was a very beautiful lady, and I asked her did she fancy the idea of coming out for a beer sometime? She said, 'I'd like that.' Well, that was sorted. We arranged to meet and that was that. It was a long walk home with the intention of Christmas morning, but for some reason it didn't seem so cold!

I met her on Sunday. We both went to Mass in St Joseph's on Highgate Hill, and then popped into the Old Crown opposite the church. We sat and talked for ages. She told me about her mum and dad, and her older brother and sister. And then, when she felt comfortable with me, she told me about David. David had been her boyfriend for quite some time and he fancied this barmaid in his local pub and said to her that they should break it off for a while and if it didn't work out with the barmaid they would get together again! I just could not believe the words she spoke. I am not saying for one second she was lying to me; no, what I meant was how could you do that? And why did she fall for it? I just could not get my head around it. But that's people! I think he took a real fucking liberty! She was clearly upset about it. I wonder why! But we started to see each other and I really liked her. She was fun to be with. We would walk over the heath and talk for England, but most important – we laughed all the time. We even had proper meals out: prawn cocktails for starters and even a bottle of Blue Nun! This was the high life!

Then one night she said could we go over to a boozer called the Royal Standard. 'Yeah, why not? You wanna go, that's fine by me.' So I get suitably attired for the evening and we go to this boozer. Why I don't know, but she wanted to go. So we are in the boozer and I see her sister and her boyfriend sitting at the other end of the pub. I smelt a rat. Then I saw her ex-boyfriend and the new love of his life! I turned to Bernie. 'What's the score here?' and her eyes started to fill. I felt for her. She was a real nice person, but why did she set herself up for this? Was it to show him she had a fella too? Fuck knows, I'll never know. But at least I saw him. He was a big lump of a bloke in a chubby kinda way, not muscular build, just a large lump of a bloke; and this is not meant in a derogatory way, but that's what he was. I had nothing against him; he was no Robert Redford, but neither am I! Bernie told me he was a trainee for one of the country's leading department stores and he went to work in a suit and had a briefcase. I was sooo impressed... big fucking deal!

Maybe that impressed her, or her parents. 'Our Bernie's going out with a trainee buyer for Fuck and Sons.' I don't know. I was a builder-labourer and that was that, and I didn't give a fuck. I was me, like it or lump it! We became close, and I even got introduced to her mum and dad; things were looking up. Her dad worked in the buildings and, like most dads, wanted the best for his daughter, but I had a real feeling I was not quite up to their expectations on the career prospects front. But I was me and we were happy with each other, and that's what matters. Well, it does to me! So once more I found myself walking around the city showing her the places of interest, and she loved it; we spent many a summer evening feeding ducks in Waterloo Park. I was even beginning to get good at duck feeding. And then we'd walk up to the village and sit outside the Flask and have a drink. It felt easy and nice.

Then one evening we met, and when I saw her I knew something was not right the minute I clapped eyes on her. I just knew it; I felt it in my blood! Then she tells me she's seen David, and he wants to give it another go and she was going back with him! Fuck – what could I say? I was sooo pissed about it, but there was nothing I could do. I could not change the way she felt and that was that. Maybe she expected me to grovel, but I am too tall for that. It's not in my nature. Besides, I would have to shave the next day, and it would be hard to look in that mirror. So I said, 'OK. Keep safe and be lucky' and walked away – and then went on the piss! It's a bloke thing!

The following Saturday night I am in the King's Head, which was my local, and I am having a drink with some of the chaps. The pub was a very busy pub on a Saturday night, and one of my mates said, 'Is that Bernie over there?' And I looked over and yep, it was, and with her geezer – David. I got the raving camel (I was not a happy bunny).

Now my mates saw my facial reaction and it told them I was not best pleased, and true to form they started to wind me up. This was taking the piss, bringing her to my boozer! That was well out of order; it was taking the piss big time! I had made my mind up: I was going to smack him in the mouth and that was that. So I stayed off the beer. If I was gonna have a tear-up, I need to be sober! So they are all sitting in the far corner, her sister and her boyfriend, Bernie and Dave, all very cosy. So as they go to leave I just walked up to him and punched him as hard as I could in the mouth, and he goes reeling back over a small table, and I said, 'That's for taking the piss.'

I only intended to punch him and walk away, but I don't know why: I was going in for the kill, as you do! It's the way I was; just make sure he don't get up! Well, out of nowhere my mate Steve grabs me behind the neck, and Barry and Mick grab an arm each, and Steve said, 'Just fuck off!' to them, which were wise words, and they took his advice and left. The gov'nor of the boozer was a real smoothy, an Irish bloke called Norbert, and the story goes that he had been a monk for years and then he saw the light and became a publican, as you do! He came over to me and said, 'Any more of that and you're barred.' Well, that's a fair one. Mind you, if he did bar me, he would lose a lot of custom, which equals money, and that was the end of that. But not quite.

I felt real bad inside after what I had done; it did not sit easy on my heart. So I phoned Bernie at home and asked to see her and David next Saturday night in the King's Head at seven. She sounded uneasy about it. I wonder why? But I gave my word I would not harm them, and Bernie knew that if I gave my word, you could carve it in stone!

So Saturday night comes around and yes, I am in the boozer, and they walk in; it seemed every eye fell on them. I had said nothing to anyone about asking them down for a drink, but the gov'nor of the pub looked at me with a raised eyebrow and I just nodded with a smile, sort of saying it's gonna be OK. So I walked over and invited them downstairs to the restaurant, and I had booked a table for two. The waitress, Teresa, looked at me: table for two, but there's three? I told her it was OK, and we sat down. David was still not sure about it; it was written all over his face. But Bernie knew it was gonna be OK; I could tell by her smile. I said, 'Look, the reason you got a bang in the mouth was not because you asked Bernie out while I was with her, it was because you came into my local and you tried to make me look a fool, and that's not gonna happen to me! No fucking way!' He then said, 'Sorry, mate, I didn't think of that.' So I said, 'OK, mate.' Then I got up and stuck a tenner on the table and said, 'This meal is on me,' and Bernie's eyes looked into mine and I nodded and walked away.

Later that evening I am standing at the bar sticking a pint of beer down my neck and they both came up to me and thanked me for the meal. I said it was my pleasure and then he said, 'We are gonna get married.' I looked at Bernie and she smiled, and it just didn't look right. I am thinking 'married!' So I wished them the best of luck and said to keep safe. Fucking married; married! I think it was something to do with her older sister, who was engaged, but married! Married! For fuck sake, a bit early in the game of life for that!

About a month later I was in the 'office' and I go to take a leak, as you do after a load of beer, and as I am walking back down the stairs there's a lobby, and just as I turn down the stairs I see Bernie. What a surprise! 'Hi,' was my reaction. 'Where did you come from? And don't say your mum and dad found you under a cabbage at the bottom of the garden!' She laughed and said, 'Can we talk?' 'Yeah, sure.' Then she looked me straight in the eye and said, 'I love you!' and hugged me around the neck so tight. I had never had a hug like that before.

I didn't know what to say. I said, 'Bernie, David's your man, not me. You chose him.' Then she hugged me tight again. I liked her very much, but I was not going to set myself up again, no way. And I said, 'Bernie, it's best this way. You're gonna get married, and I am not the marrying type. He's your man now.'

I never saw her again. I don't know if they ever got married; I don't have a clue. But I did like her and I wonder what ever did happen to her. I just hope she is happy.

I never went 'on the pull', so to speak. I would go to clubs with a few mates, but that was because they had a late licence, and it would always make me smile when you went to the bog. You would see blokes combing their hair in the mirror. For fuck sake, you're a man, not a teenage girl! For fuck sake, they will be singing into their hairbrush next while looking in the mirror! My mindset was, if it's gonna happen it's gonna happen, and there's fuck all you can do about it. It's called destiny, and there's no escape; it's meant to happen! But sometimes it does need a helping hand!

Working with my dad was great, but all things come to an end, and it did. Dad and Arthur had a blazing row with Joe, and Dad said, 'Stick your job up your arse,' or words to that effect. My dad was never any good at diplomacy, but you knew where you stood, and I think that's a good thing in a person. I am not just saying that because my dad was like that, but in my life I have been around the block to say the least, and I have seen some real fucking snidey, two-faced people: nice to you one minute and stab you in the back the first chance they get. I have seen people talk to their employer about a mortgage and been made redundant two weeks after they get the house. The bosses fucking knew what was coming but they never said a word, wankers. And I have seen people promoted in a job and given a new contract, which makes it easier to get rid of them. I have seen that happen; no word of a lie.

So I was out of work and I needed to get a job. I had thought of going back to Tradition but that would be my last resort. My dad's mate, called Norman, worked for a company down King's Cross called T G Lyons – it was like a wholesaler of nuts-and-bolts type of stuff, and he said they were looking for a strong lad in the warehouse. So I find myself back on the No. 14 bus going for my first job interview. So I turn up, and I got to see this geezer called Bob; he was supreme commander of the warehouse. Well, in other words, he was the warehouse manager, and he had his own office. It was a big cupboard with a window and a door really. So I go in and take a seat as I'm asked to. This bloke was something else; he looked like Peter Wyngarde, who played Jason King in the TV series *Department S*. He had the hair, the droopy moustache, the fuck-off shirt with massive long collar, a matching fuck-off tie, a suit, and a pair of shoes that Elton John would like to have. He was so up himself. Well, that's the impression I got. It was a very in-depth interview. He asked me some real hard questions like my name and when could I start, and that was that. I started the following day.

We started at 8 a.m., sorting out various big sacks of various types of nuts and bolts into their correct place in the racks of bins, which covered the whole side of the wall. It was not rocket science, that's for sure. It was then I was asked did I need a sub on pay day. What the fuck was a sub? Never heard that one before. 'Well,' Jason King said, 'we work a week in hand', whatever that meant, but I was soon told I would not get any wages until the following week. OK, I had some dosh anyway, so I was OK and declined his offer of a sub.

The work was mind-blowingly boring; it was endless shit. I worked with about ten other lads about my age, and the only thing they ever, ever talked about was football. It was football and football and more fucking football. I could not take much of this. We had to clock off at tea break, and clock back; the same at dinner time, and afternoon tea break. I spent more fucking time clocking in and out. The conversation with my colleagues would sometimes slightly digress from football to work, and it would be, 'I got some D26 today!' And the response would be something like this: 'Well, I haven't had a D26 for ages, but what I did get last week was G45.' Never. 'Yep, a G45!' This was a type of engineering component that they sorted; for fuck sake, give me strength! The days never seemed to end, long boring days. There's got to be more to life than this, there just had to be!

I worked with the company for a month and then I had a bit of luck. On the way home I met a pal of mine called 'Bathroom'. That was not his real name of course, but everyone called him Bathroom. It's a long, long story, but no one called him that to his face, because he was a real fucking hard case and would not think twice before turning you into a pile of snot and blood! He was built like a brick shit-house and was very strong, but I had known him for a long time and he was a good mate. So we are chatting on the bus, and he tells me he's working in the brewery just up the road. It was called Robert Porter's and he said the money was good; he said it was £40 a week! Fucking hell, £40 a week! That was good money, and I asked him were there any jobs. He said he would find out and give me a bell! Sorted.

Well, true to his word he phoned and said to pop around and see the geezer in charge, so at dinner time I did. The geezer asked when could I start and I said in the morning? Yep, that was fine. So I got back to work and said I was leaving there and then, and I walked out. It was such a relief knowing I would never have to sort out D26 or G45 ever again! It was like being released from jail: fucking brilliant! Nice one, Bathroom!

I started at 7 a.m. and was on the loading bay, loading lorries with wooden crates full of beer. Fuck, it was such hard work, on the go all day. We only stopped once a day for a twenty-minute break. God, it was hard work, I can tell you! My arms were aching all the time, and the sound of the old wooden conveyor belt going clatter, clatter all day... Fuck, no wonder the pay was so good; you earned every penny of that money. I think, looking back, it was the most labour-intensive work I have ever done! During the course of the day you were allowed to take a beer out of a crate and have a drink, which was quite nice – free beer; can't be bad. Some of the other blokes would drink all day, and never seemed to get pissed. How did they do that? But they did.

For the first couple of weeks I would go home and just relax. I was fucked. But I soon got used to it, and I was as good as the rest of the boys. The big thing was to try and get a job on the lorries that deliver the booze, but that was very hard to do; it was almost a closed shop. The benefits were you drove around delivering, got an early start and an early finish and you could make a nice few quid on the side, with an extra crate of beer on board, and for which we would get a quid, so everyone was happy. Our day finished at five. It was a very long, hard day, but it was a million times better then sorting out fucking nuts and bolts for Jason King!

Our foreman was a tall geezer called Bunny, and I am sure he was related to Elsie Fuck-Fuck. Every other word was fuck, all the time. 'Load that fucking lorry.' 'What fucking time is it?' He had the biggest feet I have ever seen on a human being. They were enormous things; I think he got his shoes from Coco the Clown! I worked at Porter's for a good while, and it was an OK type of job; no career prospects whatsoever, but that did not bother me. I was happy with my lot. Well, for the time being anyway!

One Saturday night Bathroom and I decided to go up town and go on the piss. Good plan. So we are well suited and booted, and off we go, and we end up going into loads of pubs and so on. Well, it's almost closing time and we are not pissed; that can't be right; can't go home sober; what's the world coming to? So we decided to go to a nightclub. Yep, that sounds good to me. So we end up at the door of some club called Cleopatra's, just off Soho. So we pay the ridiculous money to get in and head to the bar. Then we are told we have to put our coats in the cloakroom and of course that was more money. Well, we didn't give a shit; we were loaded. So that was done and then we head back to the bar and have more beer, but the place was full of what seemed to be foreign students and Arabs – well, it was the West End – so about closing time we decided to beat the rush at the cloakroom. So we hand in our tag, which was No. 66. The bird was yapping away to her mate and hands over to Bathroom a beautiful full-length men's leather coat and a full-length leather sheepskin. So what does he do? He just said thank you very much and fucked off. What a result! They both fitted and must have cost a fortune! The cloakroom bird gave us the coats to 99, not 66. That's what's known as a result. I think it might have been interesting when the proud owner of tag 99 turned up! Well, they would find them-selves the owner of two crap jackets!

Then I was in the boozer with Bathroom and we met some of the chaps from the Rise, and they are telling us they are working on a big building site just up the road in Hornsey Rise Gardens. It was a massive job, and they were paying good money. How good, was my question. £45 a week, £45 a week! Hello, that sounds good to me. Hmm, £45 a week. They got any vacancies?

'Yep, you need to speak to a geezer called Robbie who drinks in the Favourite.'

'So what do you reckon, mate?' I said to Bathroom.

'Hmm, £45! Yeah, fuck it. Let's go and see this geezer called Robbie.'

After work on Monday we go into the Favourite to see this geezer, so we walk in just after they open at 5.30, and the place was rammed with blokes from the site, and I asked one of the familiar faces whereabouts is this geezer called Robbie, and he said, 'He's the gobby one at the bar.' 'Cheers, mate.' So we amble over and say, 'I hear you're looking for some blokes.' His response to that was, 'If you like.' What sort of answer is that? He laughed and said, 'Yes, mate, I am. Are you looking for work?' Well, kind of. He said, 'If you want the job, see you Monday.' Yeah, that will do us; sorted!

Robbie was the head foreman for a firm called Paine and Kelly, and they had the contract to redevelop a load of huge old Victorian houses in Hornsey Rise Gardens. Robbie was a bloke that once you met you would never forget. He was a tall lean man with a long Mexican-type droopy moustache. He had very few teeth, and the ones that he still had were full of gold. He was covered in tattoos all up his arms and neck, and he wore loads of gold jewellery around his neck and at least one ring on each finger. He was brash and funny. I liked him straight away! The following day we handed our notices in and left Porter's on Friday.

Fifteen

On a bright and early Monday, Bathroom and I reported to the office of Paine and Kelly. The office was situated in one of the old houses and it was there we handed in our names and addresses to some bloke called Lou, and that was that: no application forms, no interviews, other than that with Robbie in the boozer. We were told to go downstairs and ask for Dublin, a small Irish bloke with a hat on and a well-lived-in face. Well, to be truthful it had squatters in, if you ask me!

In a very broad Dublin accent, Dublin told us to pick up some tools, so we grabbed a handful – a shovel, a pick and a couple of sledgehammers and, of course, a broom. I was put to work with a geezer called Gary, which was a bit of a pisser – I wanted to work with Bathroom – but he was sent up the road to work. So Gary and I are in this fucking great house and we follow Dublin, and he takes us up to the top floor and says, 'I want all this off all the walls. See you later.' And he pissed off. So Gary and I start knocking the plaster off the wall, and he put gloves on. Gloves! For fuck sake! Was he frightened he would break his nails? He was an OK bloke but he never stopped talking bollocks. He was a bit of a hippy type and he was not up for this type of work, but he needed a job; so did I. We were left alone all day – no one came near us until about 3.30, which was about the time the Favourite closed, and then Dublin turns up stinking like a brewery, looked at what we had done, grunted and walked away. I think it was his seal of approval. So we ended the day and handed our tools back to the store by the office.

The next day I am told to go and take some stuff to Robbie, if I could find him. Well, as I did what I was told, I got the chance to walk all around the site, and fuck my old boots they must have employed every scallywag, in North London. It was like the French Foreign Legion, not because of the multinational diversity of the Legion, but because in the early days of the Legion, it offered to some degree, a safe haven to petty criminals, which is miles away from the modern Foreign Legion of today. And as a member of the Foreign Legion Association, I speak with a degree of knowledge on that matter.

But the upside was I had loads of mates working there too, which was great. I was still working with Gary, and Dublin comes up and then told us to take every ceiling down, and fill the skips outside, and then fucked off. Gary's only experience in building was his Lego set, so I suggested that what we do is take up the floorboards and bang the ceiling down from above and get all the plaster off first, and then shovel all that away, and then go at the laths with a pipe, I had done this loads of times and told Gary to trust me! I said he could start, but I was gonna sort out the skip run. This was important, as the last thing you want is to go arse-over-bollocks with a wheelbarrow of crap. I'd done that before, and it was not funny!

By the end of that day we had done the entire top floor, ceilings down, and cleared up, skip full, done! We were covered it shit but the money was clean, and after work we would all gravitate to the pub to quench our thirst with vast amount of beer! Robbie was always the centre of attention; he was a real funny bloke. One time, and for the life of me don't know why he did it, he stood on the bar walked along the bar and kicked all the drinks off it! Why? But he did. He was always buying the beer and making people laugh with his funny stories.

It was a pub culture. Each night most of the blokes would go there and some would stay till closing time and then go home. The pub was a place to get the 'start', just like me and Bathroom. Someone was always looking for labour, or someone would say that so-and-so is looking for work. That was the way it was: the job centre. Well, back then it was the labour exchange.

It was at this time that people would be paid by cheque, which was great for the company, because it bought them time and they never had the worry of being 'had over', which was quite a common practice in those days. Security vans were always the target for armed robbers; it was always happening, so we got paid by cheque. That was a real pisser, because very few people I was aware of even had bank accounts. The firm made an arrangement with the local publican; in this case it was a large, rough Irishman, from County Galway, called Peter. The plan was simple – you would go down the pub with a load of other blokes and try and cash your cheque, but of course he never carried that sort of money behind the bar, so it was the old story. 'OK, lads, you can drink on tick.' How kind and how generous of him. Yeah, right! When you're not handing over the folding stuff, it don't seem like you're buying anything, but you are, and a lot of people spent a lot of money that they would not normally have done. But that was the plan. I can still remember some blokes' wives turning up at the pub, wanting their housekeeping money before it all ended up on the pub toilet walls. Ah, the good old days!

It was common practice to go down the pub at dinner time and stick as much beer as you could down your neck in the time that you had, but I didn't bother; I always wanted to go to sleep after four or five pints. Then something occurred to me: money could be made here. So Bathroom and I had a word with Alan, who was a hard grafter. Did he want to come and join us and try and get some piecework? Well, as far as Alan was concerned, if it meant more money he was up for it, so that was sorted. Then one morning we go down the office and speak to Robbie and he said, 'I'll let you have a go at it.' The plan was quite simple in its concept: we would be given a number of weeks to completely cut out a house, and I mean cut it out, and clear all the crap out, but if we did it in a faster time we would be paid the difference. The only worry we had was that we did not want to waste time waiting on skips so we could fill them, and Robbie said he would sort that one out.

We worked like lunatics, non-stop, and we did the house in eight days – every day, Sundays, the lot; and we cleared £200 each in our wages. That was a complete fortune to us, but we had to keep going: if we kept the momentum up, we would be millionaires one day! So we kept going for about three weeks and then we decided we would take a weekend off. We needed to, even if just to spend our loot, and everyone was happy with that.

Payday was like something out of the Wild West: money meant pub, pub meant drink, drink meant trouble! And there was always a fight around over something or other. But on that weekend off, I decided I was gonna spend the lot; well, I might be dead tomorrow! So I did what I had promised myself a long time ago, but had never got around to: I was going down to Jermyn Street, to get myself kitted out. Well, that's what I did. I took myself off to Turnbull & Asser and bought two shirts, and then I went mental and spent a fortune on a classic-cut, Chester Barrie suit and a pair of brogues, black of course, from Churches, and a silk tie. I looked the bollocks and I felt it. Well, I should do with the amount of money I spent that sunny Saturday morning! Then it occurred to me, where am I gonna wear this clobber? Not the Favourite. But I was not always gonna be a demolition labourer; I just felt it.

We had money to burn, so I decided I would take myself off to some of the nicer bars of the West End, and my favourite place was the Press Bar of the Piccadilly Hotel. I would get pissed and get a taxi home, my good man! This was the life! I was doing hard, manual, physical work, dirty work, sweated for my money, but come Saturday night I was in town with a pocketful of money, sorted! But all good things come to an end sooner or later, and we worked ourselves out of a job, but it was fun while it lasted. I had a wardrobe full of really nice, expensive clothes, and it didn't all go up the pub wall. As for savings, nah! Might be dead tomorrow.

So I find myself in the job centre, the Favourite, and I found myself talking with a couple of brickies about how a labourer had come off a ladder and broken his leg and I was offered the start, as they say. His misfortune = my gain. Well, it was good money and no more pulling down ceilings, but more than that no more sorting out fucking nuts and bolts for Jason King! That was the main thing!

I was working for two bricklayers. One was an older boy called George and he was about fifty. He wore a flat cap, just like the newspaper character Andy Capp, and he was always smoking roll-ups. He had massive rough hands that spoke of years of hard work. He was a real Londoner, came from Canning Town, the East End of London, but he now lived in Camden, and was a real nice geezer. He always called me son. To tell the truth, I think he didn't know my name!

Then there was the other bricky, who was called Ricky, and he was known by all as Ricky the Bricky. He was a real character, about six feet four inches tall, with blond cropped hair, and he had lost his front teeth in a punch-up. He was just like the character Oz in the TV series *Auf Wiedersehen, Pet*. He was a real laugh; he never stopped talking, and he had views on everything. It was the world according to Ricky!

It was Friday and was payday, and he did not turn up for work, which was not like him. He did like a drink, and boy, could he put it away, but he always made it into work, no matter how rough he was from the night before. He would make himself sick and drink a bottle of milk, and away he would go! So at dinner time he turns up for his wages, but he was walking very slowly and was obviously in a degree of pain, and to add to this he had a big fuck-off hospital dressing on his head. I thought he had been in a fight. 'What the fuck happened to you?' 'Nothing,' was his reply. 'Did you get filled in?' 'No, fuck off!'

I was determined to find out what had happened to him, so I said, 'Come on, mate, what happened?'

'OK, but don't you tell anyone!'

'My lips are sealed. I am the very soul of discretion!' OK. I lied!

This is what happened. He lived with his mum in this big fuck-off house off the Holloway Road. It was a house that had three floors and a basement. So he's in bed asleep – and slept naked I might add – and in the middle of the night he hears a noise coming from the basement of the house; it was a clatter, bang, clatter, wallop. So he jumps out of his bed and goes to investigate this noise. He tiptoes down the stairs and the noise is still going on. When he gets to the front door he picks up a large club-hammer from his tool bag, and the noise is still coming from the basement.

So he creeps down the stairs to the scullery door, which was in the basement, and holds his breath and flings open the door and has the club-hammer at the ready! And what greets his eyes is this: in the corner of the scullery kitchen was a old square butler sink, and under that sink was a curtain, and behind that curtain was a metal bucket. Well, behind that bucket was a cat and a mouse! The cat was chasing the mouse around the bucket, hence the racket. So Ricky squats down, grabs the cat and throws it to one side, and then goes to sort out the mouse.

But while he's doing this, his scrote or sack – take your pick – is, one might say, dangling in the breeze, and what does the cat do? It takes a swipe at his sack! And of course it had an open claw! Fuck, the pain! So his natural reaction was to stand up quick, but he bangs his head on the edge of the old sink – ouch! And to add to this, he dropped the hammer on his toes! He said, 'Fuck, I didn't know what to grab first! My head, my sack? The pain!'

I could not stand up for laughter. I just could not control myself; I nearly died of laughter! So as a result of his love for animals, he got two stitches in his head, a broken toe, and a very sore scrote!

He did not see the funny side. I wonder why? And he made me promise I wouldn't tell anyone! OK, I lied! But it was so funny!

Ricky was a big powerful bloke and as rough as a badger's bum, and he could handle himself. He was a real hard worker, a hard drinker, and he took no shit from anyone! One day he gets a private job in Oxford. It was a good earner, and he wants me to labour for him. Why not? Never been to Oxford before; do I need a passport? So we drive down to Oxford in his old van, and after ages we find the job. It was a big fuck-off house. Fuck knows why we are doing this job; don't they have bricklayers in Oxford? But I am not to reason why, just to knock up and bump out! (In English: mix cement, and make nice neat piles of bricks ready to be laid.) So we are nice and early, and knock out the job, and, job done, go home. Well, that was the plan, but like most plans it goes bollocks!

So the job's done and Ricky says, 'Fancy going on the piss down here? We can crash in the van and drive back to England in the morning?' Yep, that will do me! So we end up in this nice little pub by one of the colleges, and as it was a Saturday night the place was packed with student types, and we get stuck into the beer big-style, as one does. Well, there was this bloke at the bar, real student type, scarf, floppy hair, the full student look, and Ricky tries to strike up a conversation with him and the conversation was as follows:

Ricky:	So what school are you at, mate?
Student: (in a very posh, cultivated accent)	I am at Christ Church.
Ricky:	Sounds like a church to me, mate. What yah studying?
Student: (who did not seem comfortable)	I study philosophy.
Ricky:	So what's that all about then?
Student: (stopped and gave it some thought)	Well, if Cleopatra's nose was a half an inch longer, the course of the world would have changed!
Ricky:	Are you taking the piss, pal?
Student:	No, no please let me explain.

The poor fucker was shitting himself and I will give him his due: he managed to apply logic to Ricky, and Ricky accepted his point. Thank fuck for that. I really thought Ricky was going to turn him into a pile of snot and blood, and I think the student thought the same!

Well, the job drew to a close and I was out of work. The two lads headed off to work in South London; well, I don't do south of the river. I found myself down the job centre, i.e. the Favourite, and I got a start on a massive building site, on St Johns Way. It was a whole new estate being built, so there was loads of work, which was fine by me! Just up the road, sorted! It was like working in the trenches of the First World War; the mud was outrageous. At that time they built the buildings, then the roads; now it's build the road, then the house or whatever. It was like walking in glue, and it drained you, carrying timber, doors... It was a real shit, mud all over the place, and it always seemed to be raining, but it was better than sorting out nuts and bolts, that's for sure.

Well, this day, one of the chippys comes up and asks me for some kitchen units. Yeah, no problem, mate. Ah, but it was for his own place, so I said, 'OK, Dicky, I'll sort it out for you.' So I stripped it down, tied it up and dumped it over the fence so Dicky could pick it up and take it home, no problems. Well, it worked a treat, and before I knew it every fucker wants some kitchen units. Well, then Stan comes up to me and says could I get him this? 'Fuck, Stan, that's a whole kitchen!' Yep, it was a challenge, to say the least, but I said I would see what I could do. Well, I had a plan, and that plan was a bold plan, but sometimes you just gotta do it!

The day was set: it was gonna be Friday. I told Stan to be ready with his van around the corner at lunchtime. So what I did was at dinner time I loaded up the dumper truck with the order, and I waited until it was time to get paid and all the lads would be queuing up for their wages. So I drive towards the gate with a full load of kitchen units. My heart was pumping, and just as I was about to drive out of the gate, the general foreman comes out and says, 'Where you going with that lot?' And I said, 'They need it in phase one!' Which, as luck would have it they were on the second fixing, i.e. fitting the kitchens, thank God! I said, 'I am in a hurry, and it's dinner time!' He gave me the thumbs up and shouted, 'I'll pay you for your dinner.' I gave him the thumbs up over the sound of the dumper engine and just drove out of the gate around to Stan's van. Stuff in, doors bang shut and he drives off! I had done it, and I earned my self thirty nicker – and got paid for my dinner break! I dared and won! But I would not do that again; that would be pushing my luck!

Then I had another close shave. On Thursday I was skint, and it was payday on Friday. I needed a few quid. So, we were supposed to finish at 5.30, but as soon as the bosses left, everyone fucked off home. However, they needed to be clocked out, so what I did was get 20p off each of the lads to clock them out and then they could piss off as soon as the boss had gone. Good plan.

So I head down the pub and get a real bellyful of beer, and bimble back to the site, and I think it would be nice to have a kip for an hour or two. So I head off to one of the finished flats, put a load of dust sheets in a bath and get comfy, and go off to the land of nod! Fucking hell! I wake up and it's dark! FUCK! What am I gonna do? In those days all the big sites had guard dogs roaming loose around the site as security, and these were real mean fuckers. That all changed when some children were mauled and the law was changed, but that was much later, and it looked like I was gonna get eaten alive by a load of mad fucking dogs. But that was not the end of my problems: I had not clocked all the boys out!

With a lot of luck and thought, I managed to get out of the site in one piece, and headed around to the main entrance and banged on the old door. My mate's dad was the night watchman, and I told him the score, and he said that John, his son – my mate – had worked out it had gone lumpy on the clocking-out scam and had come back and clocked the boys out. God, that was a close one!

On the Monday I saw John and thanked him, and that was the last time I did that! A few weeks later I am in the Favourite, and my mate's sister is getting married, and having her reception in the Favourite. She is asking for trouble, and she gets it! So my mate's sister is in her wedding dress, and she's passing around the sandwiches – all very civilised stuff. Well, she offered her brother a sarnie, and his name was Philip. He was on leave from the Parachute Regiment and was very pissed, and as she offered him a sarnie he said, 'You can stick that up your arse!'

Well, we could not believe our ears: what did he say? Before you knew it, it was off. It was like a bad night in Dodge City. Everyone started fighting; punches, blows – it was a real balls-out tear-up! Me and my mate kept out of it, but what I remember was that the band got beat up. Why? Fuck knows. But the Old Bill turn up and it was like a battlefield. Well, it was the Favourite; what did she expect?

Sixteen

I was beginning to spend a lot of my time in Crouch End, and I made a circle of new friends. They were a different type of people from my mates in the flats. Bob was studying medicine at St Bartholomew's and was at university in Lancaster, Nick was at Portsmouth, and the others were at college. This was the first group of friends I'd made that, for want of a better word, had done further education. They were different; I felt at ease with them. It was kinda strange but nice. They never got into fights, none had been nicked, and they even spoke different.

I became comfortable here; it was nice. Yet just over the hill was 'Hungry Hill', which was like another planet! I was still on the building site, and it was much the same day-in, day-out. I didn't feel it was for me; I wanted something different, but I didn't know what. I just did. I had no burning ambition for money; I just needed something different, and it came by way of the *Islington Gazette*.

I was looking in the job section, and there was an ad for a splint technician. Training would be provided, so why not? Give it a try. The worst they could do was say no! Then one morning a buff-coloured envelope found itself on my front doormat, inviting me for a job interview. Interesting. This was my first proper job interview ever. I was quite nervous, but I did well, I think, and a couple of days later another buff envelope found itself on my doormat; and they were pleased to offer me the position of splint technician! Got it! Yes!

The big day came and it was my first day at my new job, and I was introduced to a real lady. I had seen her at my interview; her name was Annie Dummett. She was the head of the Occupational Therapy Department. She welcomed me to the hospital and then introduced me to the head of the Physiotherapy Department, a nice lady called Miss Price, and the pair of them were my bosses. Working for a woman! This was going to be different! My immediate boss was an old bloke called Ben, who was the resident splint technician. He had been there for twenty years and he was retiring in a few weeks, and I was told I had a lot to learn in a very short time before I went solo!

I was given some books on anatomy, such as *A Diagnosis of Orthopaedics*. I had to learn all the names of the bones in the body, what type of joints, how they worked, and the muscle workings of the joints; all this was homework! But I loved it. I'd been shit at biology at school; I didn't have the slightest interest in the muscle of the inside of a frog. But this was the human body, and that gripped me. I had such a thirst for knowledge, and I enjoyed it, but I had such little time to learn so much. When I was at work, I was shown all the different types of material at my disposal, how to use it, how it worked, and all this stuff I gave 100 per cent. It was a real challenge.

After a few weeks at the Whittington, I was sent on a course to Stanmore Royal National Orthopaedic Hospital to watch the masters at work. This was the place to go and learn my job. Stanmore was miles away, but I had to go, and I wanted to. It was there that I learned how to make springs, plaster casts and loads of other stuff. My time at Stanmore flew by, I can tell you, but I still had so much to learn in so little time.

I didn't even go to the boozer. I wanted to do well, but I had to work at it, and I was given a favourable report, to the best of my knowledge, and Miss Price said I had done well. Well, I had worked hard; no pain, no gain.

Then I was sent on another course at the London Hospital, and this was only for a week and I hated the place; it was a very long week. The people were so up themselves.

Well, the big day came and Ben retired, so it was sherry all round, and they presented him with a gift. He had been there a long time, but would I be?

On Mondays I would attend the fracture clinic and sit in with the doctors and just watch them, look at the X-rays, and look at the different fractures, and it was fascinating stuff. I was left to my own devices, and that was great. I had a job to do and I got on with it. The wages were shit, but you can't have it all! (Why not?)

The social life of the hospital was great; there were always nurses' parties and the local pubs were always full of off-duty staff and people on their breaks. It was like one happy family, and I made some new friends and life was looking good. But, as always, things change and our department was relocated to the new building. I hated it; it was like working in a submarine. I was much happier in the old building, but that's what they call progress.

I recall one memorable incident. I was summoned to the intensive care unit to do two jobs. This was rather unusual: two at the same time? What it was was that a man under the influence of drugs had jumped off the Archway Road bridge and survived. He was so lucky. If the jump didn't kill him, the traffic should have done, but it didn't, and he ended up with us.

His fractures were multiple, as one would expect, and a lot were compression fractures. He was in a very bad way, but he was strong and he was young, and I had to make him some splints to ease his condition in bed. It was no big deal; I done it no problem.

In the other room was an elderly Irish man. He was a family man, and his family stayed by him all the time. What had happened was he had had a few beers and was on his way home, which involved walking up a flight of stone stairs. He lost his balance and somehow fell backwards down the flight of stairs and sustained multiple head injuries, as well as other fractures on his leg and back. He was in a bad way, and once more I made the splints and it was no big problem; job done.

It was strange. I could not stop thinking about that old geezer and his family. A couple of days later I decided to pop up to ICU to see how he was getting on, but he had died that night.

It just did not make sense to me: one tries to commit suicide and lives and then you have a man that loved life and all the wonderful things of life and dies. It didn't add up! But the jumper made a full recovery, thanks to modern medicine, and a lot of help from God!

In my flats lived a woman called Dorothy. She had two children, a boy we called 'Chalky' because he was mixed race, and a girl – Chalky's older sister – called Beverly. She was a nice person, as was Chalky; just nice kids. I don't know what the trigger was but – and I think this is the best way to describe it – Dorothy had a crisis. She went up to the top floor of the flats and climbed over the balcony. Why, I don't have a clue; it was a cry for help, I think. But only God knows.

The upshot was she fell. I don't think she meant to do it, but she fell. I actually saw her fall and hit the ground with such a thud. It fucking shocked me to the bone. Her eyes were open and she was alive; she had a straw-coloured liquid come from her ears. I didn't know what that was then, but I did later. It was awful. I didn't know what to do.

Then her daughter arrives at the scene and she was hysterical. Fuck, it was her mum! No one touched Dot. We waited for the ambulance to come; it took ages.

Then Chalky shows up; it was his mum! He just stood there. He never said a single word, not a word! But in all my life I have never, ever seen someone cry like that. The tears just rolled down his little face. He was only a kid, but the tears just poured out. I had no idea that a person could cry so much. My heart broke for him. What do you say? Nothing! Then one of the neighbours took them in, when the ambulance took Dot away. Dot died that night.

In my life I have witnessed three suicides, and lost three people. Witnessing such a thing tends to leave you with a sense of your own mortality, and in my case a sense of sorrow. When I heard the news of my friend's suicide, it shocked me to the bone. I just could not get my head around it; it was such a shock! Why? In all three cases, I don't know. And I am sure that men with a greater insight into the working of the human mind, and far more eminently qualified than me, ask the same question.

Is it a moment of madness, or some form of mental break-down, as they reach a point of hopelessness, and this is the only way to escape this mortal toil?

In my life I have had some long, dark nights, and a great sense of hopelessness, but with the help of a higher power I came through those long, dark nights. But it never entered my head to end it, ever!

Some years ago I watched a Parkinson interview with the great actor Richard Burton, and he described it as a lonely dark place, an awful place. Well, I know that place; I have been there. I know that feeling and what that place is like. It's hell.

But when I was in that dark place in my heart and mind, I remember these words: 'In our darkest night there is a promise of a bright new dawn.' And it's true. Just hang on; that dawn will come, and trust in that higher power! It kept me going. Where there is life, there is hope! But never, ever give up!

The method of suicide my friend chose was that of hanging. He went to bed, and in the night came down the stairs and hung himself in the kitchen and was found by his son when he came back from a nightclub. I can't think of a more painful way other than maybe by setting fire to oneself, but that's what he decided to do. The thing that crossed my mind was, what must have gone through his mind? What if, at the last seconds, he changed his mind and frantically struggled to gasp his last breath. This was not like being hung, when the atlas vertebra is snapped and the spinal cord is snapped too and death is almost instant. No; this was death by strangulation. It does not bear thinking about! Mick, rest in peace.

The next time I saw someone take their own life was on a Saturday morning, I was walking up Archway Road. I was just about to come to the bridge, when I thought I saw a dummy fall from the bridge. But I am sorry to say it was not a dummy; it was a human being. And he landed on the roof and bonnet of a red car. I just could not believe my eyes!

He was laying there motionless, eyes closed. I think he was killed on impact. The car almost collided with the crash barrier; the driver was in an awful state, and I just stood there looking. I think I was in shock, to tell the truth – Fuck, that's a human being, and a dead one at that – and the sound of the ambulance became audible. I just walked up the road and straight into the nearest pub, which was the Winchester, and the barman, called Tom, said, 'You OK, Dave?' And I told him what had just happened, and he gave me a large double brandy. I downed it in one! I needed that! That got me!

The last time – and I hope it's the last – I saw a person die by their own hand was some years later. I was working at the world famous children's hospital, Great Ormond Street. I will not bore you with the details of the circumstances of the events that led to this particular incident. It was in what was known as the South-ward Building, which had eight floors and a basement, and this chap jumped from the top floor down the stone stairwell to end his life. I was at the scene within a matter of seconds. He was still alive, and once more he had that straw-coloured liquid coming from his ears. His feet were still twitching, and he died very soon after. What got me was that on his way down, his head had hit the corners of the stone staircase. There was blood all over the place!

The other person I knew personally who took his own life was a bloke that went to the same school as me and had became a junkie. He decided to end his life by jumping off the Archway Road Bridge, which to many people is known as Suicide Bridge. Well, that speaks for itself!

Then the other person I knew who decided to take his life had, going off what he had done to prepare, really thought it through. He lay on his bed, left a letter for his mum and brother, made himself comfy, candles lit, favourite CD on, and took a real load of tablets and a bottle of whisky, fell asleep and never woke up. He must have had his mind set on that, to take such prepara-tion. May they rest in peace! May God keep their souls, and I hope they found that eternal rest that they must have craved for, above the very precious gift of life.

It was Christmas time at the Whittington and the place had a great atmosphere. There were always parties, functions; it was a real nice time. Every department had its own little party, and the place had a buzz about it. I had made firm friends with a geezer called Les. He was a porter and a real laugh, but he met a young lady, ended up loved-up, and that was the end of that! But that's life.

I had a real strange thing happen to me in a pub in Highgate. I am on my own standing minding my own business, and this geezer looks at me and says, 'You cunt.' I think he can't be talking to me, so I ignore him, but he says it again with such venom I looked at him, bewildered; but he's up for it! So I look him in the eye, and try to assess the situation. He's with a gang of blokes; he's a real fucking hero! So I look at him and walk outside, and just walk around the corner to give myself time to think what I am gonna do next? As I am standing around the corner, he comes out with a few of his mates, giving it where's he gone? Looking for me! I had never seen any of these geezers in my life before. Why me? This was not Hornsey Rise; this was fucking civilised Highgate! This don't happen in this neck of the woods. But I was so wrong!

I am mega pissed off, so I think I'll go down the Rise, get some of the chaps and come back and get it sorted. I jump in a cab and head straight down the Favourite. I knew some of the firm would be there. The cab pulls up outside, I pay him and go and see the boys. I was right: there was Alan, Joe, Barry, Paul, Rob, AJ and Sammy. I tell the chaps what the score is. They didn't even finish their beer and the cab was called. As we get in the cabs, Alan said, 'Let's go via the King's Head; some of the lads are over there.' Good plan, Alan. And true enough there was a couple of the boys and a couple of odd marks who wanted to come along. I didn't know these geezers, but what I did say was, 'We are going up the village for a fucking tear-up. If you don't wanna come, OK, it's up to you; but it's gonna be a real tear-up.' Twelve geezers in less then half an hour, not bad!

We pull up outside the pub and we all pile out. All the cab doors go clunk, clunk, and we are all outside. And I say to the boys, 'I am gonna have a straightener with this geezer. If his mates want some, so be it!' I just wanted to have a one-to-one with that wanker. My blood was up, and I was ready for it!

So I walk in the boozer and see this 'face' and said, 'OK, let's have it outside then, me and you!'

Well, fuck me, he walks out of the boozer, but he's got a load of blokes with him, fucking loads. So I said, 'Just me and him!' It was a very tense moment, and as he walks to me I punch him in the mouth as hard as I could. Bang! He goes flying back. And then all hell broke loose; it was like a rugby scrum. I got a bottle on the back of the head, and I had blood pissing out the back of my head, but I am locked into some geezer. I saw Alan getting stuck into some bloke, and the same for Joe and Paul. We were well outnumbered, but we gave a real good account of ourselves, but the odd marks from the King's Head ran away. I remember saying to myself, I'll sort them out later, wankers! I was livid, even though I was in a real balls-out full on tear-up.

But when they ran away, a good few of the blokes we were fighting ran after them, which, thank fuck, took the pressure off us that were left. It was a very fierce brawl. Joe was like a fucking lunatic; bottles flying; it was real scary stuff!

Somehow Alan and I backed our way into the pub doorway, fighting every inch of the way. I got blood pissing out the back of my head, and I was soaked with it. Alan had a bloody nose. The people in the pub were absolutely terrified and rightly so! A beer crate was thrown through the window and glass flew everywhere. There were women screaming! But Alan and me are now trapped. It was back up against the wall stuff, but by some miracle there was a lull in the fighting, and we looked at each other and kinda read each other's minds – you go that way, and I'll go this way – and we were off! Each a different way, but there was no sign of Joe or the others. Where were they? I am trotting up the road with blood all down my back, and then this car comes to a screeching halt, and a few geezers get out and come after me! Fuck, they are mobile! I ran as fast as I could and jumped over a fence. I could hear the sound of police sirens in the distance. Fuck, that's all I needed was the Old Bill on my case as well! I got back to the Rise and safety!

The pub had an outside toilet where I cleaned myself up. I had a real lump on my head, so I sorted myself out. I was fucked! My head was killing me, but I knew I could not go to hospital in case the Old Bill were there, so I had to get myself sorted. As I walk out of the bog and walk around the corner, I see Alan, Joe and Paul. Fuck, it was great to see them! We had all made it back in one piece!

Joe said, 'What the fuck was all that about?' with that grin on his face. My reply was, 'Fuck knows; I thought you did?' We all laughed; I think it was out of relief. I knew I could rely on the Firm; they would never let you down, ever. True mates. But I was still pissed with those odd marks from the King's Head; there was some unfinished business there. I would sort that out tomorrow night, for sure.

So the pub was still serving and I bought the chaps a beer. Joe died in prison some years later, and I was shocked when I got the news. He was a real smashing bloke, and he will be missed by a lot of people.

The next night Alan and I go down the King's Head, to see these odd marks, the ones who had fucked off when it got lumpy. As we walked in they were giving it large about the previous night, so I just walked up to them and punched each one of the three in the mouth and told them to fuck off! Which they did!

When the word got out what had happened to us, 'the Come Back' was sorted. Names are not important: they know who they are. They go up to Highgate, where the so-called 'hard cases' hung out, and a car pulled up, a sawn-off was pointed and some meaningful questions were asked, but they knew fuck all about it. It had nothing to do with them, they swore it!

But in the nicest possible way they were asked to find out. They said they would. Well, a couple of days later the word comes back. It was a rugby club on a stag night! Fuck, my luck! That was some fierce fight, I can tell you, and I still carry that scar today, thirty-three years later.

But on Monday morning I was Mr Splint Technician. I loved my job; I felt I was doing something worthwhile. It was valuable, creative and very rewarding. A great sense of job satisfaction, but the money was shit!

I got to the stage where I needed more money, as we all do. The job would have been ideal for someone who's retired, looking to supplement their pension, but it was not enough for me. I am not a greedy person, but a few quid would be nice. Don't need a job title; I don't want power; I don't want position, I just wanna be me! I don't want to be nice to people I don't like, or be nice to people in the hope they might be able to elevate me in one way or another, whether in the workplace or in my social circles. It's all a load of bollocks! I am me.

I spoke to my boss, Annie, about my wages and she said there was nothing they could do. The department only had provision for one splint technician, and not a chance of employing another one, which, if they had, would have meant I would have become a higher grade, which equals more money. So in a nutshell I had more chance of getting pregnant than getting a pay rise!

But what did occur to me was, was there any chance of working as a normal porter over the weekend? I put this to Annie, and I saw a light come on! She asked would I mind doing that?

Of course not: I had suggested it! So she had a word with the head porter, a real gent, called Mr Baker. I had little to do with him, but whenever I did I always addressed him as Mr Baker, and he was held in high regard by all who worked under him, which was kinda nice.

So, true to her word, she spoke to him and he said yes, not a problem, but the downside was I would be on a lower rate of pay than a technician, but that was fine by me because I would be on time-and-a-half on a Saturday, and double pay on a Sunday, so I was quids in. I had to work seven days a week, but that's the way it goes.

So I changed my white coat for a grey jacket and portered away on my weekends. The other porters were a nice bunch of geezers and that made it so much better, and the time flew by. Well, it does when you're having fun.

So it was Christmastime once more, and yep, more large dead bird for Christmas, and the table was once more moved into the front room, but this year I had a beer with my dad; I was a man now! Mum was in the kitchen, with the bottle of whisky, sipping away!

Seventeen

And so started 1975. This was the year Margaret Thatcher became the leader of the Conservative party. It was the year of the terrible underground train crash at Moorgate, which took forty-three precious lives. John Stonehouse was nicked in Australia. Saigon fell to the North Vietnamese army, and a Japanese woman was the first woman to climb Everest. The Irish statesman De Valera kicked the bucket, and so did a bloke called Chaing Kai-shek, and the world was introduced to Spielberg's *Jaws*, the story of a cello-playing shark.

When I was a technician I had a real funny thing happen to me. Depending on the day of the week, you could gauge the type of patient you would be likely to see, according to the clinics. Well, it was a Monday, and that usually meant collars, depending on the consultant. So this old lady turns up at my door, with her yellow referral card. I take the card from her and ask her to take a seat. Now, she's in her seventies and was deaf as a post, so I said very loud and slow and clear, 'Can you take your clothes off down to the skin please; top only.' So she gets her kit off down to her shoulder; hat off, hat pin out, coat off, jacket off, cardigan off, blouse off, and was down to her bra and her string vest. Yep, string vest! So my desk looked like a jumble sale! So I proceeded to make her a collar out of a material called plasterzote; and it was ideal for a bespoke collar. She had a nice neck, and the collar fitted like a glove. She was happy and so was I. Job done! Sorted.

So the blouse goes on over the string vest, then the cardigan, then her jacket, then her topcoat, then her hat, and last but not least was the Mary Poppins hatpin! She made her way to the office door and said, 'Thank you, doctor.' It was the white coat that did it that. And as I go to open the door for this sweet old lady I looked at her referral card, and it said, in large bold writing, 'hand splint'! Fuck, and I had made her a collar! Fuck fuckidy fuck! I had made her a collar, and she had let me! Blind faith! I had to try to waffle my way out of that one and I did! But the funny side would have been in three months' time when she had her next appointment. Imagine the scene: 'Hello, Mrs Smith, how are you? Is your hand OK?' 'Yes thank you, doctor, my hand is fine, thank you; but my fucking neck is killing me!' That was a close one!

Another eventful incident happened to me, and that was on a Monday too. I fucking hate Mondays! I get this referral from the casualty department, which was quite unusual; it did happen, but not often. What happened was this geezer turns up with a referral card, and he's well suited and booted and had a real condescending tone about him. It was just the way he spoke; I think he thought I was working for him! Wrong!

So he has this temporary neck collar, which was issued by the casualty doctor the previous day as an interim measure due to his neck injury, which happened when he was standing talking to 'his men'. He was the transport manager of a large multinational company. I was so impressed; big fucking deal! But I sounded suitably impressed. I was taking the piss, but his head was so far up his arse; well, it would have been if his neck wasn't fucked! So the heavy door of the artic lorry swings open and hits him on the back of the neck and sent him flying. I did my very best not to laugh! So he's got this neck injury of course, he's come to casualty, and he is examined by the doctor and given a collar and told to come back on Monday, which he did and ends up at my door. So I make him this collar, as I was asked to do, but he was not satisfied at all. He said he needed more support for his head. Now, the head is a very heavy organ! I have actually held a decapitated head, and it is very heavy, but when the head is still attached to a living person it requires a degree of muscle support to keep it up. But no, he was not having any of this; he wanted more support. Well, as they say, the patient is always right!

But I tried once more to explain that it was not the best thing in this case. Believe it or not, he was still my patient. But he was not having any of it. I kept saying the more support you have, the more severely will movement be restricted leading to more pain, but would he listen? Would he fuck! So it was then that the fuck-him factor came into play. You want it, mate, you got it. I made him the collar of his dreams and it would have looked good on Frankenstein, so I fitted it. He puts on his shirt and then tries to put his tie on! He's got a surgical collar on, for fuck sake! And then the jacket goes on. So he leaves my room. Not a thank you, fuck all, nothing. Well, at this time I was still in my old room, which happened to be on the first floor.

So I hear a AH! AH! Clatter bang wallop, and then a loud groan. So I dash out and he's flat on his back, and he says, 'I didn't see the stairs.' Well, I just fell about; I could not stop laughing. I was in absolute hysterics; I was gone! And through my fits of laughter I said, 'Are you OK?' as if I gave a shit!

He was not a happy bunny, I can tell you. He was OK; the only damage done was to his pride, but he reported me. Yep, just as I thought he would! So I was called in to see Annie, my boss, and I told her the whole story, but what 'Neckie' had the camel with was me laughing. But what got me was that as Annie was telling me off, she was laughing too! It was go-through-the-motions stuff. Besides, what could they do to me? Can't make me pregnant!

Soon after that I was asked to make a splint for a below-knee amputation. I won't bore you with why an amputee needs a splint, but anyway, I was to make this splint under the supervision of a physio, which was a mixed blessing in a way! When you have to make a splint like this, you are very restricted with the type of material you can use, because of the effect it has on the patient. It can't be too hot, et cetera. You might have to make a plaster cast. It's so diverse. With amputees it's very difficult to judge the senses and they could be prone to burning and not even feel a thing, so caution is the key on this type of splint. And that's what happened to this patient. He ended up with a real bad burn on the stump of his leg, and it hit the fan big-time. Fucking hell, didn't it just, and rightly so!

But I was doing what the physio said! I was not happy about it, but who am I? And all the index fingers were pointed at me! Some things never change! So I get interviewed about it, and I said, 'Well, if you ask me, I would have used that, I would have done this and reinforced it with that.' Then the penny dropped, so to speak, and it was the less said about that the better. There was a full inquiry and it was sorted, but I felt so uncomfortable about it and said to myself, I don't need this, and resigned, and that was the end of that.

So I was out of work again, and I didn't care. I would get a job, no problem, and I didn't care where or what. So I find myself working as a porter at University College Hospital, London. It was a nice cushy number: no dirt, no sweat, and the pay was OK. Besides, it was wintertime, and it would do until the summer came and I could go back on the sites and earn some proper money. Well, that was Plan A. I was spending most of my free time in Crouch End. I would go to parties with Bob at Bart's, and just have a good time.

My mate Mick was the barman in the King's Head, and he was known to everyone as Corky Mick, because he was from County Cork. Well, that makes sense. He is one of my oldest and closest friends. He now lives in Thailand, got married and has a family. He works teaching English in the Arab states for part of the year, and the rest of the time he puts his feet up. Nice one, Mick!

When I first met Mick he was a serious drinker and ended up an alcoholic and found the AA, which in my opinion saved his life, for sure!

Alexandra Palace was the venue of a beer festival, and a gang of us go up for a look-see, and a bellyful of strange-sounding beers that, once consumed, would have the desired effect: off your tits! So we pay the entrance fee to get in and head for one of the many bars. I had never seen so many beers, but I would do my very best to try them all!

There was six of us, and two of the lads were on leave from the army prior to their deployment to Northern Ireland with the Parachute Regiment, and the object was to go on a real bender. Well, that was the plan! So my mate, Colin, was the first to notice that our beer was going. You would put it down and it would just disappear. The term was 'mine sweeping'. Someone was nicking the beer, which was a double pisser, as the place was rammed and it took a lifetime to get served.

Then Steve clocked this small bloke 'mine sweeping', so we all watched him. He was a small geezer, wore glasses, and he had a tweed jacket on and was carrying a newspaper, which he used as a cover when lifting a lone pint at the corner of a table. A smooth operator, but this was a dangerous sport! Well, it was gonna be for him! So Colin and Steve go off to buy a round of drinks, and they are gone ages. I was beginning to dehydrate. Where the fuck have they gone, fucking Norway? Well, after what seemed a lifetime they come back with seven pints. Hang on, there's only six of us. And Colin said, 'Don't drink that!' I thought, they're up to something, them two! But what? So we leave the spare beer at a strategically placed location; the only thing missing was a sign saying 'drink me'. So we shuffle off, keeping one eye on the target beer. And, right enough, our little man comes up, spots the beer and starts to close in on the target. The plan is working. He surreptitiously lifts the pint up and moves off to drink his ill-gotten gains!

Then wah! oh! wah! huguie! wha! He's downed the pint in a couple of mouthfuls and he throws up. Boy, does he throw up! This was projectile vomit. It was like his body had a hose in it. I have never ever seen anyone vomit like that, ever. I didn't think it was possible. Now he's on all fours, his glasses are off, in the vomit of course; then his false teeth are on the floor in the vomit. He was in a real bad way!

We turned to Steve and Colin and they are doubled-up with laughter. I could not work out why. They could not even speak through their laughter, and then they said, 'We shit in it.' They had shit in the glass, and he had drunk it and it must have hit his bottom lip and his eye met the turd! His reaction was plain to see by all!

He was taken away in an ambulance. I must admit we all laughed, but fucking hell! What a thing to do to someone! I bet he never did that again!

Having said that, it brings to mind a rather similar incident that happened to me some years later. It was at a piss-up with the Royal Marines at some naval club.

I am at the bar, waiting to get served, and I meet a mate of mine called Mark, and we start having a 'yarn' (navy-speak for engaging in conversation), and I noticed he had a bottle of beer in front of him. I had never seen its like before, so I said to Mark, 'What's that, mate,' pointing to the bottle of beer, and he said, 'Nutty, that's Trafalgar ale; you can only get it on HMS *Victory*, and it's real strong stuff. You want some?' I said, 'Cheers, mate,' and took a gulp, and it was handsome! 'That's a nice drop of ale, mate!' And then he said, 'You might as well finish it off; I am on the Pusser's.' (Good navy rum.) So I said, 'Cheers, mate,' and drank the lot, as you do!

Then the world's biggest marine comes up to the bar and said, 'Which bastard nicked my beer?' and picked up the empty bottle of beer I had just drunk! I looked at Mark and he said, 'Well, I never said it was mine!' Cheers, mate!

I was working at the hospital as a porter, which was OK-ish. I had no ambitions; I just wanted to be happy! It was Christmastime once more and I found myself working, which I didn't mind, as it would soon be spring and back on the sites. Working in a busy hospital at Christmas was novel, but I still had fucking turkey!

So started 1976. It was the year that Patty Hurst was found guilty of armed robbery. Why? She was loaded anyway. Must be the buzz.

James Callaghan became prime minister, the Israelis mounted a daring raid at Entebbe, Jimmy Carter became the president of the United States, *All the President's Men* was the big movie, Robert De Niro was the star of *Taxi Driver*, and Alex Haley published *Roots*.

The world said goodbye to Montgomery of Alamein, and Paul Getty kicked the bucket. As did Howard Hughes, one of the world's richest men, who died of malnutrition. Work that fucker out. Well, he had lost the plot completely. If you ever get the chance, read the book, *Howard Hughes: The Hidden Years* by James Phelan.

As soon as spring came I was back on the sites. I loved the freedom. No application forms, no politics, just do your job. I loved the feeling of the sun on my face, shirt off, the sun on your back, the sweat on my skin, and feeling strong. I loved it!

I was always out – never in. I was drinking in Hampstead; I liked the easy atmosphere, nice people. I would often go out on my own, and when you're on your own it's quite surprising the people you end up talking to. Life was great! But on a Sunday night I would always be found in one of the boozers in The People's Republic of Crouch End! I would meet some of the lads and catch the Gresham Special, which was a No. 41 bus that ended up at the Archway, and walk or stagger down the road to the Gresham dance hall, which had a late licence – a magnet for every drunk in the area in varying degrees of sobriety, heading for a late drink or even romance!

The Gresham had a dress code, which was quite amazing as the place was a piss-hole. It didn't make sense; you could be monged off your face, but if you had trousers on and shoes, that was OK. But what I did like about the Gresham was it was a well-lit place, and you could even hear yourself talk, unlike some of the other places.

The Gresham was the mecca of the fat-knacker bands – all of which had varying degrees of popularity with the Irish community, which at that time was huge! You had bands like The Indians, who were a bunch of Paddys dressed as American Indians. Yep, Red Indians. Why? Then you had a geezer called Brendan Shine, and some bird called Margo, but the megastar of the day was a geezer called Joe Dolan.

Most of the blokes didn't give a shit who was playing; it could be the National Bagpipe Band of Nigeria as long as the bar was open till late! With regards to the aspect of romance, two of my mates met their wives there, but me – nah! I just could not be arsed with that. Life was too short to be tied down!

The Gresham was a very popular place for nurses from the local hospital, and in those days most of the nurses were Irish. It seemed that all the Irish blokes were in the building trade, and no one was just a carpenter, or just a bricky; they all seemed to be subbies (subcontractors), which I think gave them a higher degree of social standing with the women, and every bloke had land at home – every one! Well, as for me, I had land on the moon, and I drive a submarine! It's all bollocks; you are what you are!

One Sunday night me and Mick were propping up the bar. Well, there was this woman who was a nurse at the Whittington, and she was so up her own bum you would not believe it. Well, she was with a group of people, and she decides to go and powder her nose. It was quite early in the evening and the place was not packed yet.

So as she walks back, all the blokes turn and look at her as she walks by to join her friends, and I am thinking she's not that special; but she walks past us with her nose in the air. I noticed she had tucked her dress in her knickers! That's why all the eyes fell upon her! I almost choked on my beer! There is a God!

After a few minutes it was mentioned to her, and I have never seen anyone so embarrassed. Never saw her in the Gresham again.

It was about this time a lot of the pubs in the Archway area and the Holloway Road were frequented by Irish men, and the 'tin' was passed around, which was for the 'boys' – the IRA. And my response was always fuck off! Which did have an element of danger. But if I or any of the local lads got filled in by these geezers, the pub would be turned over, no problems.

A lot of the Irish pubs would have live fat-knacker bands, and at the end of the night they would play the Irish national anthem, which pissed a lot of people off that it was allowed to be done. We were at war with the IRA. I was not too bothered if I was standing; well, that was OK. But on one occasion it did piss me right off.

I was seeing a nurse from the Whittington Hospital, who was a nurse and Irish, so she wanted to go and see a band in the Holloway Road, in the boozer called the Cock. So off we go to see this band called The Barleycorn, who start playing Republican songs, which did not sit easy with me, as I was wearing an old Para smock. It was big and baggy and really comfortable, and I just happened to be wearing it. So I go to the bar, and after what seemed a lifetime I am served. And as I am at the bar, the governor of the pub down the road, whose name was Terry, looked at me. He recognised me from using his pub. I knew a lot of his regulars, and some of them were, one might say, a bit of a handful. And he looks at me – he's half-pissed – and says to me, 'You're treading on dangerous ground wearing that in here, boy!' He said it so it could be heard. So I said, 'They would be on dangerous ground singing them songs in some of the pubs I use!' I got the drinks and left him to it!

At the end of the evening, they played the Irish national anthem, and I am sitting down; everyone stands. I don't. My attitude was fuck them!

I feel eyes burning into me. The girl I was with grabbed my shoulder for me to stand, but I just could not do it! As we leave, I go to the door and I open the door for her, as you do for a lady, and as we are walking up the road she says, 'There's something on your back.' I can't see anything, as I don't have eyes in the back of my head, so I take my jacket off and examine it; it was covered in spit! I did my bollocks to say the least. The bastards had spat on my back. The gutless wankers. They never said a word, just spat! Wankers!

I was in the Favourite one night, having a beer, and there was this local called 'Dublin'. He was a local pisshead, who got really gobby when he had a bellyful of beer. He's sitting at the bar, having a beer, and this geezer walks in the boozer. I had never seen him before, and he just walked up to Dublin and said, with a smile on his face, 'Was that you singing the IRA songs last night?' And Dublin says yes, with a degree of pride. Well, this geezer punches Dublin straight in the face and knocks him flying off his stool and on his arse. One punch; fuck, what a corker that was!

This geezer never said another word just walked out of the boozer, and no one lifted a finger to help! Dublin had it coming, was the general consensus.

Things were changing on the sites. We had to start paying tax, and I needed a change, so I got a job with a local security company and was sent to a site in London's West End in an office block of a famous advertising company. It was night work, but it was a change, and I thought it was worth a go.

I worked with a small Irishman called John Mac. He was a right nice geezer, and boy, did he like a drink, and I don't mean tea! One night, not long after I started, he asked me did I like a drink? My reply was do bears shit in the woods?

Well, this place had upstairs an all-singing all-dancing bar, pumps, the lot; it was like a private pub. Well, it was at night for us, but I did not feel like a beer most nights, so we had an agreement: he would lock down the building and go on the piss, and I would hold the fort, so to speak. Well, it was fine by me. He would go off, and I would read to my heart's content. The only thing I regret was I had no idea about adult education. It would have been the ideal place to study, but I didn't know any better. It's not that I knew and could not be arsed: it was that I didn't know. Over the years I have known two blokes that have studied for law and made it. I wish I had. But that's life!

But that was all about to change. It was my birthday and I was down my local boozer with a few of the chaps, having a light ale, as you do. It was a Saturday afternoon, and one of the lads said, 'Let's go to a football match.' Me? football? Nah. But there was a good few of us, and it was the majority that won, so I decided to go along. Well, I hadn't been to a match before and it was somewhere to go while the boozer was closed, so off we go!

The venue of the match was miles away in Chelsea. I don't even know who they were playing! What I didn't know was that that day would change my career prospects for many years to come.

So we get to the ground and I felt like cattle being herded in. We were almost at the back of the stand, and I was not best impressed I can tell you. I felt like a sardine!

Then, quite near where we were standing, a big fight breaks out and it was chaos. The crowd swayed back and the sea of people fell upon each other, and then the police showed up in great numbers. They fought their way into the sea of people and made their way to the scene of the mass brawl, and then out of nowhere my mate Colin was grabbed around the neck by a copper and dragged away. He had done absolutely nothing, nothing whatsoever, and he was being dragged away. So I made my way over to this copper and said, 'You pulled my mate out and he's done nothing!' I did not shout; I was quite calm about it, but I was firm. And then this copper said, 'You had better go with him, hadn't you?' And then he made a nodding gesture to a copper that was behind me, and then he grabs my arm and puts the other arm around my neck and dragged me off too! I was livid, I can tell you. I had done fuck all!

The more I struggled, the tighter he held me and twisted my arm, and it was hurting me as he pulled me backwards, but there was fuck all I could do! I am thinking, Well, that's it then; I am gonna be chucked out of the ground, big deal! So off we go!

When we get to the ground level by some gates, I look around and see Colin, and he has blood pouring down his face, from his nose. Well, when I saw him a moment ago he didn't have a bloody nose – it was obviously done while in police custody. And then I saw a copper punch him in the stomach, I might add while another one was holding him around the neck and holding his arm around up his back. He was defenceless and restrained, and this copper punched him. A real fucking hero! Wanker!

So I shouted, 'I seen what you done!' I just could not help it; it was out before I could think. I was livid! The next thing I know I am slammed up against the side of a waiting police van, and it kinda stunned me; it took the wind out of me. And then when I was getting to sort myself out, I was bundled into the van and driven off. The van was full of other football supporters, who were all looking rather dejected. We were taken to a local police station near the football ground.

As soon as we got there I was put in a cell with other blokes and just sat there. No one said much. We all sat there feeling sorry for ourselves, and after what seemed ages a copper took a bloke out, and then there was just the three of us. And again, what seemed like ages later, the metallic lock on the door was opened and I was called out and led to a small room, and was charged with threatening behaviour! Me! Over football! Nah! But yep! I was so angry. I had done nothing, absolutely nothing! As God is my judge! I had done fuck all!

So I was released from custody. I had about £2 on me, and I am stuck in the middle of nowhere; my joy knew no bounds! So I made a phone call to a woman I knew called Jean – she was a mate's wife – and told her the score, and could I get a taxi and could she pay for it when I got to her place, and I would settle up with her when I got sorted? And as Jean was Jean she said yes, not a problem. TAXI!

I get to Jean's and she gives me some dosh to pay for the cab, and I tell her what had happened. She found it sooo funny, me getting nicked at a football match. Me! But she then said something that made me think: she said, 'Well, there was a few times you didn't get caught. Maybe it's God's way of punishing you.' Hmmm.

Jean was a wonderful woman. She was a voluptuous woman and had two lovely daughters, real nice decent people, and Jean had a heart of solid gold. She was my mate's wife – well, kind of, they lived together. I was always fond of Jean. She was a lovely lady, and she was a jock! And, I might add, very proud of it!

So the day comes for me to go to court, which was Horsferry Road Magistrates' Court. So I am dressed in a suit and tie and shiny shoes and looking as respectable as possible. As I walk in the court I go to check my name on the list and I can't see it on the court list, so I go down to the jailer's office and I tell him my name is not on the list. So he goes 'humm', and said, 'Come this way.' So I do, and I am led straight into a cell! Hang on? As he closed the door he said I should have been there yesterday! What?

What had happened was the day and date were written down wrong, and I was adrift for a day! So I am sitting in this piss-hole of a cell, in a very expensive Chester Barrie suit, and I was not a very happy bunny! Then I ask to see the duty solicitor. I waited for ages and ages, and at last my cell door opened. I was led out to see the duty solicitor. She was a very attractive young lady and she was Scottish, and she introduced herself as Helena Kennedy.

I told her what had happened, and she said I was also charged with failing to appear! What? 'Yep, you did not appear, so you have been charged.' But she said it was no real biggie and she would get me bailed to appear at another date, and I would be out of here in a couple of hours at the latest. She was true to her word. I was bailed again to appear on another date. I would make sure the date was right this time!

So it's the day of the race, and I am back at the magistrates' court, and my name is on the list. Sorted. It was the full monty – court appearance attire, and wait and see what happens. But I was told I was in front of a real fucker of a magistrate, called McDermott. So as I am waiting to walk into the lion's den; I am waiting to see the copper who arrested me, but I don't see him. Maybe he's sick? Maybe he's dead? But then this copper comes up and tells my solicitor he's the officer on the case. Hang on, that was not the copper who arrested me! I have never seen that man in my life before! I can't work this out.

I am in the dock and pleading 'not guilty' and this copper whose name is burned into my memory, PC Moser, starts to give his evidence. He lied, lied, fucking lied through his teeth! I could not believe my ears!

I think it's important to mention that this was the height of football hooliganism in the country, and people were pissed off with it, and the policy was to take a very firm hand with anyone involved with it and to punish them accordingly. Well, that was the plan, and it looked like I was gonna be in for a rough ride!

No matter what I said, it might as well have been in Swahili for what good it did. No matter what I said, I was a football hooligan, and that was the label I had firmly pinned to me. There was fuck all I could do about it. My brief did her best, and the three wise men retired to make the decision on my fate.

Then they come back, and he goes into a one long one. 'This sort of behaviour is totally unacceptable, blah, blah, blah…' Prison three months. Fucking what! Me, inside for three months? I could not believe my ears! I looked at Helena, and then the words 'suspended sentence' came out. At least I still had my freedom. I had done nothing, but I had a criminal record now. I was so pissed off with that! But Helena did say, I was rather lucky; a lot of other people came off a lot worse then me, I got a result, yep, but I didn't do it!

Well, as for PC Moser, I hope you die alone and in pain! You are a fucking lying bastard! He fucked me big style. I had never seen him before, never done him a bad turn, and yet he lied though his teeth, and I will never forget that. I just hope we meet one day. That will be interesting!

Eighteen

A moment can change your life. A tiny decision and your life is changed for ever. I will tell you about two mates whose lives changed for ever in a split second!

This is Steve's story. Steve was a 'chippy' (carpenter), and one hot summer evening he decided to pop into a boozer on the Holloway Road and have a couple of pints on the way home from work. So Steve is sitting at the bar with a beer, and after a couple of pints has to go and empty himself, as you do, and when he retuned to his stool there was a bloke sitting on it. And Steve pointed out to the geezer that he was sitting on his stool, but this son of the Emerald Isle ignored him and then laughed at him.

So Steve is well pissed off, but realised that it was not worth the hassle and gets himself another beer. Then the 'Paddy' goes for a piss and Steve reclaims the seat, and the Paddy comes back and sees Steve on his seat and gets the right camel (not a happy bunny). Words are exchanged, probably lots of four-lettered ones, and a row develops, which led to a fight breaking out. But Paddy has got a few chums with him and they get stuck into Steve too. So what did Steve do? He went and grabbed a hammer from his toolbag and buries it into Paddy's head!

In the meantime the Old Bill have turned up and arrest Steve. He's taken down the local nick and is charged, and the Paddy is taken to hospital in an ambulance, and later that night he died as a result of the hammer blow to his head. In the early hours of that morning, Steve is charged with murder. He was denied bail and at the trial he was 'lifed-off' for murder! All this over a bar seat. What a waste of two lives, not to mention the waves of the ripples that affected the lives of both men's families. A fucking bar stool!

Barry's story is a sad one. Barry liked a drink, as one might say, but he was no Beer Monster. So this night he's in the boozer in Hornsey Road, and he's having a right nice drink with a couple of geezers, and at closing time they decide to get a carry-out and go back to this geezer's gaff and have a right good session. Well, I think we have all done that.

So, copious amounts of mind-bending lager are consumed, and people crash out, and some go home. Barry crashed out, and is woken in the early hours by some geezer making sexual advances on him while he's asleep. Barry wakes up and goes into one! In a semi-drunken rage, he picks up a chair and hits the bloke over the head with it, and knocks him down and then in a rage of anger he grabs the chair leg and rams it down his throat and it kills him!

He then panics and legs it. It's in the very early hours, and he's panicking. Then he goes to see Twink and tells him what happened. Then Twink's neighbour, Del, gets, for want of a better word, involved. Well, Barry's covered in blood and he tells the boys what has happened, and they advise him to give himself up. A wise bit of advice. And Barry took their advice and gave himself up. A wise move, but the result of the case was he too was 'lifed-off', and the last I heard of him was that he had developed a flair for art and actually had his work out at an exhibition. But he was still in the nick doing a long one!

So I am out of work, but Jean's Peter gets me a job on the site that he was working on, which was great. It was then that I realised that Peter had a drink problem. We started work on the site at eight in the morning, and he would be drinking cider. It's eight in the morning! It was such a shame; he was such a nice bloke, but the drink got a grip of him and never let go. But as he got me the job, I would cover for him as best I could; I felt I had to. The foreman, as he was called – I think the modern term is line manager, but then it was foreman, a position of rank and power! – his name was Densie and he was as rough as a badger's bum! He was from Galway, in Eire, and there was something strange about him. I could not put my finger on it, I just felt it. He was the real deal when it came to being a real navy. He would cook his breakfast on his shovel over an open fire. I had heard of this but never seen it, but yep, that's what he did. Fuck knows why he never went to the cafe like the rest of the civilised world.

I was working with Peter, and an Irish geezer called Martin.

He was so quiet, but his claim to fame was he had met Elvis while he was working in the Fatherland! He kept a photo of him standing next to Elvis in a faded envelope in his wallet. It was a precious possession.

We were gutting out these old flats for refurbishment, and it was hard dirty manual work, but I did not mind. I enjoyed Peter's company. He was a well-travelled man. He had been to a lot of far-off places and done all sorts of stuff, and always had a tale to tell. It was then I was getting the wanderlust!

Peter was drinking a lot at this time. After he had done his cider in, he would work like a lunatic, and come noon his thirst would get the better of him, and he would skulk off down the boozer and go on the beer. Peter had limited funds. I think he was kinda given pocket money by Jean, I think for his own benefit, but he would always find money to piss up the pub wall. He would often borrow off people to fund his drinking, but he would always manage to pay them back somehow, and then start all over again. When he had his few beers at lunchtime he would then come back to work, and once more work like a lunatic to make up time. The work was hard and physically demanding, dirty work, but it was a job, and it had its upside. Well, if you ask me, anything was better then sorting fucking nuts and bolts out; anything!

Peter's drinking was a problem – well, for him not me. It was then that I realised he was an alcoholic, and like so many others I had always harboured the illusion that alcoholics were confined to a park bench and that's the way it was. But during the course of my life I have seen it all at one time or another. I worked in the City. I was not a reversible Bound Trouser Dealer, but I would often spend time in the City boozers, and I am a people watcher. I like to watch people; it's just a thing I do. I wonder what they do for a living, what they are really like, and what they are talking about. And believe me, I have heard some serious bollocks spoken, I can tell you! No word of a lie!

But I would watch these 'Suits' knocking it back big time, large gin and tonics day after day. They were the same as Peter, but they had suits on, and more disposable income to put up a pub-bog wall. I was covering for Pete and this was not doing him any favours, but he was a mate, and he done me a good turn, and I would never forget that, ever. I wonder whatever happened to him. I just hope God has been kind to him.

Nineteen

I turned up for work on Monday morning and was sacked with all the other blokes, and that was the end of that. I think the firm went bust, and it took ages to get my money, which turned up weeks later by the way of the Royal Mail, but at least I got my dosh! I then got a job at a hospital in Liverpool Road, and it was a right cushy number. Sorted!

I had a good mate; his name was Marco. His mum was Italian and his dad was Polish. I met him at St Peter's in Chain Church youth club, and we became real good mates. Marco was in a long-term relationship with a really nice girl called Cathy, who was a very good friend then and even now. But for some reason or other the relationship went lumpy and they parted. It was a real shock to me. I really thought that they would go the distance, but no. These things happen in life.

So Marco had managed to save a few quid and he decided to take off to Africa. He had seen an advert in *Time Out* magazine and found himself a member of a group of like-minded people and headed off in an ex-army four-tonne truck, and headed off to Mombasa.

I was so pissed off I didn't go because I was skint. I lived for the day and never saved a penny. I always had a few quid but nothing like I needed to join Marco, but it did get me thinking! So I said goodbye to Marco, and he headed off to the Dark Continent, the lucky bastard. But I found myself thinking about taking off.

One of my mates was getting married. It's a funny thing; it was that time in my life I was always going to weddings and christenings, and in later life I found myself going to nothing but funerals, and when I was a kid I was always in the last car. But the older you get, the closer you get to the front car, and a few funerals ago I was behind the lead car! Made me think!

I remember a mate of mine was getting married and, in true

male tradition, he had a stag night, and the Beer Monster was on top form and ended getting monged, pissed, wankered, and off my face, and even drunk; all of the above. I did not make it into work; I was fucked!

So, on Monday morning I am called into the office to see the boss, who was a lady called Babs Frost, and she was a really nice lady. So I am on the carpet and asked why did I not come to work. So I said, 'OK, I could say I had a tummy bug or I had a real bad headache, but no, I went on the piss and got hammered. It was my mate's stag night, and I was fit for nothing, never mind work, and that's the truth.' She looked at me and smiled and said, 'I am gonna give you that, for being so honest.' I was surprised. Honesty does pay! Well, sometimes.

So my mate gets married. Now, his fiancée was from a large Irish Catholic family. Anyway, come the big day, her dad has a couple of large whiskys in the morning to steady his nerves, so a generous dose of the old firewater did the trick! So the time of the arrival of the wedding car is drawing closer and closer, and time was ticking by, but no car! So the time came to go. Well, her dad could not drive because he had been on the firewater, and her mum could not drive. I think the only thing she ever drove was a pram. So they phoned for a minicab: sorted!

So me and some of the lads are waiting outside the church, puffing away as you do, and fuck my old boots, this blue Escort turns up, with a yellow door I might add, and it looked like an explosion of silk in the back. It was the bride-to-be! And her dad! And for good measure the driver was called Winston, and came complete with furry dice and a coat hanger as an aerial! Laugh? It was hilarious! But they carry on with the service, and the vintage Roller turned up just in the nick of time!

While I was working at Liverpool Road, I heard one of the funniest stories ever! There was a couple that I became friendly with. They were Pam and Alistair; nice people and all that, but they were so boring, and I mean boring. Their idea of a good night was to do a jigsaw! For fuck sake! But sometimes they'd really push the boat out and go rambling off around the countryside, complete with bobble hats! So they're off to some far-flung place in darkest Wales, and Alistair comes across a hole in the ground, and decides to satisfy his curiosity by finding out how deep the hole is. So he picks up a stone and drops it down the hole and counts out. The theory was if you count down the time it takes the stone to reach the bottom, it should tell you how deep the hole is. Well, that's the theory!

So the stone does not make a thud, so he goes off and gets a larger stone and repeats the exercise, and still silence. So now he's getting pissed about it, so he bimbles off and gets a boulder – muddy hands, mud all down his nice new kagoul – and lobs the boulder down the said hole! And nothing! So now he's got the right camel and walks off to find something he can lob down the hole. By this time, Wendy is getting really pissed with this scientific experiment. It's raining, it's cold, and she does not see the point of this nonsense!

So the next thing she sees is Alistair pulling a fucking great railway sleeper; have you seen the size of one of those things? They are enormous! So he's dragged it into place and manages to stand it on end, and edges it into position near the hole, saying with a great degree of pride that this will do it, and lobs the wooden sleeper down the hole. As it plummets down, he leaps back, and then he notices there's a chain attached to the end of it, and it clatters down behind the sleeper as it falls, and the chain is falling fast. And then, to their horror, they see a goat! Which is attached to the other end of the chain, and speeds past them and down the hole!

For fuck sake, there was this goat minding his own business, munching away on the grass, and then whoosh, he's pulled down a fucking great hole! I was doubled-up with laughter, but what made me laugh more was they were proper vegetarians. Well, one thing's for sure – they will confuse some archaeologists in a couple of thousand years from now! But the upside is they're lucky there was not a potholer down there!

Outside the porter's lodge was a bench, which was the home of the hospital cat on a sunny day. So it was a glorious day, and I was sitting down by the hatch – which was directly over the bench – and I am rubbernecking (half asleep). Well, the hospital was the headquarters of the local hospital maintenance department, and one of the chaps who worked there was a geezer called Harry. Harry was a right laugh. He wore these glasses, which looked like the end of milk bottles, and he always wore a flat cap, always, and he never had a fag out of his gob, and in his bottom lip was like a groove, as if it was part of an ashtray, and for all the world he looked like the Benny Hill character Fred Scuttle. Well, that was Harry.

So as he walks past me he picks up the sleeping cat and throws it at me, and it startled me as well as the cat. And the upshot is I land on my arse and the cat goes bonkers. I took it in good humour – well, I had no choice – but I don't think the cat did. Harry the hat found it so funny, as did the rest of his workmates. But I said to myself, I will get you for that, you fucker! I didn't know when but I knew I would somehow; but not in a spiteful way.

About a week later I was walking around the back of the hospital and its outbuildings, and was by the ablutions (toilets), and I see Harry go in! YES! Got ya! So I tiptoe up to the old ablutions and peep inside. The layout was as follows: it had six traps and opposite the traps was a long urinal, but one of the traps is closed! That will do me!

So I bestow myself with great speed to the porter's lodge, silently, hoping the cat would be fast asleep on the bench as usual; my luck was in and Tiddles was dead to the world, sprawled out in the hot midday sun. So I grabbed him by the tail with a very firm grip and ran as fast as my legs would take me to the ablutions, swinging the cat around just to enhance the momentum, which I hoped would give the required effect once launched.

So I run into the ablutions and lob the very pissed-off Tiddles over the closed trapdoor, and heard the ruckus. Job done, I am thinking. As I leave the ablutions I see Harry! What the fuck? Well, who's in the toilet? So I run back to the porter's lodge and calm myself down, get-a-grip type of thing, and wait and see what happened. I did not wait long. The phone made a sharp shrill as it rang, and I answered, 'Hello, Front Gate.'

'Hello, it's Mr Brown's office. Do you have a first-aid box there?'

I said, 'Yes, we do; what's up?'

'It's Mr Brown; he's had a slight accident. Can you pop it over?'

'Of course.' So I walked over to his office, and noticed he was walking rather funny. I wonder why! Mr Brown was a very senior member of staff! Fuck, fuckidy fuck! But I got away with it. It was a close one!

When I was not at work I would spend my time around the Angel and around Upper Street. It was a nice place – it had a kinda nice feel about the whole place; it had an easy atmosphere. This was before it became a trendy place, with continental coffee bars and trendy wine bars. But sometimes I would go back to my roots in Hornsey to see some of the 'faces' and shoot the shit with the old firm.

Now this is straight out of *Only Fools and Horses* and no word of a lie! I am walking up the Hornsey Road, and I bump into a geezer called Bosher. His name was John, but to everyone he was 'Bosher' O'Grady. Bosher was a real character, once met never forgotten! He was a year younger than me and went to the same school as me, but he had left at an early age, as he said, 'Fuck it. I've had enough of this school shit. I am off.' And that was that. He started to work in demolition. He had massive hands, very rough, the result of many years spent swinging a heavy sledge-hammer and a pickaxe. He was a little bit shorter then me, about six foot, his neck started at his ears, and he was powerfully built. He was just a very strong man, and a real hard fucker.

John earned the name 'Bosher' because he was always getting into fights, and would say 'I give the geezer a right bosh!' Hence the name 'Bosher'. He kinda had a personal code of honour, if that makes sense. He never took drugs and hated them with a true passion; he was not a tea leaf (thief), just a bit of a scrapper, but he did like a drink and was not frightened of strong drink in any amount. Come to think about it, I don't think Bosher was frightened of anything or anyone!

As I said, he had like a code of honour. He would not let anyone take, as he would say, 'A diabolical liberty' with anyone. One night, a couple of the lads were at one of the Paddy dance halls; I don't remember which one, but this is what I was told happened.

A couple of the bouncers were giving this drunk a hard time; they were out of order. Anyway, Bosher turns up and says, 'There's no need for that, for fuck sake, he's pissed!' And one of the bouncers told him to fuck off! So what does Bosher do? He punches the pair of them, bosh, bosh, and knocked the pair of them flat on their arses; job done! They knew what was best for them, and left it out! I wonder why. Bosher was one of life's nice people, and I am sorry to say he was killed by a hit-and-run driver.

Not long before he was killed he was given an award for his courage. A person either fell or jumped, or was pushed, under an Underground train, and Bosher jumped down, got under the train and stayed with the person until professional help came. He was that type of geezer.

When I got the news he was killed, it gripped me. He was a smashing bloke, and I was glad he was my mate. I still miss him, even today. Rest in peace, mate.

So I meet Bosher and we pop in the Fox and Hounds boozer, and we meet two of the lads, a geezer called Beano and Long Barry. Beano was a bit of a lad, and he was called Beano because he looked like one of the characters out of the *Beano*'s 'Bash Street Kids'. He looked like Plug. Why they didn't call him Plug fuck knows. It's one of life's great mysteries, like where did people go on bank holidays before we had garden centres?

The other geezer was Long Barry. Well, he was tall, hence Long, and his name was Barry, so that makes sense. But he was also on what was known as a Long Firm (they carried out fraud), which was fucking amazing if you ask me, because he was far from the brightest colour in the colouring box of life!

When he was younger he did a lot of bird. He was locked up at an early age, and when he was in the Boob (prison) he had his knuckles tattooed with Mum and Dad, and they looked shit! So what did he do? He removed his own tattoo with acid on a matchstick! Fucking painful or what? But he stuck with it and burned them off! He was so very lucky that he never died from blood poisoning; so lucky. So guess what he did then? Your starter for ten. And if you like, you can phone a friend or even ask the audience! As the scars on his hands were so bad, he had tattoos to cover the scars! As I said, he was not the brightest colour in the box!

Anyway, I am having a yap with Beano, and I ask how's it going? And he tells me he's had a right result! So what's that, then? He then picks up a holdall which was at his feet and says, 'Have a butchers at that lot.' So I pick the bag up and sit down and open it, and there are two packages, very neatly wrapped in like a grey sugar paper – the type of stuff you drew on when you were a kid at school with your crayons. So, I unwrap it and fuck me! It was a bundle of birth certificates, a load of them, brand new, never issued! 'Fuck me, Beano, you struck gold here, mate!'

'Yeah, sure did.'

'Where did you get them from?'

'Packi (his younger brother) had it off when he went creeping (burgled a place and had some good fortune!). Yeah, it was some government building, fuck all else; tea money and that was about it. Then he picked those up!'

And the other bundle was a load of blank death certificates. This was a real result!

So I ask him what he's gonna do with them, and then he said two words: 'Rubbish Tony'. Fucking Rubbish Tony! Rubbish Tony was a fence in the local area, and he could get you anything, at a price, and was usually top price, but when you were trying to knock stuff out (sell stolen goods) he always paid shit money. But as I was not a thief, I had little to do with him; I did not trust that man as far as I could spit a piano! If I shook his hand I always counted my fingers after! But he had one redeeming feature: he would have nothing to do with drugs, which was fine by me; and, funnily enough, a lot of the real villains never had anything to do with them either. But that was in those days; the world has changed. There's big money in the drug trade, and you never hear of bank robberies any more; they've had their day. Although you still get the odd dinosaurs who walk into banks with a gun.

So Rubbish Tony is gonna give Beano a grand for the lot; not bad – nice earner, as one might say! As Rubbish Tony walks in the pub, Bosher and I leave and let them do their business. About three weeks later I am in a boozer, and Long Barry walks in, and we exchange greetings, as one does, and I ask him, 'Well, how did it go with Rubbish Tony and Beano?' And he said, 'For fuck sake, he had Beano's pants right down!' I looked at him and said, 'What happened?' And he said, 'The fucker paid Beano in funny money!' – in other words, it was counterfeit. Well, I could not help myself: I had to laugh!

Long Barry didn't see the funny side of it. I wonder why!

When I was not up the Angel, I was over the hill in The People's Republic of Crouch End, and the King's Head was my office. I seemed to know everyone, and everyone had a nickname, like Corky Mick, Esso Pete, Bob the Doc, Fishy Mick, Archway Pete, Bathroom, the Honey Monster, Wallet, Sporran Gob, the Neff, Tricky Dicky, Long Barry, Oddball, to name just a few.

The Gov'nor was a geezer called Norbert, a real fucking smoothy, and he thought he was the dog's bollocks. Well, he was the only one that did! This night I am in the pub with a pal of mine called Jim Boy, and he was going out with one of the barmaids; she was a real cracker! Anyhow, Norbert was playing poker with a couple of blokes in the snug bar, and whenever he wanted a drink he would click his fingers, and it was getting right up Jim's girl's snotter! And this in turn gave Jim the raving camel. So I am standing by the front door, and then she loses the plot completely and goes into one with Norbert, and Jim goes fucking potty, I think he was on Paracetamoxyfursenbenroneocyin (Check the net – it makes you good at fighting!), and in his frustration he punches through the glass door, so I grab him around the neck to calm him down. He was strong as an ox, but me and another pal sort him out and calm him down. The pub closes and we go home.

The next day I walk in the pub and park my arse on a stool by the juke box, and Marco comes over and said, 'I hear you're barred, mate?' So I said, 'No, can't be me, mate. You mean Jim Boy.' So that was that. Well, then Norbert comes over and puts his arm on my shoulder and says, 'You're barred.' And I think, fuck it, I might as well make it worth my while then! So I punched him as hard as I could on the nose, and he reeled back, and I said, 'It's OK; I am barred now!' And fucked off.

Well, the following night I walk past the pub, and there are loads of people drinking outside; it was a real summer evening. And one of the boys brought me a beer out, and they seemed quite pleased that Norbert got a smack in the gob! After a short while the Old Bill turn up, and tell the people to either drink up or go in. This had never happened before. So they said to me to move on, and I said no, and they got right stroppy about it, and, as I was talking, one of them punched me right in the face, and it really fucking hurt! And then I was bundled into a van and carted off down the local nick. I was not a happy bunny.

So I am charged with loitering, for fuck sake, a £2 fine. Big deal. But I am pissed that I got a bang in the mouth for fuck all! So I said to the custody sergeant that I wanted to make a complaint against the officer that punched me, and that I had witnesses. Well, that caused a reaction, I can tell you. The magic word was 'witnesses'. Get out of that, you fucker!

So it goes ahead, and then I get a phone call from Corky Mick saying that Norbert would like to have a word. OK. So I said I'll pop down and have a word. So I go down the boozer and it was about 5.30. It had just opened, and Norbert said, 'If you drop the charge of assault, I won't bar you.' So I said OK. That's that done then. I am back in the office, sorted, and Norbert was still wearing sunglasses!

Well, that night something happened that really affected me for a long time after. I am standing by the bar, and a couple of blokes walk in and get a drink and stand by the jukebox. These geezers weren't English; they were maybe Greek or Turkish. They did not speak English, that's for sure. Then a few hours later a team of geezers come in the pub. I just smelt trouble; it was a feeling I had in my blood and that never lets me down. They are all pissed-up, and I knew some of the faces from over the hill, but they had what was known as odd marks with them. There was about ten of them, a lot of geezers. Then one of the odd marks put some money in the jukebox, and that was that. But one of the foreigners sits on the jukebox, and the odd mark's record jumps. A couple of words are exchanged, and right out of nowhere one of the odd marks – and it was like slow motion – he smashes a pint jug into the main column of the pub and smashes it into one of the foreigner's faces. He hits him between the ear and throat. Fucking hell!

The blood is gushing out of this wound, and in a split second I grabbed a bar mat and grab him and cover the wound with the towel to try to stop the flow of blood that was pumping out of his neck, and I mean the blood was all over the place. My left hand held his head and my right hand was over the wound, and I pressed as hard as I could. I could feel the blood pump through my hand. The blood was so sticky, and it seemed so much darker than other blood I had seen. The blood was running down my arm. I am saying to him, 'OK, it's gonna be OK,' and between saying he was gonna be OK, I was shouting, 'Get a fucking ambulance! Get an ambulance!' I was terrified, and then his eyes started to roll back in his head, and I am thinking he's gonna collapse any second!

His mate was hysterical, shouting, crying; it was awful. Sporran Gob was trying to calm him down with Esso Pete. The team of blokes fucked off sharpish; the place was in an uproar! I am praying in my head, where's that fucking ambulance? Come on, come on! At last it turned up, and they took over, thank God, and he was away in that ambulance in fast time, and the sirens gave it whompo up the hill and away!

I walked out of the pub into the fresh night air, and it was such a feeling of breeze on my sweating brow, and I light a fag and I was shaking like a leaf; I just could not stop shaking. And as I looked down at my nice new white shirt I got from Jermyn Street, it was covered in sticky blood! Thank God it was not my blood! And that intake of nicotine was just what I needed.

And then Esso Pete came out and said, 'You OK, mate?' I just said 'Yeah,' and he said, 'Well done, son. You probably saved his life!'

So I went to the bog as the police turned up, washed myself and went home. And when my mum saw me she nearly fainted, but I said I was OK. I washed myself off and fell on my bed and fell asleep. I was fucked!

I could not get what had happened out of my head; it was a mindless unprovoked attack, a vicious attack on an innocent defenceless man. I was horrified. The Old Bill went potty – asking lots of questions, but no one saw anything which the Old Bill were not happy about. They wanted the animals who did that, and quite rightly so! I went over the hill and spoke to some of the faces that were there that night and told them the score: that the Old Bill were mega pissed off, and to keep low. And Joe said, 'It was not us; it was those fucking odd mark hangers-on, who were a bunch of fucking nutters.' Yep, I can vouch for that.

That was the end of that, but I wonder had I not been there, at that exact time, at that place… don't know. Was it synchronicity? What they say is so true: 'What we do today echoes in eternity.' No matter how small an action we take, it can have a profound impact on others we have never known, or will know!

The Maynard pub had just been refurbished and was a very popular pub at the time; everyone wanted to take a look-see. I love the smell of new pubs; they have a kinda special smell – new paint, new carpet, and the aroma of ale, and cigarette smoke. It's a nice smell.

It is said that the sense of smell invokes the memory more than any other sense. When I took my little girl to her first day at school, I smelt that school smell. It's a smell of polished floors and pencils, and it brought back that memory of that first day at school for me in Wales a hundred years ago!

Well, the Maynard had been transformed from a smelly old piss-hole of a boozer into a real nice pub. I liked the place. Yep, this will do me, and this was gonna be my new office!

Then I meet her. Her name was Jane. She was one of the new part-time bar staff, and I started to chat with her. She shared a flat in Crouch End and worked in an office in the West End as a full-time job. We seemed to get on well. She had worked in a kibbutz in Israel for a few months, and she was from some place north of Watford. She loved animals, and I said I loved animals too. Roast beef, roast lamb – and roast chicken. And she kinda looked at me sideways and she started to laugh. So I asked her if she would like to go out for a beer when she was off, and she said that would be nice. Sorted.

That Sunday evening we headed off to Alexandra Palace and had a few drinks, and talked for ever. She talked all about her life and why she came to London, and all that sort of stuff, but what got me was her eyes. They were so blue and deep you could drown in them, and her smile… well, it lit her whole face. We did a lot of laughing too, which is so important! Before I knew it we were seeing rather a lot of each other, and it was nice. She was older than me by three years, but age is just a number. Besides, most of my mates were older then me. Why? Don't know, but that's the way it was.

It was the time when a lot of pubs had live bands, and I don't mean fat-knacker bands either! We would go to Dingwalls in Camden Lock, and other venues to see bands that had just not quite made it, bands such as The Tourists, Darts, and the Tom Robinson Band, and we had a load of fun. And then one night we sat on the back step of the house she lived in and talked till sunrise, and she had told me she had just kinda come out of a long relationship, and it could be seen in her eyes that it still cut deep into her heart. You can't take the pain out of a person's eyes – well, they are the windows to your soul. In her room was a photo of her and a bloke in a frame by her bed, and I looked at that photo, and it was not her brother, because she did not have a brother, just two sisters. So by logical deduction it was her ex-boyfriend, and it was sort of strange. They kinda didn't look right together; I don't know why but they didn't. He was not at all what I had expected somehow. He was really thin and really tall with a beard, and long hair. On a personal note, I fucking hate long hair on men, and earrings. For fuck sake, they will be wearing high heels next, shaving in hot water, using Nivea for Men, for fuck's sake; give me strength!

But somehow they did not look right together. Some couples look right together, and if they kinda look right together, they usually are, but they looked like chalk and cheese. But that's the way it goes.

I knew she still loved him; you get a feel of it. What is love? It's such a very small word, but yet once said, and not said with an empty heart, there is nothing on this earth more powerful to mankind, in any language. It makes a human being complete, or it can destroy them like nothing else can. Love is a look; it's when two souls touch; it's a knowing touch; it's an embrace that makes a person tremble with emotion. It's empowering. It's love.

Love seems the right word. I mean if it were another word, it just would not be the same. I mean if I said to someone 'I paracetamoxyfursenbenroneocyin you!' Well, it would not have that feel about it, would it? But I think the best way to describe love is this – and I read it once – love is not the person you see yourself with, it's the person you can't see yourself without! And that's about the size of it!

It was on a warm summer Monday evening and I popped around to see her, and there was something not right. What, I didn't know, but I just felt it, and I was not wrong either! She says to me that her girlfriend and boyfriend had invited her to go and see the Harlem Globetrotters, and her ex-boyfriend would be there. I smelt a rat. I did not like the sound of this, but I said if you wanna go, do; no biggie. But my mind was racing, and I could not feel easy with it. But I had made my mind up: I am not going down this road. Been there once before and not doing it again, no fucking way!

So when we go back to her place, I said, 'I just can't do this. He's still deep in your heart, and it's best we end it here, now.' Her eyes knew I was right, so I pecked her on the check and said, 'Keep safe, be lucky.' And I walked away and never saw her again. Shit happens! As I walked away, I bit my lip hard! I would have never done that to her, but I will say one thing: at least she didn't say she was washing her hair!

Thank God it was Monday night! Corky Mick was off and we go on the piss big-time up the Gresham, and the Beer Monster was out! It's a bloke thing!

In the morning, when I stumbled out of my bed with a hangover the size of a small African country, I found a postcard on the mat from Marco. He was in Mombasa, lucky bastard! But that really got me thinking!

I was off work for a few days and decided to go down the King's Head for a livener, and as I walked in the boozer I noticed something I had never really paid any attention to before. As you walked into the pub there was a large alcove on the right, and it was commonly known as the elephant's graveyard. This is where all the old blokes sat and drank their halves of bitter. So I got my beer and went over and sat down with them and started to talk to them.

They had all lived; they had all done something. Many had

fought in the war, and though it was the 'during the war' they had been to places and done something!

None of my mates had been anywhere, except the ones that were in the army, but my feet were beginning to get very itchy, and it really got me thinking about my life and what I wanted to do with it. I looked around me. There had to be more to life then this; there had to be!

About a week later Marco was home and it was great to see him. He told me about Africa and the places he had been. He had crossed the Sahara Desert. Fuck, the Sahara Desert! He had been across France, Spain, Morocco, Mauritania, Mali, Niger, Nigeria, Cameroon, Congo, Zambia, Tanzania and Kenya. I was fascinated and so impressed, I can tell you!

I made my mind up that night: I was gonna go! And I would save up as much as I could as soon as possible. I sold my hi-fi. I just knew I had to go, because if I didn't I would end up in the elephant's graveyard, and done fuck all with my life. I had a shit job, so nothing to lose on the career side of it, that was for sure. I just had to go and the sooner the better.

I got as much dosh as I could as soon as I could. I got about 400 nicker and took myself off on a cold wet Saturday morning, with my Bergen on my back. I was going on my own, and I would be the master of my own destiny, and that was the way I wanted it!

I made my way through France, Belgium, across Germany, down through Yugoslavia, into Greece, and ended up in Beirut. Well, that's another story. I was nineteen.

I sincerely hope this has made you smile at least once, and if it has my endeavours will not have been in vain. And if it didn't, tough. Get a life!

Sue, thanks a million. I mean that!

Printed in Great Britain
by Amazon.co.uk, Ltd.,
Marston Gate.